Social Skills
for Students

With **Autism Spectrum Disorders**

and **Other Developmental Disabilities**

Laurence R. Sargent

Darlene Perner

Toni Cook

Council for
Exceptional
Children

Council for Exceptional Children
2900 Crystal Drive, Suite 1000
Arlington, VA 22202
www.cec.sped.org

Printed in the United States of America

Library of Congress Cataloging-in-Publication data

Sargent, Laurence R.
Social skills for students with autism spectrum disorders and other developmental disabilities /
by Laurence R. Sargent, Darlene Perner, and Toni Cook.
p. cm.
Includes biographical references.

ISBN 978-0-86586-468-9

Cover and interior design by Carol L. Williams.
Illustrations on CD by Marion Jackson III, Colorado Springs, CO.

First edition

10 9 8 7 6 5 4 3 2 1

Table of Contents

Acknowledgments

The authors wish to extend appreciation to the Board of Directors of the Division on Autism and Developmental Disabilities of the Council for Exceptional Children for their continued support for this book on teaching social skills and the previous editions that began over 20 years ago.

Foreword

There is a bit of a "been there, done that" sense in the field of special education when it comes to social skills instruction. The earliest special education textbooks, dating back to the first decade of the 1900s emphasized social skills instruction. Do we really need another text on social skills instruction?

Yes, of course we do. Teaching social skills to students with autism spectrum disorders and other developmental disabilities has been on the agenda of special educators for a century because they are really important skills for people to learn; that is as true in 2012 as it was in 1912, and perhaps more so. Hanley-Maxwell and Izzo (2012) identified foundational skills for preparing students for the 21st Century workforce and not surprisingly, social skills are identified by these authors as critical components of job success. Eisenman and Celestin (2012) point to the importance of social skills for postsecondary education, independent living, community participation, friendship development… in other words, to a good life.

So, let's take it on faith (and fact) that social skills are important and we need to pay attention to promoting them. Given that, do we know how to do so? Allwell and Cobb (2009) conducted a metasynthesis of the social skills intervention literature for youth with disabilities. Their conclusion? That social skills training interventions improve the social skills they target and also improve the acquisition, performance, and generalization of prosocial behaviors necessary for positive transition outcomes. So, promoting social skills is important and we know how to do it. Do we need a new text to provide methods, materials, strategies, and lessons to enable us to do this?

Yes, of course we do. Why? It's not 1912 or 1952 or 1998—which was when the first edition of Social Skills for School and Community (Sargent, 1998) was published— it's 2012. What hasn't changed in the past 100 years is that teaching social skills is important and that we know how to do it. What has changed dramatically, is the context in which such instruction must occur. In the past, social skills instruction was implemented to achieve improved social skills; today, that is not enough, evident in the long awaited update to Social Skills for School and Community, now titled *Social Skills for Students With Autism Spectrum Disorders and Other Developmental Disabilitie*s. As noted in the preface, this edition places a greater focus on teaching social skills in inclusive settings. That's the 21st Century context that matters . . . inclusive school and community settings.

This two volume edition of *Social Skills for Students With Autism Spectrum Disorders and Other Developmental Disabilities* changes more than just the focus on where social skills are taught; it explicitly and implicitly changes the intent of this instruction. Social skills are important in the development of social competence. Social competence is important for social inclusion. The objective of instruction introduced by these books are not only to improve social skills—it is to enhance social inclusion. Without enhanced social inclusion—at work, in the community, in schools—social skills are only isolated behaviors. Friendships. Job and school success. Independent living. Meaningful relationships. Those are the outcomes that are targeted by this new edition. As well *Social Skills for Students With Autism Spectrum Disorders and Other Developmental Disabilities* provides educators with the tools they need to enable students to achieve these outcomes and lead a better life. Methods, materials, strategies, and comprehensive lesson plans. Is it really that important? Well, of course it is.

Michael L. Wehmeyer, Ph.D.
Chair, Publications Committee, CEC Division on Autism and
Developmental Disabilities; Professor, Special Education
Director, Kansas University Center on Developmental Disabilities

References

Alwell , M. , & Cobb , B. (2009). *Social and communicative interventions and transition outcomes for youth with disabilities: A systematic review. Career Development for Exceptional Individuals*, 32(2), 94-107.

Eisenman, L. T., & Celestin, S. A. (2012). *Social skills, supports, and networks in adolescent transition education.* In M. L. Wehmeyer & K. A. Webb (Eds.), Handbook of adolescent transition for youth with disabilities (pp. 223-232). New York, NY: Routledge.

Hanley-Maxwell, C., & Izzo, M. V. (2012). *Preparing students for the 21st Century workforce.* In M. L. Wehmeyer & K. A. Webb (Eds.), *Handbook of adolescent transition for youth with disabilities* (pp. 139-155). New York, NY: Routledge.

Preface

Many descriptions of autism and Asperger's describe people like me as "not wanting contact with others" or "preferring to play alone." I cannot speak for those other kids, but I'd like to be very clear about my own feelings: *I did not ever* want *to be alone . . .* I played by myself because I was a failure at playing with others.

John Elder Robinson
Look Me in the Eye: My Life With Asperger's, p. 211

The purpose of this social skills teaching framework is to address the social competence needs of students with autism spectrum disorder (ASD) and other developmental disabilities. Today, many students with disabilities are educated alongside their typically developing peers in general education classrooms, with limited pullout for specialized instruction. Many of today's students receive support from special education teachers and paraprofessionals serving students with a wide range of disabilities. A typical elementary special education teacher might serve one or two students with ASD, two students with significant support needs, four students with mild/moderate intellectual disabilities, four students with behavioral disorders, and additional students with learning disabilities—all part of a 20-plus student caseload.

This updated edition of *Social Skills for School and Community* (Sargent, 1998) places a greater focus on teaching social skills in inclusive settings. Strategies for teaching students with ASD often are also effective in addressing the social skills needs of students with other disabilities and those who are "at risk." The earlier versions of these materials have been used successfully with young children considered to be at risk, students with emotional and behavioral disorders and learning disabilities, and students in juvenile detention centers. In addition, many of the strategies continue to be useful for teaching social skills in settings where students with similar disabilities are clustered in special classes.

In this volume, geared toward the social skill needs of elementary school students, we present a framework which incorporates a rationale for teaching social skills, a broad perspective on social competence, and methods and content for enhancing social competence. Chapter 1 provides practitioners with an overview of the various strategies and a perspective on the complex processes we refer to as *social skills instruction*. The remaining chapters discuss procedures for addressing inclusive practices (Chapter 2); teacher- and peer-mediated strategies for engaging students (Chapter 3); and direct instruction of social skills (Chapter 4). The social skill lesson plans in Chapter 5 incorporate specific follow-up activities for facilitating maintenance and generalization, as well as recommendations of technology resources (apps, software, and web links); the Appendix contains assessment and progress monitoring forms.

Together, the two volumes of this publication provide 100 different lesson plans to support students in acquiring social skills (see Table 4-3, pp. 60–62); although half are geared toward elementary school students and the others toward middle and high school students, any of the plans can be adapted to suit the needs of a different age group. The accompanying CD includes the 50 elementary school lesson plans; templates of the lesson plan; forms for assessment, progress monitoring, and home-school communication; line drawings and images teachers can use in creating comic strips or social stories; and an Excel template for progress monitoring and graphing.

The social skills lessons in this publication should be used on the basis of need and do not necessarily represent a sequential or developmental curriculum. We encourage teachers to apply the seven-step lesson design described in Chapter 4 when teaching social skills that are not specifically addressed in this publication.

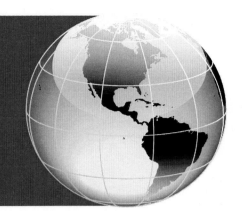

Chapter 1
Proactive Instruction for Social Competence

Teaching social skills to elementary students with autism spectrum disorder (ASD) and other developmental disabilities can be both a vexing and a rewarding endeavor for educators. *Social skills instruction* is a complex process requiring individual and group strategies, repetition, and persistence. Despite its challenges, social skills instruction holds promise for improving the social competence of children and youth with ASD and other developmental disabilities; sufficient evidence demonstrates that social skills can be taught and the lives of these students enhanced. Although the title of these books focuses on students with ASD and developmental disabilities, these lesson plans are also extremely effective and appropriate for students with intellectual disability and are thus referenced throughout the text.

Rationale

For most children, social competence develops through incidental learning and intellectual maturation. Unfortunately, children and youth with ASD and intellectual disabilities are notoriously inadequate in their incidental learning ability (Freedman & Silverman, 2008; Gumpel, Tappe, & Arki, 2000; Hume, Bellini, & Pratt, 2005; Simpson, 2005). They commonly exhibit learning deficits in areas of reciprocal communication, discrimination, attention, memory, and generalization (Ellis, 1963; Fisher & Zeaman, 1973; Zeaman & House, 1963) which contribute to impaired social affect, social skills, and social cognition. Consequently, children with ASD and intellectual disabilities fail to accrue acceptance by peers and adults. Moreover, many children with these disabilities incur social rejection as a result of exhibiting awkward, interfering, and socially unacceptable behaviors.

The long-term consequences of social rejection and poor social competence are many. Early studies indicated that individuals identified during childhood as social isolates were likely to have difficulty during adulthood (e.g., run-ins with the law, alcohol, divorce, and other social ills; Gresham, 1981). Further, rehabilitation literature indicates that most individuals with intellectual disabilities who lose jobs do so primarily because of a lack of adequate social skills and other socially inappropriate behavior (Gumpel et al., 2000). In addition, individuals with ASD are prone to develop social anxiety, which exacerbates their isolation (Bellini, 2004; Bellini & Hopf, 2007). Due to the great importance and lasting effect of social competence, programming provided for these students must include efforts to build this skill set—and that programming should be carried out in positive and nonpunitive ways.

Proactive Instruction

Proactive instruction provides learners with opportunities to gain acceptance by others, develop friendships, and lead healthier and happier lives. Improving social competence helps people with ASD and other developmental disabilities to avoid debilitating social rejection, poor self-concept, social anxiety, inappropriate or potentially offensive social behavior, and a diminished quality of life.

Proactive instruction is preferable to reactively treating perceived social deficits. Addressing social competence from a proactive perspective, students learn new skills in a positive milieu through positive techniques before any negative consequence of social rejection occurs. In contrast, a reactive approach waits for individuals to fail and then tries to fix their problems. Too often, reactive responses to social inadequacy result in punishment as a way to suppress undesirable behavior.

Students with ASD and developmental disabilities often have difficulty recognizing and interpreting social cues and nuances that are integral to social interactions. In addition, some of these students are unable to discriminate acceptable social norms. Because of such deficits, their individualized education programs (IEPs) throughout their years in public education should include goals to improve their social competence.

Before undertaking proactive instruction, it is helpful for educators to grasp the concept of social competence. What is social competence? What are the goals of social skills instruction?

Conceptual Framework of Social Competence

It is critical for professionals trying to address the needs of students with ASD and intellectual disabilities to understand the notion of social competence. *Social competence* is a mix of interacting and overlapping variables. A conceptual framework (Figure 1-1) assists in making sense of these variables, as well as helps guide how to address

Figure 1-1

Conceptual Framework of Social Competence

Inputs { Cultural determinants

Processes {
Social affect

Social skills

Social cognition

Outcomes { Desired outcomes

socially related problems. This basic framework—consisting of inputs, processes, and desired outcomes supports formulating actions that will enhance the social competence of students with ASD and other developmental disabilities.

Inputs: Cultural Determinants

Cultural determinants are individuals' values and social standards. They are the dynamic "raw materials" of social competence and vary according to community size, ethnic mix, geographical region, and community traditions. Failure to function within these cultural boundaries can inhibit both social acceptance and development of self-efficacy. Major cultural determinants include community values, standards for adult/child relations, family member role expectations, privacy standards, standards of decency (e.g., taboos), work ethic, standards of fairness, independence expectancy, temporal standards (e.g., how long to chitchat, how late is acceptable), standards of social responsibility, community tolerance of differences, aesthetic conventions and values, and situational conventions (e.g., table manners, classroom manners).

Cultural determinants are the ingredients of social competence which must be acted upon to arrive at the desired outcomes. These actions occur through the three process elements of the model; individuals adjust and match their behavior to these myriad values and rules.

Processes

The three *process components* of this framework are social affect, social skills, and social cognition. Each component warrants attention, and failure to address all three areas represents inadequate effort to achieve desired outcomes.

Social affect is not only an overt process component of social competence; it is also an *outcome*. In our framework, *social affect* relates to how the individual appears to others. Positive social affect includes cheerfulness, enthusiasm, confidence, optimism, risk-taking, independence, good posture and grooming, sense of humor, affection, and assertiveness.

There are a number of teaching materials and methods designed to improve student affect (see, e.g., *Hot Wings Skills and Activities* from www.wingsforkids.org, *Games and Activities for Children with Autism* from Children Succeed); these can be incorporated throughout activities and instruction. Most of the components of social affect are best addressed during teachable moments. It's important to note, however, that attention to affect alone does not create a more socially competent individual.

Social skills are behaviors, the most obvious aspect of social competence. Behaviors can be learned by being taught directly or taught through infusion into life experiences, or can be acquired incidentally through modeling of competent peers and adults. There are hundreds of social skills in a variety of categories: interaction initiation activities (e.g., starting a conversation), interaction responses (e.g., responding to a complaint), personal social behaviors (e.g., dealing with embarrassment), and setting-specific skills and behaviors (e.g., riding a school bus, waiting in line). Specific settings include school, home, and public arenas.

Instruction on the observable aspects of social proficiencies holds great promise, but is insufficient if it is the only element of social competence on which the instructional team focuses. Techniques used to teach social skills must incorporate strategies to enhance social cognition.

Social cognition encompasses an individual's ability to understand, interpret, and take appropriate actions relevant to different social settings, personal interactions, and complexity of situations (Greenspan, 1979). Greenspan (1979) identified *social cognition skills* as including role taking/empathy, social discrimination and inference, social understanding/comprehension, understanding others' motives, moral and ethical judgments, referential communication, and social problem solving. Whereas many typically developing students acquire these abilities as they mature, this process component is by definition the most difficult area for students with ASD or intellectual disabilities.

Despite the inherent difficulty in this area of personal growth, students with ASD and developmental disabilities can make progress when provided interventions. They can learn strategies for social problem solving and gain social discrimination skills from arranged experiences; it's important to reinforce their moral and ethical judgments, and to provide opportunities to practice social problem solving.

Outcomes

The outcomes from successfully developing social competence are some of the most positive aspects of life itself: self-esteem, self-confidence, peer acceptance, acceptance by family and others, friendships, strong personal relationships, community acceptance, social independence, and a supportive social milieu. They represent the fulfillment of the needs and desires of the individual with a disability as well as the aspirations of parents, professionals, and care providers, who'd like to see that individual become a productive and happy adult.

These outcomes are attained through the interaction of life experiences and the efforts of professionals acting on the lives of students with ASD and other disabilities. To achieve success, interventions must occur during the student's entire developmental period, from preschool through secondary education settings.

Preparing for Inclusive Settings: What Works Best

One significant reason to support students in developing social competence is that modern educational practices are focused on providing instruction in the least restrictive environment, which for many students is the general education classroom. Social competence is essential for success in inclusive school and community settings. Another reason for addressing social competence is that structured learning activities are educationally more fruitful than previous instructional techniques, which relied on skill acquisition through tangentially related experiences (Lloyd & Carnine, 1981). Thus, programming for social competence should not be left to chance if it is to be effective. Social interaction skills are learned and mastered through practice and performance, and they must be taught (Bellini, 2006b).

There are a variety of approaches to teaching social skills. Although there is no single "best" way to teach social skills for all students with disabilities, structured procedures and sequences hold promise for supporting developing social competence. After reviewing research on academic instruction, Stevens and Rosenshine (1981) concluded that the most successful teachers were those who selected and directed activities; approached the subject matter in a direct, businesslike manner; organized learning around questions they posed; and occupied the center of attention. Since that time, a number of education researchers have agreed with Stevens and Rosenshine's findings (Marzano, 2007). Further, researchers have concluded that the most efficient process for teaching is a three-step sequence of demonstration, prompting, and practice. During the practice phase students must experience a high level of success to sustain learning gains, and learning is enhanced when pupils receive feedback on their efforts. This structured sequence is often referred to as *direct instruction*. Several researchers have reported successful use of direct instruction approaches to successfully teach social skills to students with ASD (Flores & Ganz, 2007; Kroeger, Schultz, & Newsom, 2006; Lopata, Thomeer, Volker, & Nida, 2006; Webb, Miller, Peirce, Strawser, & Jones, 2004).

Research has also illustrated that academic instruction for students with disabilities is often best offered in a systematic, sequenced format. Close, Irvin, Taylor, and Agosta (1981) found that *instructional assistance* (verbal cues, modeling, and prompting), systematic feedback, and repeated correct practice ensured learning. They used a variation of direct instruction techniques to teach life skills to individuals with intellectual disabilities. Similar structured learning approaches (e.g., introduce the skill, model the skill, practice skill, and facilitate generalization) appear to be successful with pupils with varied disabilities when teaching social skills (Gresham, 2002).

What to Teach

One of the major determinants of social acceptance appears to be perception of *interfering behavior*. Greater social rejection occurs for misbehaving children than for children with mild disabilities who are simply perceived as intellectually challenged (Gottlieb, Semmel, & Veldman, 1978; MacMillan & Morrison, 1980; Siperstein, Leffert & Widaman, 1996). Similarly, children with learning disabilities who tended to be rejected by peers were found to emit negative verbal behaviors in general education classrooms (Bryan, 1974). Some of the behaviors most important to gaining social acceptance in the general education classroom are attending, complying, volunteering, following directions, speaking positively about academic material, and remaining on task (Cartledge & Milburn, 1980). The National Association of School Psychologists (NASP; 2002) provided a list of important social skills that include listening, following directions, ignoring distractions, sharing, asking for permission, joining an activity, waiting your turn, asking for help, apologizing, accepting consequences, dealing with teasing, losing, accusations, being left out, and peer pressure.

In addition to facilitating acceptance among peers, positive behaviors encourage greater acceptance on the part of general education teachers and other school personnel, and result in the child with a disability having more positive interactions with these adults. Therefore, learning teacher-pleasing behaviors is an important part of developing social competence. For young children, a good place to start is with one of several lists of "kindergarten survival skills" (Brigman & Webb, 2003; McCormick & Kawate, 1982). To set the stage for personal growth, negatively perceived behaviors—such as aggression and acting out—must be reduced through teaching children how to interact in a socially acceptable way.

Personal interaction skills are equally important to ensure success in school settings; in fact, Bellini (2006b) asserted that these are the most important skills for students with ASD to develop friendships. Other authors have identified behaviors such as helping, sharing, smiling, greeting, joint attention, speaking positively to others, joining in conversations, and controlling aggression as necessary for adequate social interaction (NASP, 2002). In addition, recognizing emotions, complimenting, positive physical contact, asking for information, extending invitations, giving information, taking turns, listening, positive eye contact, participating, expressing enthusiasm, and good grooming have all been found to contribute to positive social interaction (Cooke & Appolloni, 1976; Gottman, Gonso, & Rasmussen, 1975; Gronlund & Anderson, 1963; Mesibov & La Greca, 1981; Odom & Asher, 1977; Travis, Sigman, & Ruskin; 2001).

Individuals with ASD, developmental, or intellectual disabilities are often perceived as egocentric and therefore require concentrated training in *social cognition*—understanding what others are perceiving, thinking, and feeling. A major characteristic of individuals with ASD is that they lack the ability to perceive and understand the thinking of others (Simpson, 2005). Students with intellectual disabilities are often deficient at *social inference*, the ability to interpret what is happening around them, decision making, and problem solving. Students with ASD and other developmental disabilities also may lack understanding of social processes such as friendship (Greenspan, 1979).

Elias & Maher (1983) recommended a social-cognitive problem-solving skills framework as a foundation for school-based programming. They contended that social skill competence comprises a specific set of skills: an expectation by individuals that they can take personal initiative in a situation and gain a favorable outcome; sensitivity to others' feelings and perspectives; the ability to set a clear goal and consider various possible consequences, to plan specific steps to reach a goal, and the behavioral repertoire needed to implement their plans; and the persistence to continue using their problem-solving skills in the face of obstacles, and the ability to refine their problem-solving strategies in light of experience.

Vaughn, Ridley, and Cox (1983) identified several skills that fit into the social cognition category, and designed an instructional program around them. Their instructional program for young children includes

- Fundamental language concepts (e.g. *same*, *different*, etc.).

- Cue sensitivity: Awareness of key factors in social situations and how to react appropriately to the situation.

- Goal identification: Proceeding from goals to action.

- Empathy: Taking the role of another.

- Alternative thinking: How to predict likely outcomes for problem situations using alternative problem-solving strategies.

- Consequential thinking: Strategies for predicting likely outcomes of problem-solving methods.

- Procedural thinking: How to get from a chosen alternative to a desired goal.

- Integrating skills: Incorporating all of the components of the interpersonal problem-solving approach into a single process.

It's clear that there are many skills and behaviors that must be taught to increase the social competence of individuals with ASD and intellectual disabilities; the timing of instruction is also important.

When to Teach

In some form or another, social competence must be taught at all times in a child's life. Reinforcement of social affect and socially appropriate behavior will always be warranted. However, not every social competency must be addressed as soon as it is perceived as a deficiency. Decisions on when to teach a particular skill are related to the characteristics of individual children. Browning and White (1986) emphasized that instruction should be matched to children's ages and their cognitive abilities. For example, a child with a mental age of 4 is not likely to have a well-developed concept of what is "fair" and what is "not fair." Young typically developing children often acquire these concepts with little intervention. In contrast, some students have so many deficits that it is necessary to tackle the most obtrusive problem or the potentially most valuable skill first. In other words, it's important to establish a system of priorities.

For students with ASD, *social communication* must be a priority at all levels of development. The SCERTS model (Prizant, Wetherby, Rubin, Laurent, & Rydell, 2006) posits that children with ASD develop in three stages of social communication: (a) social partner stage, (b) language partner stage, and (c) conversational partner stage. Many of the lesson plans we provide and the strategies we discuss in this book assume students are at the language partner or conversational partner stages of social communication development.

Determining when to teach a particular skill can be accomplished by responding to a series of questions. Affirmative answers to these questions may lead to the conclusion that the skill should be taught immediately; if an answer is negative, the skill may be taught at a later date. In some cases, the response to a behavior may have to be shaped through the use of behavioral analysis techniques rather than through instruction that requires the learner to apply cognitive strategies (see box, "When to Teach").

When to Teach
✓ Is the skill deficient or inadequate?
✓ Does the student have the cognitive ability to learn the skill?
✓ Has the student developed sufficient language to engage in the skill?
✓ Will the student have an opportunity to practice the skill?
✓ Does changing the student's behavior have importance to significant others in the student's life?
✓ Is the skill needed in current or future environments?
✓ Is acquisition of the skill essential to the individual's ability to remain in his or her current environment?
✓ Does acquisition of the skill help to gain acceptance and friendships among peers?

How to Teach

No single approach to building social competence appears to be totally satisfactory. The approaches selected for use depend on a wide range of variables including age, mental ability, practice opportunities, communication skills, and a host of concerns related to the student's unique needs. Further, improving social competence is a longitudinal matter: Efforts must be made throughout the student's entire school career. It is unlikely that a lesson or two on how to make friends will result in the individual establishing close personal relationships. Children must have sufficient self-esteem, confidence, and risk-taking ability to make friends. At the same time, they must have the ability to understand how their friend feels and thinks, the moral and ethical judgments to be respected by a friend, and the ability to solve social problems that assist in sustaining friendships. To state this more broadly, the individual must attain sufficient social affect, adequately perform social skills, and exercise social cognition to become socially competent.

Improving Social Affect

In the mid-20th century, authorities believed that simply dealing with the self-concept of children with mild disabilities (by removing them from the frustrations of general education) would result in socially maladaptive behaviors disappearing (Kirk & Johnson, 1951). Several studies have indicated that students in special education class settings tend to have somewhat better self-concept than similar students with similar disabilities in general education classes (Bear, Minke, & Manning, 2002). However, this does not mean that they have better social skills or that they are better liked by others; it only means that they think better of themselves.

With the current federally legislated mandate to educate children in the least restrictive environment, it is very important to approach social affect in a variety of ways. Because affect is part of all social behavior, this aspect of social competence is best taught when integrated into all instructional areas, as well as being taught directly. Many sound practices may be infused into everyday academic and personal development instruction.

Building a healthy social affect begins as soon as a child enters school. Attempts to shape effective behaviors such as cheerfulness, good posture, good grooming, independence, and optimism should be ongoing throughout the student's school career. General and special education teachers can positively impact social affect in a variety of ways, including providing instruction and activities in which the individual student can be successful, reinforcing smiling, making eye contact, expressing enthusiasm, and demonstrating assertiveness. Further, simple corrective feedback on behavior such as posture and grooming assists in developing an affect which contributes to social acceptance.

In many cases, efforts to build social affect require the efforts of more than just a single special education teacher. Success can be achieved by through peer reinforcement and prompting interactions (Strain & Odom, 1986), adult confederates (Sargent, 1983), and classmates (McGinnis & Goldstein, 1984). Strain and Timm (1974) were able to increase cooperative play of children with disabilities and their typical peers by reinforcing the children without disabilities for initiating interactions and cooperative play.

Simply integrating students with ASD and intellectual disabilities into general education classes is unlikely to improve social affect and social skills (Bellini, 2006a; Gresham, 1982; Jenkins, Speltz, & Odom, 1986; D. Johnson, Johnson, & Maruyamma, 1983). However, interventions can facilitate interaction and improve self-concept. A procedure that works well in general education class settings is *cooperative learning*, where students engage in cooperative goal setting. Students with intellectual challenges engage in twice as much interaction in cooperative learning environments than in competitive learning situations; they also have better self-esteem and maintain relationships during periods of free play (R. Johnson & Johnson, 1983; Pierce & Schreibman, 1997). Another benefit of cooperative learning is that typically developing students become more accepting of their peers with disabilities (Ballard, Corman, Gottleib, & Kaufman, 1977; Cushing, Kennedy, Shukla, Davis, & Meyer, 1997). To be successful in cooperative learning activities, however, students with ASD often need to learn how to behave in those settings (Bock, 2007).

Using peer tutors is another approach to teaching social skills. McMahon, Wacker, Sasso, Berg, and Newton (1996) demonstrated that peer-mediated social skills instruction impacted learning of social interaction skills. Sasso, Mundschenk, Melloy, & Casey

(1998) found that peer-mediated instruction worked best in dyads rather than in triads. (See Chapters 2 and 3 for further discussion of grouping students for instruction in inclusive settings and peer-mediated instructions and interventions.)

In most cases, direct instructional techniques to improve social affect are combined with attempts to improve social cognition. A variety of materials were published in the late 1960s and early 1970s to teach children behavior such as understanding feelings and being optimistic. This older methodology for teaching skills such as social problem solving usually adhered to a story-followed-by-discussion format (Goldstein, 1974); current practice is to follow any classroom discussion with role-playing and modeling to reinforce the desired skill. Using video and video modeling with students with ASD has proven successful due to students' strengths in visual learning; Browning and White (1986) were among the first to use interactive video media to deal with affect concerns including "being positive" and "being responsible." The methodology of teaching social affect directly resembles other aspects of direct instruction. This often includes presentation of a story or video and then discussing the important learning points of the media used. Role-play and practice typically follow discussion.

Impacting Social Cognition

Social cognition and social affect are so closely linked that most authors do not separate the two. Much of what the professional literature describes as *affective instruction* is what we define as *social cognition*. Interventions in the area of social thinking are worthwhile, but research indicates that they must be accompanied with specific skill instruction to be successful and have long-term benefits for individuals with ASD and intellectual disabilities (Bellini, 2006b; Castles & Glass, 1986). Although not as powerful as social skills training, instruction in the arena of social cognition addresses some important elements of social competence untouched by most specific-skill training approaches. An additional positive attribute of training in social cognition is that students are given strategies for dealing with a wide range of problems and conditions. In contrast, specific-skill training tends to focus on narrowly defined operations. The majority of the research has been conducted in areas such as role-taking ability and social problem solving.

Elias and Maher (1983) developed a model for teaching social-cognitive problem solving skills. To teach these skills, they used videotapes, discussion, and role-playing. They stressed the importance of knowledge of children's cognitive ability at different ages. According to the authors, use of video and film is especially valuable because:

- Video activates a range of sensory modalities; it also stimulates motivation, attention, and is easily recalled.

- A synergistic learning effect occurs when video is combined with discussion that promotes learning of a general cognitive strategy.

More recently, researchers have used video modeling, self-video, and computer-based strategies to improve social skills and social cognition of students with ASD and intellectual disabilities (Bernad-Ripoll, 2007; Bernard-Opitz, Sriram, & Nakhoda-Sapuan, 2001; Browning & Nave, 1993; Crites, & Dunn, 2004; Embregts, 2003; Nikopoulos & Keenan, 2007; Wang & Spillane, 2009). In addition to book-video combination resources (e.g., James Stanfield, 2010; Knapczyk & Rodes, 2001), there is a variety of video programs specifically designed for teaching social skills. Videos work well with a variety of learners and many are specifically designed for students having ASD and intellectual disabilities. Ogilvie (2011) provided a step-by-step model for using video modeling to teach social skills to students with ASD. Wang and Spillane (2009) performed a comparison meta-analysis of promising practices and found that video modeling qualifies as evidence-based practice.

Vaughn and colleagues (1983) validated their problem-solving training with children with intellectual disabilities and preschoolers. The procedures included discussions, modeling, and rehearsal. Through these processes, students demonstrated significant gains in interpersonal problem solving compared to controls. Students increased response repertoires to include trading, sharing, getting assistance from others, and waiting.

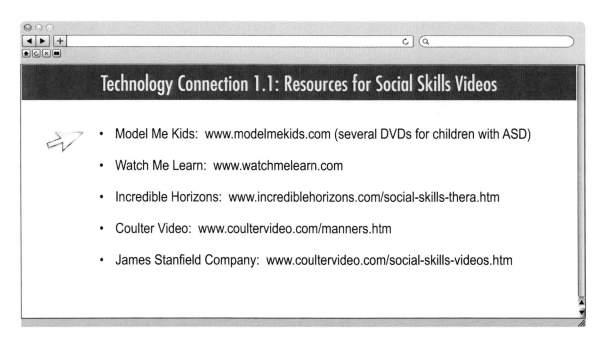

Technology Connection 1.1: Resources for Social Skills Videos

- Model Me Kids: www.modelmekids.com (several DVDs for children with ASD)

- Watch Me Learn: www.watchmelearn.com

- Incredible Horizons: www.incrediblehorizons.com/social-skills-thera.htm

- Coulter Video: www.coultervideo.com/manners.htm

- James Stanfield Company: www.coultervideo.com/social-skills-videos.htm

Another useful approach for enhancing social cognition is cognitive behavior modification; Meichenbaum (1977) recommended a five-step approach (see Figure 1-2). Similarly, Bash and Camp's (1980) *thinking aloud* procedure encouraged children to verbally rehearse responses and alternative solutions to social problems.

Teaching response strategies that students can apply helps students gain social problem-solving skills. Students learn the strategy of verbal self-instruction to deal with problem situations by verbalizing their thinking during simulated problem solving and decision making sessions. Strategies are rehearsed and then applied when needed. Browning and White (1986) used this procedure in conjunction with videos focused on areas including "being positive," "relating to others," and "being responsible." In addition to verbal rehearsal of strategies, they used self-talking, workbooks, homework, role-playing, and expansion games. Rosenthal-Malek & Yoshida (1994) found that meta-cognitive strategies could be used to teach social problem solving to students with intellectual disabilities. The difficulty with these procedures is that they are highly reliant on language that many individuals with ASD and cognitive delays have little skill using. However, with adequate practice, cognitive behavior modification can be used successfully with students with ASD and mild intellectual disabilities.

Bellini (2006b) recommended using self-monitoring techniques to assist students with ASD acquire and practice appropriate social behaviors. He indicated that these strategies were effective for a number of externalized behaviors such as work completion and disruptive behaviors.

Teaching Specific Social Skills

There is some evidence of success using direct instruction methods when teaching social skills (Cartledge & Milburn, 1980; Kroeger et al., 2006; McGinnis & Goldstein, 1984; Mesibov & La Greca, 1981; Sargent, 1983; Stephens, 1978; Strain, Shores, & Timm, 1977; Strain and Wiegerink, 1976; Webb et al., 2004). The procedures used for the various direct instruction approaches are all very similar. They rely heavily on modeling, role-playing, practice, and feedback.

Social skills differ slightly from *social thinking*: Social skills are overt behaviors related to specific social needs such as making an introduction, sharing, or staying out of fights. The instructional procedures for the lessons included in Chapter 5 are, in effect, direct instruction of specific social skills with adaptation and consideration for the characteristics of learners with ASD and intellectual disabilities (see Chapter 4). Albeit powerful, direct instruction is most effective when accompanied by additional instruction and practice.

Figure 1-2

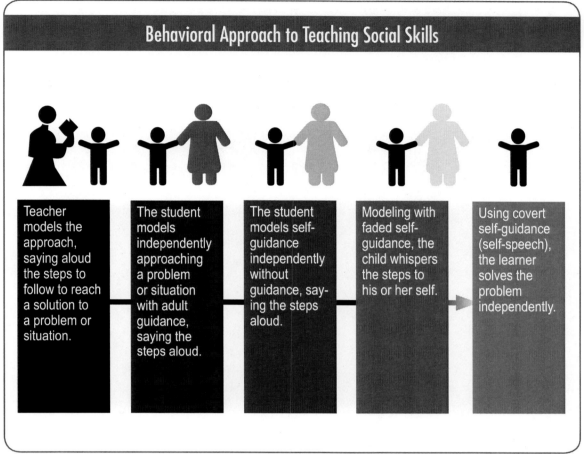

Behavioral Approach to Teaching Social Skills

Teacher models the approach, saying aloud the steps to follow to reach a solution to a problem or situation.	The student models independently approaching a problem or situation with adult guidance, saying the steps aloud.	The student models self-guidance independently without guidance, saying the steps aloud.	Modeling with faded self-guidance, the child whispers the steps to his or her self.	Using covert self-guidance (self-speech), the learner solves the problem independently.

Individualized Social Skills Instruction

Several approaches are available to teachers wishing to provide individualized treatment for a social skill deficit (see Chapter 4), such as social stories (Gray & Garand, 1993), scripts, power cards (Gagnon, 2001; Spencer, Simpson, Day, & Buster, 2008;) and individualized behavior plans.

Gray and Garand (1993) introduced the process of using stories to teach social skills to students with autism. In this model, *social stories* involve four basic types of individually prepared sentences used to guide behavior change, written for a specific student and related to a specific behavioral need (Gray, 2000):

- **Descriptive** sentences provide information about the setting, constellation of people, and what they are doing.

- **Perspective** sentences describe the state of other people to encourage students to learn how others might perceive a situation.

- **Affirmative** sentences refer to a law, rule, or common belief to reassure the student.

- **Directive** sentences tell the student what to do to be successful.

Using the social stories strategy, researchers have reduced crying, screaming, and hitting by young children (Adams, Gouvousis, VanLue, & Waldron, 2004); increased participation in novel events (Ivey, Hellin, & Aberto, 2004); and reduced disruptive behavior (Crozier & Tincani, 2005; Graetz, Mastropieri, & Scruggs, 2009; Kuttler, Myles, & Carlson, 1998). In addition, Kuoch and Mirenda (2003) demonstrated positive effects beyond initial training. Although Scattone, Tingstrom, & Wilczynski (2006) improved appropriate social behaviors using social stories, participants did not become fully competent; they concluded that social stories were effective for some children with ASD. Although many successful uses of social stories have been reported for selected groups of students, this technique has not yet achieved classification as a research-based strategy across the entire autism spectrum (Test, Richter, Knight, & Spooner, 2011).

Some social skills are so intensely important that we must address them in the most sophisticated and scientific means that we have. The use of function-based assessments and individual behavior support plans (see Chapter 4) may be appropriate for some students (for a teacher-friendly description of behavior intervention strategies, see Jones, 1998).

Follow-Up: Coaching

For typical populations, coaching as a teaching method has proved to be as effective as modeling (Odom & Asher, 1977), although La Greca, Stone, and Bell (1983) found that modeling was more successful than coaching alone for teaching social skills. Although slightly weaker as an initial teaching strategy, coaching remains a powerful maintenance and generalization strategy. Based upon the Teaching Family Model (Phillips, Fixsen, Phillips, & Wolf, 1979), the Boys Town curriculum and teaching strategies originally focused on improving the social behavior of institutionalized adolescents. The Boys Town social skills curriculum and training model (Black, Downs, Bastien, & Brown, 1984) incorporates some components that can be effectively adapted for use with students with ASD or intellectual disabilities. The Complete Teaching Interaction component is a structured and useful tool for facilitating maintenance and generalization of learned social skills, using feedback and reteaching (see Figure 1-3). This

Figure 1-3

Boys Town Model for Teaching Social Skills

Expression of affection (e.g., smiles, physical contact, use of the student's name, statement of affection

Initial praise/empathy (a positive statement related to the student's accomplishments or a statement of concern about the student's feelings)

Describe inappropriate behavior, telling the student exactly what was inappropriate.

Describe appropriate behavior or demonstrate an alternative behavior.

Provide a rationale to the student, pointing out the benefit or consequences for engaging or not engaging in certain behaviors.

Request acknowledgment to check for understanding—some steps may need elaboration or repeating if the student does not understand.

Practice to make sure the student truly understands how to perform the skill.

Provide feedback to the student to reinforce and/or correct performance (during the practice component).

Provide consequences to teach students the relationship between their behavior and the results of their behavior.

Offer general praise to end the session positively and reinforce the student for participating in the teaching/learning experience.

procedure can be used as part of a follow-up to direct instruction for students with ASD and intellectual disabilities; it is too reliant on verbal instruction, however, to be used as the only approach to teaching social skills to students with cognitive and communication disabilities.

The Boys Town model is based upon the premise that teaching social skills is most effective when a problem arises. For example, when a student fails to accept criticism, that is the time to teach that skill. To be able to teach a skill, the teacher must be very accurate at observing and describing behavior, and needs to be trained in specific approaches to implementing the process.

Generalization: The Elephant in the Classroom

A major failure of many programs designed to teach social skills is that once taught to criterion, the student does not use the skills in different settings, novel situations, with changing constellations of people, or out of sight of the original trainers. Simply teaching the strategies described in this framework without addressing generalization is unproductive and a waste of effort and time. When taught in a classroom or clinic setting without follow-up support, the effect size of these training programs is very small for both individuals with ASD and those with intellectual disabilities (Barry, Klinger, Lee, Palardy, Gilmore, & Bodin, 2003; Collet-Klingenberg & Chadsey-Rusch, 1991; Gresham, Sugai, & Horner, 2001; Helgeson, Fatuzzo, Smith, & Barr, 1989; Webb et al., 2004).

Despite the issue of poor generalization, empirical evidence demonstrates that with appropriate social skills instruction, generalization can be attained. After reviewing most of the research on social behavior of children with autism, Rogers

Social Competence Components

Social affect represents appearances that the individual presents to others. These behaviors, such as cheerfulness and good posture, can be taught through infusion into other learning activities. They are reinforced through attempts to facilitate interaction and cooperation with others.

Social skills represent overt behaviors used in a variety of social contexts. They include groups of skills related to initiating and responding appropriately in personal interactions and numerous skills related to socially acceptable behavior in a variety of environments. Many of these skills can be taught directly, but instruction must include efforts to facilitate generalization.

Social cognition represents the thinking or cognitive component of social competence. Some aspects of social cognition can be enhanced through use of techniques such as role playing, training in thinking strategies, and cognitive behavior modification.

(2000) concluded that social behavior can be improved by intervention. Teaching social skills may take several weeks and should include integration with typically developing peers (Ellis, Wright, & Cronis, 1996); generalization effects for children with autism may be enhanced by facilitating interaction with typical peers and use of peer tutors (Laushey & Heflin, 2000; Roeyers, 1996; Wolfberg & Schuler, 1993). Yang, Schaller, Hang, Wang, and Tsai (2003) increased transfer of skills taught in a resource room for children with autism by having adults in general education classes mediate use of skills. Unfortunately, despite the success of students achieving generalization when the matter is addressed through instruction and follow up, some students occasionally regress when faced with emotionally charged situations, reverting to older and stronger competing behaviors (Gresham et al., 2001).

Summary

Enhancing the social competence (see box, "Social Competence Components") of individuals with ASD and other developmental disabilities is a long-term goal of special educators. This goal cannot be accomplished unless the concern is addressed broadly and longitudinally. The breadth of concern includes taking actions to improve social affect, social skills, and social thinking.

No single approach to improving social competence is sufficient, and a variety of techniques for teaching social skills—or a combination of techniques—can be effective. Educators must continually reinforce appropriate social affect, teach social skills, and instruct students on using of thinking strategies to understand and solve problems in social situations.

Chapter 2
Supporting Students With Disabilities in the Inclusive Classroom

Positive and supportive learning environments are necessary for students with and without disabilities to acquire, use, and expand the elements of social competence. The challenge is creating and sustaining positive settings and actions that support skill acquisition, acceptance, friendships, and self-efficacy for students with autism spectrum disorder (ASD) and developmental disabilities. What do effective inclusive practices look like? How can teachers develop a supportive classroom environment?

Support for Inclusive Practices

During the latter part of the 20th century, a number of approaches to serving students with ASD and developmental disabilities took hold in schools in the United States. One practice that evolved over time is *inclusive education*. Inclusive education has a philosophical, legal, and research base of support.

Philosophically, inclusive education has its roots in the normalization principle (Nirje, 1969) but came to the forefront when it became based on the principle of equality (Villa & Thousand, 2005). The *Brown v. Board of Education* (1954) case ruling confirmed civil rights for students. Many researchers took the *Brown* case principle of "separate but not equal" and applied it to students with disabilities educated in segregated environments; Zionts (2005) stated "the only way for students with disabilities to receive an equal education is to have them taught with general education students" (p. 4).

Legal mandates for students with disabilities (i.e., Individuals With Disabilities Education Act, IDEA, 2006; No Child Left Behind Act of 2001, 2006) to interact with students without disabilities and to have access to the general education curriculum have helped to support and increase inclusive education for all students. As well, research over the past decade supports inclusive education by providing evidence of the benefits of inclusive practices for students with and without disabilities. Downing and Peckham-Hardin

(2007) documented numerous studies demonstrating the importance and positive attributes of inclusive education for students with severe disabilities. Other studies also have confirmed that positive effects result when students with disabilities are included in the general education classrooms—not only for the students with disabilities but also for students without disabilities, their teachers, and their administrators (Falvey, 2004, Fisher & Meyer, 2002; Foreman, Arthur-Kelly, Pascoe, & Smyth King, 2004; Hunt, Hirose-Hatae, Doering, Karasoff, & Goetz, 2000; Idol, 2006; Katz, Mirenda, & Auerbach, 2002; Villa, 2005).

Benefits of Inclusive Practices

Through inclusive practices, students with and without disabilities can learn and practice various social skills together, within the "natural" setting of the general education classroom. Students with disabilities can learn and/or practice functionally relevant skills such as greeting others, sharing in tasks, working with others, and developing friendships with their peers (Carter & Kennedy, 2006). Cooper, Griffith, and Filer (1999) noted that students with developmental disabilities and autism have difficulty in developing friendships and social skills which they need to learn and generalize, and these skills are best taught in the general education setting. Gordon, Feldman, and Chiriboga (2005) agreed that these skills needed to be taught in the natural school environment.

Social skills can be learned both directly (e.g., teacher-mediated instruction, direct instruction, peer-mediated instruction) and indirectly (e.g., incidental learning, peer modeling). The general education classroom as a natural setting provides many opportunities for students to interact with each other and to develop the skills and relationships that are important in other settings inside and outside of the school, and which can be used currently as well as in the future (e.g., community, home, work environments). When students with and without disabilities are in close proximity, there are more opportunities for developing and maintaining friendships (Chadsey & Han, 2005). Exposure to typical peers appears to have significant effects on friendship behaviors of students with disabilities (Bauminger et al., 2008). Students with disabilities who are educated in inclusive classrooms as opposed to self-contained classrooms or resource rooms spend more time with peers without disabilities. As a consequence, they have more opportunities for peer interactions than students who are educated in partially or fully segregated environments. These social interactions can help to facilitate the development of social skills and relationships that can lead to friendships (Carter & Kennedy, 2006; Gordon et al., 2005).

CHAPTER
2

Hendrickson, Shokoohi-Yekta, Hame-Nietupski, and Gable (1996) surveyed middle and high school students about friendships with their peers with severe disabilities. The results of their study showed that students with severe disabilities included in general education classes were more likely to develop friendships with their peers without disabilities. Chadsey and Han found similar results (2005) in their interviews with 33 middle school students who felt that students with disabilities should be included in general education classrooms more often and should be provided the extra help they need in inclusive environments.

The middle school students in the Chadsey and Han (2005) study also provided suggestions to teachers to help facilitate the inclusion and friendships of students with disabilities with their inclusive education classmates:

- Place students in the general education classes but provide the extra help they need.

- Inform students without disabilities about students with disabilities (e.g., specific similar and different characteristics).

- Make sure that students do not make fun or tease students with disabilities.

- Provide classroom opportunities where students can interact and socialize informally.

- Establish volunteer programs such as peer partners or buddy systems.

- Group a student with disabilities with an established "group of friends" (i.e., a social network) instead of pairing students.

- Have students with disabilities share information about themselves and their disabilities.

- Include students with disabilities in extracurricular activities and encourage their participation.

- Allow students with disabilities to take the same bus as students without disabilities. (Chadsey and Han, 2005)

Although inclusive education has shown to be successful for students with ASD and developmental disabilities, it is also has been documented that placing students with disabilities in inclusive classrooms without support does not benefit them academically or socially (Hyatt & Filler, 2007; Meadan & Monda-Amaya, 2008). There are many different types of support that help students to be successfully included in general education classroom environments with their age-appropriate peers (Burstein, Sears, Wilcoxen, Cabello, & Spagna, 2004; Crawford & Porter, 2004; Giangreco, 1997; Kugelmass, 2006; National Center on Educational Restructuring and Inclusion, 1994; Perner, 2008; Perner & Porter, 2008; Sailor & Roger, 2005; United Nations Educational, Scientific, and Cultural Organization, 2004; Walther-Thomas, Korinek, McLaughlin, & Williams, 2000; Working Forum on Inclusive Schools, 1994). Although many strategies are effective in creating inclusive classrooms, there are also specific methods that have a positive influence in developing social skills, interactions and relationships, and in creating friendships. Some of these methods are teacher-directed or facilitated, whereas others are peer-directed or supported.

For inclusive education to be successful, however, teachers need to create supportive classroom environments that reflect acceptance of all students and provide opportunities for appropriate social interactions and the development of social competency. Successful inclusive classrooms do not happen without teacher thought and input in creating an environment where there is a sense of belonging by all students (Downing & Eichinger, 2003) and an atmosphere that supports a diversity of learners.

Some key elements that teachers can use to support students include creating a positive classroom atmosphere (e.g., teacher-student relationships, classroom management, student-student relationships), varying classroom arrangements (e.g., use of space, design of activities such as groupings and centers), and engaging and supportive activities (e.g., choice-making, cooperative learning activities). There are a number of strategies and choices in how these factors can be used, enhanced, or modified to support and engage students in learning.

Positive Classroom Atmosphere—A Sense of Community

Within any classroom both teachers and students should have a sense of comfort and belonging. This feeling, often referred to as having a *sense of community*, should be part of every student's and teacher's school life. Some of the essential features of a classroom that exhibits a sense of community are respecting others and diversity (including cultural, gender, linguistic, sexual orientation, and ability differences), helping and working cooperatively with others, having high expectations for students, and maintaining a positive climate (e.g., sharing positive feedback).

Respecting Others and Diversity

A major component of having a sense of community is teachers and students respecting each other. In schools where there is a sense of community teachers and students learn about themselves and each other—they share their different backgrounds and cultural practices. They understand individual differences and respect them, whether based on culture, abilities, ethnicity, linguistics, gender, or one's own being. To learn about others, one needs to know oneself; teachers' and students' individual background, experience, and cultural patterns can impact their acceptance of diversity. It is helpful to recognize one's own characteristics such as customs, mores, values, and abilities in order to learn about and understand the customs, mores, values, and abilities of others. One successful way to help students recognize their own characteristics, as a basis for understanding others, is to have students learn firsthand from each other. Sharing and learning about their own and other students' cultural and other background characteristics gives students a better understanding of diversity and its relationship to them. With this exposure and knowledge students should feel more comfortable about characteristics that are different than their own.

Each student has a uniquely defined cultural makeup; that is, individual characteristics distinct and different from all other human beings. Understanding and using this background information can help students feel comfortable and be socially accepted, which leads to a sense of belonging within the classroom and school community.

Helping and Working Cooperatively With Others

Having a *sense of community* means a classroom and school where everyone helps each other and works together for the benefit of the students, the classroom, and the school. It is more than using cooperative learning activities or partnering or grouping students for instruction within the school day; it is a way of accepting and encouraging students and teachers to work together to achieve common goals: It is based on learning cooperatively, not competitively, and thus reinforcing students for being cooperative. It also may require students to learn how to work together. Some ways to facilitate cooperation in the classroom are:

- Brainstorm with students about cooperative classroom expectations (rules).

- Reinforce students for behaviors that conform to these expectations.

Social Skills for Students With Autism Spectrum Disorders

- Reinforce students for helping each other and working together in a cooperative manner.

- Establish instructional tasks that encourage and reinforce students for working together.

- Teach students strategies that will help them to work together (e.g., sharing, asking for help, contributing to discussions, apologizing, giving a compliment, problem solving).

Having High Expectations for Students

To have a sense of community means that teachers and students regard each other as equal members of the classroom and school. Teachers model this and encourage other staff and students to do so as well. Having high expectations for students does not mean that teachers have the same expectations for all students: it means that each student's learning goals are appropriate for that particular student. Students should be involved in setting their goals and, consequently, in setting high expectations for themselves. The more teachers know about their students, the better they can help students set realistic but high expectations.

Maintaining a Positive Climate

Having a sense of community means that the climate within the school and class must be positive and supportive of students and teachers. There are many strategies that can help to foster a positive learning environment for students (see Table 2-1).

The classroom environment and its arrangement (physical and participant make-up) can contribute to a sense of community. Classroom arrangements should provide for inclusiveness (i.e., including all students within the classroom arrangement, not isolating individuals or a group of students), for comfort (e.g., seating, noise level, physical space), and for a sense of order (e.g., material storage, student work folders). Ideally, classroom arrangements are flexible and can be modified easily. Some teaching and learning activities are designed for various settings within the classroom. When making modifications, it's essential to consider the learning environment arrangement. These arrangements should permit a variety of instructional grouping approaches.

26   Council for Exceptional Children

Teaching/Learning Groups

Whole-Class or Large-Group Instruction

Whole-class instruction is the grouping pattern teachers most commonly use. When students are grouped as one and taught together, all students feel included as a part of the group. Also, there are times where whole-class instruction and grouping can serve an important instructional purpose (Vaughn, Bos, & Schumm, 2007, p. 224; see box, "Benefits of Whole-Class Instruction").

Whole-class instruction should be used carefully within the teaching and learning context. Because of the diversity of students within a class, students can, for various reasons, get "lost" in this type of instructional setting. Some students may only be physically (not instructionally) included within the whole group. Teachers need to be aware of this and adjust both instruction and teacher and student interactions to ensure inclusion of all students.

Table 2-1. Fostering a Positive Learning Environment

Have clear expectations	Classroom and school rules and routines/procedures are written in a positive manner
Provide incentives	Encourage positive behaviors
Communicate individually with students	Learn about students' interests and preferences; identify student abilities and strengths, and focus on them
Reinforce students	Provide reinforcement and positive feedback for students' individual and group work
Positive discipline	Use positive approaches (e.g., token-economy systems) and approaches to develop student self-discipline
Show respect	Students feel trusted and respected in the classroom
Model behaviors	Teach and model positive social skills such as sharing, taking turns, and listening; offer supportive responses to student ideas; communicate positively
Promote diversity	Provide opportunities for mixed-ability grouping

Small-Group Instruction

The number of students that can be instructed within a small group varies. A small group generally consists of three or more students and can be directed or facilitated by the teacher, an instructional aide, a student, or the group itself. Small-group instruction allows students a variety of opportunities to develop social and communication skills and friendships. Teachers can divide students into small groups based on ability/skill (i.e., mixed-ability/skill or same-ability/skill), interests, content, methods for presenting new material (e.g., reading a book, viewing a film, listening to a recorded book), activities used for practice (e.g., centers, study groups, partners), and/or products used for evaluation (posters, presentations, group response sheets). Any grouping arrangement must not become permanent or extend to other skills and/or skill areas. Mixed-ability/skill groupings are commonly used to help students be accepted and part of the class community.

Benefits of Whole-Class Instruction

✓ Builds classroom community

✓ Helps to establish classroom routines

✓ Permits easy introduction of new units of study

✓ Students jointly explore new skills and concepts

✓ Enables whole-class discussions

✓ Develops common experiences

✓ Provides opportunities for guest speakers, viewing educational videos

---

Paired Groups

Students also can be paired with other students for instruction. Pairing or partnering students consists of assigning two students to work together as a group. Like small groups, paired groups can be based on a variety of factors (e.g., ability, skill, interests). Teachers often use paired groups for peer (i.e., same-age or grade classmates/schoolmates) and cross-age (different age classmates or schoolmates) tutoring (see Chapter 3). In these cases, one student may be assigned the role of instructor based on ability, skill development, and/or experience. Paired groups offer students a variety of opportunities to enhance social and communication skills and friendships. As with other types of grouping it can help to provide a student with direct instruction and build self-esteem. Peer-mediated strategies are described in detail in Chapter 3.

Flexible Grouping

There are a number of strategies for grouping students for instruction, learning activities, and working on projects or products. Different types of grouping can serve the diverse needs and interests of students. *Flexible grouping* allows students to flow in and out of groups, to work in more than one group at a time, and to have some choices in selecting their group membership and roles and tasks within the group. All types of flexible grouping can be used to promote social skills, peer interactions, and peer relationships. To use flexible grouping effectively teachers must carefully select the types of grouping that best meet the individual needs of a diverse group of students including students with disabilities.

Interest groups consist of paired or small groups of students who share a similar interest in a topic, an area of study, or learning a specific skill. (Student interests can be determined through various informal assessments such as surveys and interviews.) Having students work together in sharing these interests, learning more about them, and/or using them to learn other concepts and skills can be highly motivational for students. Because friendships often are based upon sharing common interests, matching students with similar interests can help facilitate friendships. It also can encourage students with different abilities and skill levels to better appreciate each other.

Mixed-ability/skill groups comprise students of various levels of ability and/or skill acquisition. Usually these groups are formed for a specific purpose such as working on a project or a presentation, learning a new skill or practicing one recently learned, discussing an assignment, or solving a problem. In a mixed-ability group, students are assigned a single group task, but different objectives and subtasks may be targeted for individual students within the group. There are numerous advantages for mixed-ability/skill groups (see box, "Benefits of Mixed-Ability/Skill Grouping").

Benefits of Mixed-Ability/Skill Grouping

✓ Improves social, behavioral, and academic skills

✓ All students are included—part of the group

✓ Students are role models for each other

✓ Students receive assistance and instruction from other students—and provide assistance and instruction to others

✓ Everyone contributes based on individual needs and abilities.

✓ Students learn cooperative skills

Cluster grouping combines some of the students within a class into a small instructional group based on one or more common characteristic (e.g., age, ability, interest, learning style). Usually cluster groups are not short-term; students stay within the same cluster for a specific instructional reason or to reach a specific educational goal (e.g., community service project, research project) or form in the same cluster for other subject areas throughout the day and/or during the year.

Cooperative learning groups enable students to work together to maximize their own learning as well as the learning of the other members in their group. Students work together on achieving a shared goal. As discussed in detail in Chapter 3, there are many different types of cooperative learning activities and groupings (Johnson & Johnson, 1994, Kagan, 1994; Slavin, 1995).

Adult Supports

Teachers and other adults such as paraprofessionals can be instrumental in facilitating communicative interactions and social skill development in students with autism and developmental disabilities. Although students with disabilities have developed or enhanced their social skills gains when supported by programs that focused on adults facilitating, directing, modeling, and/or rewarding students (Causton-Theoharis & Malmgren, 2005; Milsom, 2006; Vaughn et al., 2003), continuous direct contact with adults can greatly reduce or hinder social learning opportunities for students with disabilities (Batchelor & Taylor, 2005; Carter & Kennedy, 2006; Causton-Theoharis & Malmgren, 2005). An overreliance on adults can be a barrier for social interactions between students with disabilities and their peers without disabilities (Carter, Cushing, Clark & Kennedy, 2005; Causton-Theoharis & Malmgren, 2005; Downing; 2006; Harper & McCluskey, 2003; Hodge, Yahiku, Murata, & Von Vange, 2003; Vaughn et al., 2003). Giangreco and Broer (2005) found that schools rely too much on paraprofessional support of students with disabilities when endeavoring to provide inclusive opportunities; employing paraprofessionals to support students one-on-one can interfere with social interactions and also create a negative stigma for the students with disabilities (Downing, 2006). Causton-Theoharis and Malmgren (2005) trained four paraprofessionals to facilitate interactions between students with severe disabilities and their peers. Based on the positive results of their study, they recommended that paraprofessionals be trained to facilitate peer interactions with students with disabilities; otherwise, paraprofessionals may "unwittingly isolate and segregate the students whom they support" (Causton-Theoharis & Malmgren, 2005, p. 442). Downing (2006) and Carter and Kennedy (2006) advised that supports to increase social interactions and communication of students with disabilities within the general education classroom could be provided more naturally by peers.

Table 2-2. Sample General Education Matrix for IEP Social Skills Goal

IEP Goals	Language Arts	Recess	Math	Lunch	Social Studies	PE	Art	Science
1. Asks teacher for help.	X	X	X	X	X	X	X	X
2. Initiates interactions with peers.	X	X	X	X	X	X	X	X
3. Follows written directions.	X		X		X			X
4. Participates in group activities.	X	X		X	X	X		
5. Shares materials with a peer.	X		X		X		X	X

Note. IEP = individualized education program.

Supporting Individualized Education Programs (IEPs)

Students who qualify for special education services and supports under IDEA require an individualized education program (IEP), which provides a framework for planning and implementing programs for students with disabilities. The IEP includes selected goals and objectives related to students' current academic, behavior, and social performance and needs. The IEP provides an overall picture of students' strengths, needs, and goals; it does not specify when (day or time), what period (e.g., subject, area, classroom activity, daily routine), where (environment), or by whom (specific individual) the IEP goals or objectives will be addressed. Using a matrix (see Table 2-2) can help the IEP team determine when and where goals or objectives might be addressed formally or incidentally within the general education classroom (see Giangreco, Cloninger, & Iverson, 1998). It also can help to define how learning objectives or goals might be addressed within the student's daily/weekly schedule; identify instructional modifications and supports to assist the student in reaching IEP goals/objectives; and provide a visual representation of the student's schedule and who may be supporting the student (e.g., teacher, paraprofessional, peer). The IEP matrix is an at-a-glance document that can be coded to show the types of instructional adaptations including materials, resources, and personal supports such as teacher, peers, and paraprofessionals for each goal/objective. (Table 2-2 provides a social skills example; see California Department of Education, 2005, for additional examples.)

Summary

Considerable evidence demonstrates that students with ASD and other developmental disabilities benefit from inclusive environments when given effective support in general education classrooms and other natural environments. The supports provided to students with disabilities include creating positive classroom cultures, adult guidance, and peer supports. The following chapter provides additional information on strategies that support students while being served inclusive settings.

Chapter 3
Engaging Students in Learning Activities and Teaching Social Behaviors

Engaging Students in Learning Activities

There are a variety of ways teachers engage students in learning and social activities. Because of the diversity of students in inclusive general education classrooms, teachers need to respond to different levels of ability. Within any one lesson a teacher may need to use varying questions, simplify some of the materials, include higher order thinking skills within the group activity, and/or break the task down into more manageable parts. Differentiated teaching strategies such as tiered or multilevel instruction can help teachers include students with autism spectrum disorder (ASD) and developmental disabilities. Teachers also can engage these students in learning by incorporating student interests, using student-selected outcomes, offering choices in learning activities, and pairing or grouping students for cooperative activities.

Specific strategies that have been identified in the literature to support students are teacher and peer-mediated procedures (Hyatt & Filler, 2007) and structured social environments (e.g., instructing a small group of students in social skills; Thiemann & Goldstein, 2004). To create supportive environments and increase the social interactions and skills of students with ASD and developmental disabilities, teachers often use a variety of these methods in their inclusive classrooms (Carter & Kennedy, 2006; Gordon et al., 2005; McDonnell, Mathot-Buckner, Thorson, & Fister, 2001; Thiemann & Goldstein, 2004).

Teacher-Facilitated and Teacher-Mediated Strategies

Teachers can create environments that facilitate positive social interactions and help to develop social skills and friendships using a variety of methods (see box, "Teaching Methods That Help Students Build Social Skills"). In their review of the literature on interventions that facilitate social acceptance and interactions between young children with disabilities and their peers, Batchelor and Taylor (2005) identified and described six types of social interventions:

1. **Child-specific interventions** (i.e., social skills are taught based on specific student needs).

2. **Affective interventions** geared toward peers without disabilities to inform them about children with disabilities (via stories, discussions, puppets, etc.).

3. **Friendship activity interventions** (i.e., songs and games that contain positive social interactions with peers).

4. **Incidental teaching of social skills** during play activities; teachers and peers model appropriate skills.

5. **Social integration activity interventions** (i.e., a socially adapt peer helps promote and maintain appropriate play activities with the student with disabilities).

6. **Peer-mediated interventions** where peers are trained to promote social interactions with students without disabilities and to respond appropriately to their initiations. (Batchelor & Taylor, 2005, p. 11)

Peer-Mediated Instruction and Interventions

There are many different types of peer-mediated instruction and interventions that have been used successfully with students with ASD. Peer-mediated instruction and interventions include peer tutoring, peer buddy systems, peer networks, and group-oriented contingencies (see Utley, Mortweet, & Greenwood, 1997, for detailed descriptions).

For all of the approaches discussed in this chapter, *peer selection* is an important component to assure success for students with disabilities. Odom and Strain (1986) recommended selecting only socially competent peers, similar in age, with age-appropriate skills, and able to follow instructions. Many of these interventions require training peer participants (i.e., describing their roles, practicing, and reinforcing them for interacting with the students with disabilities). Owen-DeSchryver, Carr, Cale, and Blakely-Smith (2008) used a procedure where students listened to a story about a boy with autism or participated in a peer social network group to facilitate their interaction with students with autism. Students also participated in a discussion about the strengths of the students with autism, and learned to use guiding questions (see box, "Questions to Guide Peer Interactions").

The premise of *peer modeling* is that students can learn behaviors from observing and then imitating another student. Peer modeling is often used in combination with other methods (e.g., peer tutoring) and during cooperative learning activities. Peer modeling also can be implemented by having the student with disabilities view a video of a peer demonstrating an appropriate behavior such as taking one's turn or sharing.

Peer initiation training has been used extensively by teachers and requires teacher involvement. This strategy involves training a peer to promote and maintain specific social and communicative interactions from a student with disabilities. The approach usually involves separate training of peers so that they learn how to promote and reinforce appropriate responses from the students they are training.

> ### Teaching Methods That Help Students Build Social Skills
>
> ✓ Providing time for students to interact socially
>
> ✓ Encouraging and reinforcing cooperative behaviors
>
> ✓ Less structured teaching activities
>
> ✓ Modifying instruction
>
> ✓ Cooperative learning activities/centers
>
> ✓ Flexible grouping
>
> ✓ Modeling and allowing students to rehearse appropriate social skills and behaviors
>
> ✓ Employing peer support interventions

Peer monitoring has been used to help students complete specific goals or tasks. A peer monitor is assigned to a student or group of students to check the performance of a task(s) assigned. The peer monitor may be responsible for a number of activities (e.g., reinforcement, modeling correct behavior, providing corrective feedback).

Peer network interventions promote supportive social environments for students and can help students increase social-communicative behaviors and develop language (Utley et al., 1997). The goals of this intervention for students with disabilities are to increase the frequency and quality of social interactions with socially competent peers and to create a supportive network of friends. The intent is to enhance peers' understanding of and involvement with students with disabilities, to promote interaction (DiSalvo & Oswald, 2002; Forest & Lusthaus, 1988). Chadsey and Han (2005) described the facilitation of peer networks among typical middle school students; they suggested that teachers assign students with disabilities to groups with socially accepted peers and to use this strategy instead of pairing students.

Questions to Guide Peer Interactions

✓ When can I play with [focus student]?

✓ What can we talk about?

✓ What can we do together?

✓ How can I help the student with ASD play?

✓ What can I do if [focus student] does not respond?

Circles of Friends (Forrest, Pearpoint, & O'Brien, 1996; Newton, Taylor, & Wilson, 1996) is a popular adult-facilitated peer support network strategy teachers use to help include students with ASD and severe disabilities in the general education classroom. When established, the Circles of Friends network can help to facilitate the development of friendships and social skills (Frederickson & Turner, 2003).

The process begins with a teacher or other adult providing some information about the student with disabilities. The teacher explains why she wants to create a Circle of Friends (e.g., to include a student in their general education classroom, to help a student develop friendships with his/her classmates, to participate more in classroom activities and extracurricular activities). The students then complete a blank handout with four concentric circles which illustrate the Circle of Friends concept (see Figure 3-1). It often helps students to discuss, after completing each circle, the similarities and differences among their responses; the teacher may want to also provide a hypothetical example of someone who may not have many individuals listed in Circles 2 and 3 (e.g., "How would you feel if your circle was empty?"). In facilitating discussion, the teacher also might also note when the focus student's circle is similar to another student's.

The teacher then asks students what they might do to make their focus student welcome in the class and included in activities in the classroom, school, and community, and to volunteer if they want to be part of the focus student's peer network/Circle of Friends and support the student in becoming involved in and part of the classroom community. This is different from asking who will be the focus student's *friend*, as friendships need to be developed over time. Initially the Circle of Friends' focus will be on helping the student participate with his or her peers in classroom, school, and community activities. With time, support from peers, and a nurturing teacher, friendships can develop. The teacher and students can brainstorm some ways they can help the focus student participate with the whole group and with selected peers within the Circle of Friends.

It is important that the Circle of Friends meet each week to discuss their and the focus student's involvement with the support network and its goals, sharing both positive outcomes and concerns. Students should be able to acknowledge and celebrate

Figure 3-1

Sample Circles of Friends Handout

Fill in the circles:

In Circle 1 put the names of the people closest to you (mom, dad, sister, brother, etc.).

In Circle 2 put the names of people you really like and are close to (good friends, relatives, neighbors).

In Circle 3 put the names of people you like but you are not as close to as in Circles 1 and 2 (club friends, a relative you might see once a year).

In Circle 4 put the names of people you pay to be in your life (doctor, teacher, dentist, etc.).

Who is in your Circles of Friends?

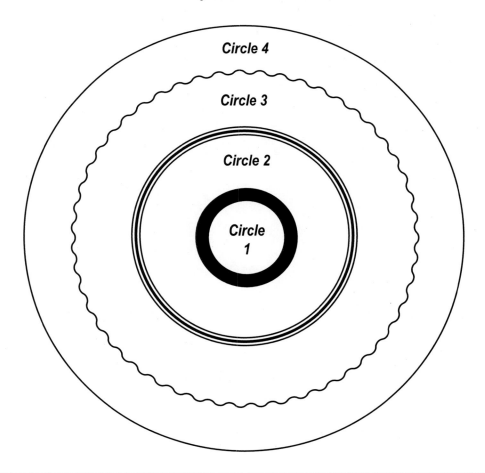

Circle 4

Circle 3

Circle 2

Circle 1

accomplishments and also to problem-solve specific issues that arise. The teacher should facilitate and structure these sessions as necessary. Circles of Friends (Forrest et al., 1996; Newton et al., 1996) is an informal and flexible concept. Students are welcome to join or leave, but the focus student must always be part of the circle.

Although Circles of Friends (Forrest et al., 1996; Newton et al., 1996) has had some success in promoting acceptance (Eddas, 2002; Frederickson & Turner, 2003), a major concern relates to the issue of reciprocity. The focus student (often a student with ASD) is the recipient of help and support (Frederickson & Turner, 2003); status as the "focus student" within the circle does not appear to change. Therefore, when using peer support networks or any other type of peer-mediated instruction and interventions, it is important that teachers facilitate the equality of status for all students by providing opportunities for reciprocal activities within the classroom.

Peer buddy programs can help promote the inclusion of students within the general education classroom and school. These programs are often developed at the secondary level and students without disabilities may receive credit for their participation in this service-learning program. Although peer buddy programs vary, the main goal of is to have students without disabilities provide instructional and social support to students with disabilities. According to Hughes and Carter (2008), "Peer buddies 1) act as liaisons to the general education curriculum and environment, 2) lighten demands on teacher when accommodating students, and 3) provide instruction and social support to their peers with disabilities" (p. 18). Peer buddy programs also help students with disabilities form social relationships with their peers and extend their time in the general education classroom. Like other peer-mediated instruction and interventions or support programs, teachers need to plan and implement training for the peers who will be teaching and socializing with students with disabilities (see Hughes & Carter, 2008)

Peer Tutoring

There are many different definitions of *peer tutoring*; generally, peer tutoring involves one peer instructing another peer on academic, social, and/or personal skills. Many types of peer tutoring have been successfully employed with students with disabilities and their peers (e.g., same-age tutoring, cross-age tutoring, reciprocal peer tutoring, classwide peer tutoring, peer-assisted learning). Peer tutoring interventions have been successfully used during instruction with students with disabilities and their peers in both general education and special education classrooms; students with disabilities also can effectively tutor other students (see Utley et al., 1997, for a review of studies).

Peer tutoring in academic subjects can have positive effects on social skill development. Peer tutoring "promote[s] the incidental learning of social behaviors through natural interactions" (DiSalvo & Oswald, 2002, p. 200). Benefits to students with and without disabilities have been documented extensively (e.g., Bond & Castagnera , 2005; Carter et al., 2005; Heron, Villareal, Yao, Christianson, & Heron, 2006; Maheady, Harper, & Mallette, 2001; Miller, 2005; Utley et al., 1997). For example, students with disabilities have shown development in social skills and increased and enhanced social interactions with their peers (Thiemann & Goldstein, 2004; Utley et al., 1997). Students without disabilities can gain knowledge about and understanding of disabilities, learn to develop empathy towards others, and appreciate diversity (Milsom, 2006).

There are some disadvantages to peer tutoring. According to Maheady et al. (2001), peer tutoring programs can be a burden to teachers especially when starting up the program—although once initiated, peer tutoring can reduce teachers' workloads (Utley et al., 1997). Downing (2001) indicated that peers may need to be taught how to interact with students with disabilities.

Peer tutoring approaches usually require training the peer tutor to use a specific set of behaviors when instructing the focus student, and training can be intensive depending on the behaviors or skills being taught. Tutors need to know how to provide feedback to other students; provide verbal/tangible reinforcement and/or corrective feedback, teach and model specific skills; supervise or monitor independent/group activities and transitional periods; and support students with redirecting, modeling, cueing, or prompting. There are a number of ways to train tutors to help them be successful in this role.

Miller (2005) identified 10 specific steps for implementing successful peer tutoring programs:

1. Define the tutoring context.

2. Define the objectives.

3. Define the curriculum area.

4. Select and match participants.

5. Identify the tutoring technique and the student contact specifics.

6. Select the tutoring materials.

7. Train the tutor(s).

8. Monitor the tutoring process and assess student learning.

9. Evaluate the program.

10. Provide feedback. (Miller, 2005, p. 27)

Miller also offered a number of helpful suggestions and ideas for teachers to consider as they implement each of the steps, and there are a variety of other strategies to train tutors.

Utley et al. (1997) summarized Deterline's (1970) goals for tutoring as (a) putting the tutee at ease, (b) clarifying the prescribed task, (c) showing the tutee how to verify his or her answer, (d) directing the tutee to read each problem aloud, (e) having each tutee respond overtly before the tutor provides feedback, (f) having the tutee verify each response, (g) avoiding any form of punishment, (h) providing verbal praise when appropriate, (i) providing a tangible reward when appropriate, and (j) evaluating elements of mastery. Although these goals were specifically related to students' performance in math, the elements can be readily applied to the instruction of social and interpersonal skills.

Polloway, Patton, and Serna (2008) provided a systematic, seven-step procedure for teaching peers to be tutors:

1. Prepare the student to learn about tutoring.

2. Assist the student in learning the steps for tutoring in a specific subject area.

3. Demonstrate how to teach the skill and have the student practice it in a role-playing situation while giving corrective feedback.

4. Have student use self-monitoring as they role-play the lesson.

5. Assist the student if the student needs correction; continue to help until the student conducts the lesson correctly.

6. Have tutors begin their tutoring sessions.

7. Evaluate the performance of both the tutor and tutee to ensure the lesson was correctly performed and the tutee improved in skill level. (Polloway et al., 2008)

In *same-age tutoring,* peers of similar age or in the same grade tutor each other. There are a number of arrangements for same-age tutoring: a peer may be assigned as a tutor based on ability level, or because he or she has mastered a skill or has difficulty with learning a skill or behavior; another arrangement is where both peers are the tutor and tutee.

In *cross-age tutoring* usually the tutor is at least 2 years older and has mastered the skills and behaviors being taught. Cross-age tutors can be from the same school or from other schools. This arrangement has many advantages. Cross-age tutors have been effective in enhancing the quality of social interactions and in developing language skills by making accommodations for the students they are tutoring (Utley et al., 1997). The use of cross-age tutors with students with disabilities can be very effective in supporting students in inclusive classrooms (Bond & Castagnera, 2005). Bond and Castagnera (2005) noted that students with disabilities, who are most often in the position of being the tutee, should be provided with opportunities to tutor younger students. Utley et al. (1997) described this as *reverse-role tutoring*, where students with disabilities tutor younger students with and without disabilities. They documented the positive social aspects of this tutoring arrangement.

Classwide peer tutoring (CWPT) is conducted in a class where the teacher has paired students to work together. The teacher then assigns the pairs to two competing teams whose goal is to earn the highest team-point total for correct responses. CWPT is a *reciprocal teaching* approach: halfway through the peer tutoring session, tutor-tutee partners switch roles. Utley et al. (1997) described the main procedures in conducting classwide peer tutoring as

- Review and introduce new material to be learned/unit content materials to be tutored (e.g., reading passages, spelling word lists, or math fact lists).

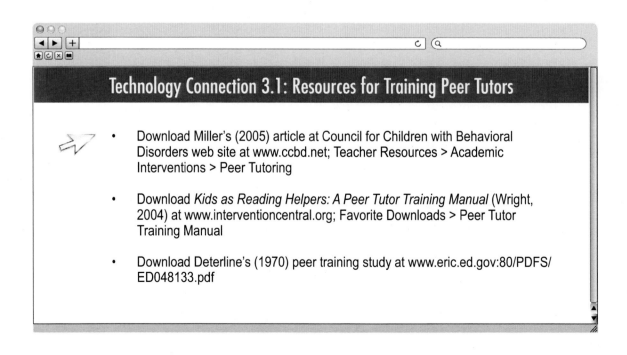

Technology Connection 3.1: Resources for Training Peer Tutors

- Download Miller's (2005) article at Council for Children with Behavioral Disorders web site at www.ccbd.net; Teacher Resources > Academic Interventions > Peer Tutoring

- Download *Kids as Reading Helpers: A Peer Tutor Training Manual* (Wright, 2004) at www.interventioncentral.org; Favorite Downloads > Peer Tutor Training Manual

- Download Deterline's (1970) peer training study at www.eric.ed.gov:80/PDFS/ED048133.pdf

- Assign new partners each week.

- Use partner-pairing strategies.

- Ensure reciprocal roles in each session.

- Tutors provide immediate error correction.

- Publicly post individual and team scores.

- Provide a social reward for the winning team.

CWPT sessions are highly structured and the teacher needs to ensure that students are staying on task, correctly implementing procedures, and focusing on instructional content (Polloway et al., 2008).

Although similar to CWPT, *peer-assisted learning strategies* (PALS; Fuchs, Fuchs, Mathes, & Simmons, 1997) use a different approach and can be linked to computerized curriculum-based measures (Utley et al., 1997). PALS has been validated through a number of studies and the results of these studies have confirmed the effectiveness of the program (Rohrbeck, Ginsburg-Block, Fantuzzo, & Miller, 2003). PALS is a highly structured program where students learn the content presented while working in pairs. Students are matched on the basis of one student of higher ability and another student of lower ability. Student pairs, however, share in the roles assigned (e.g., coach and reader). Besides its documented academic success, Fuchs, Fuchs, Mathes, and Martinez (2002) reported that PALS also increased the social acceptance of students with learning disabilities.

Cooperative Learning

Cooperative learning is another method for helping students develop social skills and be included in the general education classroom. In cooperative learning, students work together in groups to achieve a common goal (e.g., complete a task, solve a problem). The principal developers of cooperative learning are Roger Johnson and David Johnson, Spencer Kagan, and Robert Slavin, although each one used somewhat different methods (Metzke & Berghoff, 1999).

Cooperative learning involves a number of elements: positive interdependence, individual accountability, cooperative skills, face-to-face interaction, and student reflection goal setting (Putnam, 1998). *Positive interdependence* is achieved when all members can accomplish the group goal (e.g., all students agree on an answer and can show how it was solved). *Individual accountability* occurs when each member is responsible for what should be learned and contributes to the achievement of the group goal. *Cooperative skills* are skills that help students work together and support each other in achieving the group goal. Teachers assist students in learning specific cooperative skills (e.g., listening, sharing materials, encouraging each other) and explaining why these skills are important for students in reaching the shared goal (United Nations Educational, Scientific, and Cultural Organization, 2004). *Face-to-face interaction* occurs when students are allowed to directly interact with each other. *Student reflection and goal setting* relates to students evaluating their performance individually and as a group to help improve cooperative behaviors and academic skills. During this evaluation process students not only evaluate how well they worked together as a group but also identify what they can do to improve in their group functioning (Polloway et al., 2008). There is a variety of different cooperative learning activities that can be used to facilitate social skill development, increase social interactions, and help create peer support networks (Johnson, Johnson, & Holubec, 1998, 2002; Kagan, 1994; Slavin, 1995; see Table 3-1).

Strategies for Teaching Social Behaviors

Social skills and other social behaviors typically require interaction between the members of the group or dyad. Thus, most social skills instruction is conducted in group environments where the members learn to interact with each other in ways that are deemed

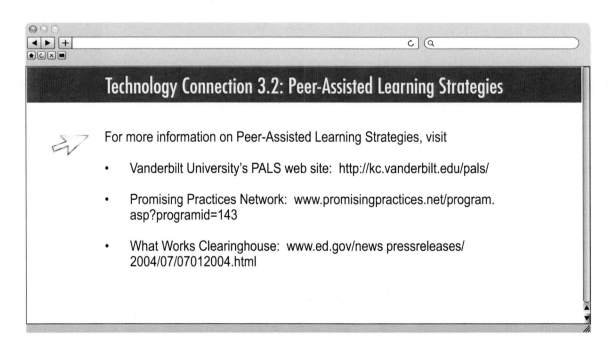

Technology Connection 3.2: Peer-Assisted Learning Strategies

For more information on Peer-Assisted Learning Strategies, visit

- Vanderbilt University's PALS web site: http://kc.vanderbilt.edu/pals/

- Promising Practices Network: www.promisingpractices.net/program. asp?programid=143

- What Works Clearinghouse: www.ed.gov/news pressreleases/ 2004/07/07012004.html

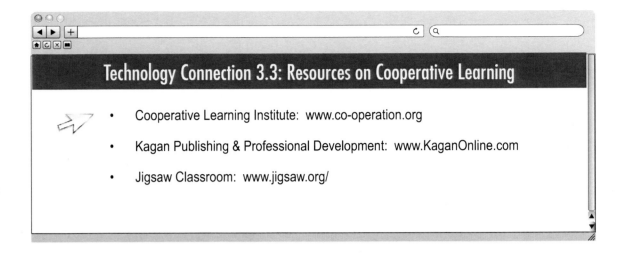

appropriate by others in their milieu. However, not all social behaviors are amenable to change through group instructional processes. Often, educators find it necessary to use more individualized approaches to increase social competence for some students and for unique problems.

Four types of research support individualized approaches to improving social skills. *Social stories* have a substantial body of research supporting their utility for children with autism spectrum disorders (ASD; Adams et al., 2004; Graetz, et al., 2009; Reynhout & Carter, 2006; Scattone, Wilczynski, Edwards, & Rabian, 2004); evidence also exists demonstrating that this technique is effective for students with other developmental disabilities. Derivations of the social stories strategy include *comic strip conversations* and *power cards*. In addition, *video modeling* has proven effective for helping students with ASD learn social skills, perhaps because they are visual thinkers/learners. In addition to research-validated instructional strategies, practitioners report a variety of approaches to teaching social skills and support development of social networks for students with ASD and developmental disabilities. Some of this anecdotal evidence will also be shared in this chapter.

Social Stories

A social story is a script that describes to a student the relevant social cues and common responses in a specific situation. It explains what happens and why the situation occurs. A social story is designed to prepare a student for an uncertain event; to share information; or to provide a strategy to deal with an event effectively, with a thought-out plan and guide. It translates a goal into understandable steps.

Table 3-1. Cooperative Learning Strategies

Jigsaw	Each person in a small group is assigned a particular task (e.g., reading a specific section of a selection, solving a problem). Each member of the group teaches the material assigned and quizzes the other group members to ensure that the group has learned this material. A variation of this activity is that students who are working on the same task across the class meet to work together in completing the task and deciding how to teach it when they return to their original groups.
Team-pair-solo	Students in a small group solve a problem (e.g., a word problem) together in their group, then solve the problem with a partner, and then on their own.
Turn-to-your-neighbor	Students discuss the lesson, a concept just presented, or an answer to a teacher- or student-posed question (e.g., "Name three other animals that are domesticated.").
Focus partners or trio	Students in pairs or a group summarize what they know before a lesson or activity. After the lesson or activity, they compile together new information that was learned (e.g., K-W-L sheet to enter What I Know, What I Want to Know, What I've Learned).
Roundtable	The teacher passes out one paper and pencil per group and describes the task (e.g., "name all the materials in your home and at school that you can recycle," completing a multiplication worksheet). Students take turns adding information on the sheet, until the teacher asks them to share.
Numbered heads together	Each student in a small group numbers off from 1–4. The teacher then asks a question for the group to answer (e.g., test review). The students have time to discuss the answer so that everyone in the group can give a response. After discussion, the teacher calls one number from 1–4, and those students respond to the question.
Think-pair-share	The teacher asks a question of student partners (e.g., "Why do we recycle?"). Each student thinks of a response and then pairs to discuss their answers. Partners team with another pair and continue discussing.

CHAPTER
3

Social stories (Gray & Garand, 1993) are typically used with higher functioning students with ASD and other developmental disabilities (see Adders, 2006) who have some reading skills, although limited reading ability does not rule out using social stories. Creative users can also incorporate comic strip drawings, pictures, picture prompts, and coaching processes to bring about behavior change.

Social stories are prepared for individual students and relate to specific issues presented by the student's behavior. Teachers or instructional teams must prepare the social story in ways that address the characteristics of particular students. The examples provided in this chapter are intended to serve as examples of the process and not for use with individual children unless their characteristics are very similar to those depicted in the model stories.

The social story should be based on the student's specific needs relating to a particular concern (see Table 3-2). Social stories can help individuals learn social skills, adapt to transitions and changes in daily routines, participate in social interactions, complete academic tasks, and understand how to respond to situations that may cause anxiety or confusion. To implement the social story strategy,

1. Identify a behavior the student needs to acquire to increase positive social interaction and break it down into sequential steps.

2. Define the target behavior concisely.

3. Collect data about the target behavior before, during, and after using the social story as an intervention.

4. Help the individual to generalize the story across situations, through different activities and experiences.

5. Gradually fade use of the social story.

Social stories comprise four different types of sentences:

1. *Descriptive sentences* describe where a situation occurs, who is involved, what the individuals are doing, and why. They are used to describe a social setting or to provide sequential steps for completing an activity.

2. *Perspective sentences* describe how others feel and react within a given situation. They are designed to reflect others' perspectives.

3. *Directive sentences* describe the responses and actions the person should make in a given situation. The desired behavior is defined in positive terms. The sentences often begin with "I can try to...", "I will work on...", or "I will try...."

4. *Control sentences* describe strategies the individual will use to help him/her remember the social story's information.

Subsequent researchers have added strategies to the use of social stories. For example, Kuoch and Mirenda (2003) added affirmative sentences to their social story interventions.

Comic Strip and Picture Conversations

Children and youth with ASD tend to be visual learners; comic strip conversations respond to this characteristic while also providing direction on improving social skills (see Figure 3-2). These conversations are a variation on social stories, but are centered around pictures rather than text; the comic strip is used to review a situation and discuss alternatives to student behavior. The teacher creates comic strip drawings or uses photographs to depict the social behaviors that are a problem and consequences and has a conversation with the student. Gradually, the role of drawing comic/picture strips is shifted to the student. Although this strategy was originally created for use with students with ASD, it also has demonstrated use with students with learning disabilities, mild intellectual disabilities, and behavioral disorders (Glaeser, Pierson, & Fristschman, 2003; Pierson & Glaeser, 2005). See Figure 3-2 for examples used to support lesson plans in elementary and secondary school.

Technology Connection 3.4: The Gray Center

- Carol Gray developed both social stories and comic strip conversations. The Gray Center: www.thegraycenter.org/social-stories is a resource for information on social stories and the Social Response Pyramid, an educational tool for teaching social understanding.

Table 3-2. Implementing Social Stories

Background	The Social Story
Tyler is a 10-year-old boy with ASD. He has reading skills that are functional for using of a written social story. His special education teacher has decided to focus on increasing his greeting peers and adults in the general school setting. He is able to perform this behavior, but only does so when prompted.	The boys and girls at Lincoln Elementary like to be friendly and say "hi" to each other. They would like to be friends with Tyler. Patricia looks at people in the eye and says "hi" when she sees them. Mark does that too. Tyler will be a friendly Lincoln student too when he looks other students in the eye, smiles, and says "hi." The other children feel good when Tyler looks them in the eye, smiles, and says "hi." They will say "hi" back to Tyler.
Maria is a first-grade student who does not participate in group activities. She does not move her desk close to other students, does not greet them or participate in assigned activities, and often gets up and leaves the group.	It is group time. When it is time for group, I put my desk with Emily's, John's, and Jaime's desks. I sit with my feet on the floor and my hands to myself. I say "hi" to everyone in the group. I listen to the teacher's directions and do my part in the group. I stay with the group. I don't get angry when I don't get a turn because I will get a turn another day. When group is over, I move my desk back to its regular place. My teacher and group will be proud of me!

Note. The pages or sentences in social stories can be numbered, or written on separate cards and numbered to help students master the sequence of behaviors.

Figure 3-2

Comic Strip Conversations

Lesson 45: Asking a Peer for Help

Lesson 81: Standing Up for a Friend*

* Lesson 81 is from *Social Skills for Students With Autism Spectrum Disorders and Other Developmental Disabilities*
Vol. 2: Secondary School Lesson Plans (51-100).

Power Cards

The power cards strategy (Gagnon, 2001; Spencer et al., 2008) is designed specifically for students with ASD and involves scripting behavior. Power cards use "visual aids to teach and reinforce academic and behavioral skills" and appeal to students with ASD's "highly developed special interests" (Autism Spectrum Institute, n.d., ¶1). The cards are a combination of text and graphics, and are small enough that the student can carry them throughout the school day (see Figure 3-3).

Self-Video and Self-Pictures

As indicated in Chapter 1, self-video modeling is an effective and research-proven strategy for teaching and improving social skills. This procedure involves taking a short video of a student engaged in an inappropriate or awkward performance of a social behavior. The student is then asked to view the video and either self-critique it or engage in a conversation about his or her performance. Self-pictures are used for the same purpose, meaning that the pictures can be used to give feedback or have the student self-critique. Videos can also be produced showing the student performing the behavior properly, to reinforce acquisition of the skill. These tools also can be used to teach student how to recognize body language and how to interpret facial expressions and gestures.

A Word About Behavior Support Plans

Structured behavioral support plans are powerful tools used to correct misbehavior, teach new behaviors, replace inappropriate behaviors with appropriate ones, and to increase or decrease specific behaviors. Social skills are among the new behaviors commonly taught using the behavior plan process and these plans are used frequently to reduce behaviors that result in social rejection for the individual student. Behavior support plans are seldom written unless the behavior of concern is somewhat serious or inimical to the student's social welfare. Chapter 4 includes information on developing and assessing behavior support plans, and the Appendix includes a template for such a plan.

Teacher-Initiated Strategies

Many of the approaches used by successful practitioners involve making careful observations and judgments regarding the behaviors (or lack of behaviors) of the students they serve. Typically, they take advantage of favorable conditions that present themselves as teaching or support opportunities; they also take advantage of naturally

Figure 3-3

Power Card Examples

1 When I work in a group, I will only talk about the topic the teacher assigns.

2 When I work in a group, I will listen to my classmates.

3 When I do a good job in group, I get to use the computer later.

CHAPTER 3

---

1 When something is hard to do, I will ask a friend for help.

2 I will think of a nice way to ask for help.

3 I will say thank you when my friend helps.

---

1 When I do school work I will not say I hate it and refuse to do it.

2 I will finish my work and do Sudoku later.

3 My teacher will like it when I finish my work.

occurring situations for helping students to become engaged with peers—both of these are examples of "teaching on the fly." To make the most of such opportunities,

1. Establish rapport with the student.

2. Suggest an action related to a social skill (e.g., introducing yourself, asking to be included).

3. Facilitate student engagement in the selected skill.

4. Reinforce correct performance.

5. Monitor the skill and behavior over time.

Teachers often know the triggers for individual student behavioral responses to a variety of circumstances, some of which result in negative experiences. There are numerous opportunities for observant teachers to intervene and provide instruction, guidance, and support for learning or using appropriate social skills, including

- Precorrection: Reminding students of the behaviors they have previously been taught prior to changing environments (Sugai, 2006).

- Prompting and reinforcing previously learned skills.

- Responding to behavioral cues: Intervening with an on-the-spot strategy for dealing with the situation the student is experiencing.

- Arranging physical features of the classroom to facilitate student interaction.

- Signing up students for activities and then providing support for participation.

Some teachers also find success with an approach referred to as the Facilitative Interactional Teaching Style (Prizant et al., 2006). This style is characterized by following the child's attentional focus, offering choices and alternatives within activities, responding to and acknowledging the student's intent, modeling various communicative functions, and expanding and elaborating on the child's topic (Prizant et al., 2006, p. 119).

Summary

Without the planned and facilitated process for engaging students with ASD and other developmental disabilities to interact with typical students there is little chance for social skills to develop incidentally or reach mastery and become generalized in natural environments. Individualizing social skills training is often a necessity for students with ASD and other developmental disabilities. The techniques identified in this chapter including teacher facilitate and peer-mediated strategies support and are essential to the process of gaining social competence. For many students with disabilities, a more direct and targeted approach to acquiring social skills is necessary. The direct instruction and supplemental strategies in the following chapter address these skill-targeted approaches.

**CHAPTER
3**

Chapter 4
Direct Instruction of Social Skills

Most children learn social skills through imitating other children, their parents, and the other adults they encounter during the course of daily living. Except for some intensive instruction and reinforcement by parents on manners, much of what children learn in the social area can be described as incidental. Unfortunately, children with disabilities, especially children with autism spectrum disorder (ASD) and other developmental disabilities, are notoriously inadequate in their incidental learning. As a consequence, they are often deficient in social skills (see Table 4-1) and fail to accrue acceptance by peers and adults. In addition, many children with disabilities tend to incur social rejection as a result of exhibiting interfering and socially unacceptable behaviors. These conditions affecting the lives of students with disabilities contributes to the need to teach them social skills.

Attending to Learner Characteristics

Whether taught in groups or individually, children and youth with ASD and other developmental disabilities have unique learning characteristics that must be addressed and accommodated during instruction. Individuals with ASD perceive the world differently from their typically developing peers, and generally are not proficient in recognizing or understanding the thinking of others. They are often visual learners who require interventions that tap into their strengths and special interests. Students with intellectual disabilities have difficulty with memory, problem solving, and generalizing learning. Teachers need to bear these learning characteristics in mind when developing small-group lessons and follow-up procedures. Strategies that respond to attention, discrimination, memory, and generalization deficiencies specifically address the needs of students with intellectual disabilities. The use of pictures, drawings, or video is generally regarded to be helpful in teaching students with ASD.

Table 4-1. Types of Social Skills Deficits

Social Skill Deficit	Description
Skill deficits	The student simply does not have the skill in his or her behavioral repertoire. *Example:* The student does not know how to make an introduction and, consequently, never makes an introduction.
Inadequate skill performance deficits	The student performs a social skill, but leaves out some critical component. *Example:* The student starts a conversation but fails to succeed as a result of neglecting a skill component (e.g., deciding on the right time to approach, establishing eye contact).
Fluency deficits	The student is able to perform a particular social skill but does it awkwardly and in an unnatural way. *Example:* The student greets everyone with the same phrase (e.g., "Hi ya Buddy!") or may use halting speech and a monotone voice to communicate.
Performance deficits	The student possesses the skill but does not use it with sufficient frequency. *Example:* The student interrupts when others are speaking, even though he or she knows that it is inappropriate.
Self-control deficits	(1) Obtrusive behaviors: The student exhibits behaviors which interfere with other students or the teacher's lesson. *Example:* The student talks in class, acts out, or wanders around the classroom. (2) Excessive behaviors: The student behaves in a way which is socially unacceptable. *Example:* The student exhibits sloppy eating, nose-picking, or self-stimulation behaviors (stimming), or talks to self in an audible voice.

When addressing social skills deficits, consider the language stage of the learner. In the SCERTS model (Prizant et al., 2006), when the student is at the "language partner" stage it is essential to establish rapport with the child before attempting to teach social communication in a context that may be new to the student. The learning of students with ASD is also impacted by situational and stimulus dependence (e.g., the student may communicate with a sibling but not with others).

Assessing Social Skills

Social skills can be assessed through a variety of procedures including teacher rating scales, pupil rating scales (Gresham & Elliot, 1990), sociometric exercises, and naturalistic and structural observation (Bellini, 2006b). For students with ASD, Bellini's Social Skills Profile (Bellini, 2006b)—which assesses student social reciprocity, social participation/avoidance, and detrimental social behaviors—is a helpful tool. The SCERTS Assessment Process (Prizant et al., 2006) is a comprehensive and useful set of tools for assessing social communication and also may be helpful when working with students with ASD.

Our process for assessing social skills is based on procedures established by other authorities in the field and uses a double-checking teacher assessment/rating system. For the first check, the teacher observes and rates student behaviors against a checklist of social skills appropriate for elementary school students; this initial general assessment and observation identifies the area(s) of greatest need for the student. The second check, a task analysis, breaks down each of these skills into its components and enables the observer to record whether an individual student is performing each of the steps in the skill. The Appendix includes both the social skills assessment form and the task analysis template. Each of the social skills on the assessment form is linked to a social skill lesson plan (see Chapter 5); each individual plan addresses all the skill components. As discussed later in this chapter, the same assessment form and process should be used subsequent to intervention to evaluate student mastery of the skill. The companion volume of this publication contains a similar appendix with lessons relating to social skills appropriate for secondary school students; the accompanying CD includes 50 of the lesson plans, along with Word templates for both the general assessment form and the task analysis form—which can be adapted for use with any of the social skill lessons.

Teaching Social Skills Lessons

There are different approaches to teaching social skills. Goldstein (1974) emphasized a problem-solving approach; Strain and his colleagues (Strain et al., 1977; Strain & Wiegerink, 1976) recommended employing antecedent manipulation and behavior modification techniques; still others have supported a direct instruction approach (Bernard-Opitz et al., 2001; Cartledge & Milburn, 1980; Mesibov & La Greco, 1981; Nikopoulous & Keenan, 2007; Stephens, 1978). Our approach to teaching social skills is based on the direct instruction model. All lessons follow a seven-step process (see Table 4-2).

Table 4-2. Process for Teaching Social Skills

Step 1: Establish the need	The purpose of this step is to help students see the relevance of the skill and understand the benefits of mastering the skill. When possible, relate the targeted skill to the student's experience and background knowledge.
Step 2: Identify skill components	The purpose of this step is to present and verbally rehearse the sequence of actions. The sequence of actions is determined by task analysis of the successfully performed target social skill.
Step 3: Model the skill	Modeling the skill facilitates learning more rapidly than other procedures.
Step 4: Role-play	This step allows students to exercise the skill and receive feedback on the skill performance.
Step 5: Practice	The practice steps generally occur after the presentation and are used to reinforce mastery of the skill. Provide feedback during practice to refine skill performance and assure maintenance.
Step 6: Generalization	This step is designed to encourage students to perform the skill in settings outside the training setting, with different people, different circumstances, and at different times.
Step 7: Evaluation	The purpose of this step is to determine if the skill was learned to criterion and generalized. Failure to generalize requires changing strategies for individual students.

Rationale for Lesson Content

The direct instruction lessons include in Chapter 5 (and those in the companion volume, which focuses on secondary school students) are similar to those designed for typically developing children (Stephens, 1978) and for students with behavioral disorders (Goldstein, Sprafkin, Gershaw, & Klein, 1980), but differ in that the lessons are tailored to the learning characteristics of children and youth with ASD and other developmental disabilities. These characteristics require special consideration for deficits in discrimination, attention, memory, motivation, joint attention, visual learning, and generalization. The 50 lessons designed with elementary school students in mind fall into the categories of teaching *prosocial skills* (i.e., skills that reflect social acceptability), *personal skills* (i.e., skills that impact self-concept), and *social interaction skills* (i.e., skills that foster development of interpersonal communication and friendships); see Table 4-3.

Discrimination

Youngsters with ASD and intellectual disabilities often lack the ability to discriminate the essential components of social skills; our direct instruction process incorporates two procedures to assist them in identifying the skill components. First, each skill is task analyzed to identify its components, and then the essential components are presented to the student. Second, while modeling skills, the teacher narrates and emphasizes the critical components (*thinking aloud*); when using video modeling, the teacher narrates or points out critical components.

Attention

Considerable research indicates that many children with ASD and developmental disabilities have difficulty maintaining attention to task. Modeling and role-playing can help enhance attention: Modeling brings some novelty to the instructional setting, and role-playing enhances attention through providing active participation and feedback incentives.

Memory

The major deficits in the memory process of children with ASD and developmental disabilities are inadequate rehearsal and verbal mediation strategies. To account for this lack of strategies, *rehearsal* can include oral rehearsal of skill components, role-playing the skills, practicing skills as homework assignments, watching prerecorded videos of the skill, review sessions, and exercising a particular skill in school situations. There are various strategies for providing *verbal mediators* for different age groups. For students with significant cognitive delays, labeling and unison repetition of skill components help to guide students through a sequence of actions; in some cases, special chants or rhyming verses can assist in verbal mediation. For older students, thinking aloud is useful for engaging in verbal rehearsal. In addition, writing the skill components as part of direct rote rehearsal, discussion to increase verbal elaboration, and reviewing the skill components as homework are all designed to encourage students to acquire the language mediators necessary for following a sequence of actions. Videos that students can watch at home are especially appealing to and may be effective for students with ASD; because these students are visual thinkers/learners, videos can help reinforce lesson plan components.

Table 4-3. Social Skills Lesson Plans for Elementary School Students

Lesson Plan	Topic	Prosocial Skills	Personal Skills	Social Interaction Skills
1	Classroom Rules: Paying Attention to the Teacher, Getting the Teacher's Attention, Asking Questions	X		
2	Responding to Questions From a Teacher or Other Adult	X		
3	Active Listening in the Classroom	X		
4	Classroom Rules: Sitting in Your Own Space	X		
5	Keeping Your Desk in Order	X		
6	Saying "Please" and "Thank You"	X		
7	Requesting a Preferred Activity	X		
8	Hallway Etiquette: Staying in LIne, Entering a Room/Area	X		
9	Riding the School Bus	X		
10	Being Patient: Learning How to Wait	X	X	
11	Using the Restroom	X		
12	Appropriate Classroom Participation	X	X	X
13	Cafeteria Rules: Going Through the Lunch Line and Sitting With Peers	X		
14	Cafeteria Rules: Table Manners and Having a Conversation	X		
15	Greeting Teachers and Other Adults	X		
16	Greeting Peers and Friends	X		X
17	Using Classroom Materials: Sharing, Taking Care of Supplies, and Requesting Materials From Others	X		X

Table 4-3. Social Skills Lesson Plans for Elementary School Students (Continued)

Lesson Plan	Topic	Prosocial Skills	Personal Skills	Social Interaction Skills
18	Active Listening to Peers	X		X
19	Recognizing and Reporting Emergencies		X	X
20	What to Do if You Get Hurt		X	
21	What to Do if You Hurt Someone Else		X	X
22	Coping With Sensory Issues		X	
23	Problem Solving		X	
24	Telling the Truth		X	
25	Being a Friend: Accepting Ideas Different From Your Own		X	X
26	Taking Turns			X
27	Asking Someone to Play With You			X
28	Joining in an Activity			X
29	Dealing With Stress and Anxiety: Calming Activities		X	
30	Reading Facial Expressions			X
31	Understanding Nonverbal Communication Cues			X
32	Understanding Figures of Speech			X
33	Understanding Sarcasm and Irony			X
34	Recognizing and Expressing Bodily Needs	X	X	
35	How to Tell a Story		X	X
36	How to Describe a Movie, Book, or TV Show Episode		X	X
37	How to Describe a Personal Experience, Memory, or Dream		X	X

CHAPTER 4

Table 4-3. Social Skills Lesson Plans for Elementary School Students (Continued)

Lesson Plan	Topic	Prosocial Skills	Personal Skills	Social Interaction Skills
38	Understanding Responsibility: What to Do When You Have to Do Something You Don't Want to Do	X	X	
39	Avoiding Inappropriate Contact	X		X
40	Playing Games with Peers: Winning and Losing		X	X
41	Playing Games with Peers: Following the Rules and What to Do When Someone Cheats		X	X
42	Classroom Participation: Managing Transitions	X	X	
43	Hygienic Behavior: Handwashing, Personal Grooming, and Cleanliness	X	X	
44	Helping a Peer			X
45	Asking a Peer for Help		X	
46	Self-Advocacy: What to Do When Someone is Bothering You		X	
47	Recognizing and Expressing Emotions: Feeling Happy, Sad, Mad, and Excited		X	
48	Managing Emotions: Dealing With Frustration	X	X	
49	Managing Emotions: Dealing With Boredom		X	
50	Being a Friend: Expressing Empathy and Sympathy			X

Motivation

Motivation is a critical part of teaching social skills, and is enhanced by teaching and reinforcing skills in natural environments. Teaching social skill lessons to clusters of students with disabilities in separate settings (i.e., special classes) can be extremely boring. Using typical peers who participate in the instruction (and serve as competent peer models) can increase motivation. These peer models can also interact with the students with disabilities during unstructured times.

Joint Attention

Joint attention is attending in unison with another person to an object or situation (Bellini, 2006b). The concept of joint attention is relevant to students with ASD, as in many cases these students do not always pay attention to the same things as their peers. Joint attention skills can be reinforced through the lessons' imbedded prompts and feedback.

Generalization

In many attempts to teach social skills to learners with ASD and developmental disabilities, students have failed to generalize the skills learned (see discussion in Chapter 1). Generalization is not likely to occur unless the teacher uses specific strategies that enhance its likelihood. Attempts to create language mediators contribute to generalization, but these are not enough. A variety of generalization procedures should accompany initial teaching of social skills: self-reporting, reteaching in different environments, transfer and fading of reinforcement systems, changing trainers, supportive cueing in different environments, reinforcement for generalization, and peer-mediated intervention strategies (see Chapter 3).

Simulation Versus En Vivo Training

Although simulation training (such as our seven-step social skills lesson plan format) has proven to be very effective for typically developing children, students with ASD and intellectual disabilities frequently fail to generalize from this type of instruction. Real-life *(en vivo)* instruction can take place in general education classrooms, on the playground, in the community, and on the job, and enhances skill mastery. Each type of training has its advantages—and both should be used.

Simulation training in small-group settings allows more opportunity than occurs naturally to provide students with practice and feedback on how they perform specific tasks. Teachers can model, correct, and reinforce behavior in ways that allow them to shape appropriate performance on the part of the student. This training can be critical, but simulation training alone is insufficient due to transfer problems between simulated and real life settings.

En vivo instruction is necessary because naturally occurring antecedents and consequences will only be present in real-life situations, although en vivo training alone may be insufficient for some students. Students with ASD and developmental disabilities have had many real-life experiences with all the natural antecedents and consequences—and yet they still exhibit social skill deficiencies. In addition, some social skills critical to social acceptance occur at such low frequencies that opportunities to teach them are seldom present in natural environments. Thus, the concentrated simulation training offers some benefit to those who require the skills to be broken down into discrete steps and trained.

Preparing to Teach Social Skills Lessons

For children in elementary school—particularly the primary grades—social status is often affected by a teacher's attitude and acceptance. Therefore, many of the social skills lessons included in Appendix A reflect teacher-pleasing behaviors (*prosocial* skills). The rationale for teaching prosocial, socially acceptable behaviors during the early years of school is to enhance these students' potential for inclusion in general education and other natural school environments. Teaching these behaviors is both a proactive approach to classroom management and a way of helping students become more successful in general education classrooms.

Personal social skills relate to behaviors that are considered culturally necessary for individuals to be accepted such as expressing enthusiasm and accepting praise. Some students lacking personal social skills tend to draw negative attention to themselves by engaging in behaviors that are outside of the cultural norms such as poor grooming, inappropriate physical contact and nonhygienic behavior. Correcting deficits in personal social skills is necessary for preventing social rejection.

Students with ASD and other developmental disabilities also need to acquire *social interaction* skills to gain friends and interact with others in their environments. The social interaction skill lessons for younger elementary school children focus on very basic social tasks such as making greetings and asking a friend to play. (Any of the topics, of course, can be revised and retaught as students move through the grades.) For students in the upper elementary grades, lessons are intended to continue to build the social interaction skills needed in school contexts. With support and intentional effort, these skills (e.g., listening to a peer) will generalize to nonschool settings.

Lessons can be presented to whole classes as a way of introducing acceptable school behaviors to all students; many schools' existing schoolwide behavior programs may even correspond to some of the lesson topics. However, although students with ASD or other developmental disabilities thus will receive an orientation to positive school behaviors, they will not likely become proficient as the result of simply participating in whole-group classroom lessons. For this reason, we also recommend teaching the lessons in small group sessions, resource rooms, or in counseling rooms either as a program of regular social skills instruction or as interventions for selected students.

Preparation: Form Instructional Groups

Attempts to teach social skills lessons to homogeneous groups of students with disabilities too often results in students acquiring additional inappropriate behaviors and not those of the intended lessons. Therefore, we recommend that teachers involve competent peers in portions of the initial instruction (e.g., discussions, modeling, role-playing).

After assessing needs, group students according to their need to acquire or refine specific social skills. Lessons generally work best when students are aware of the sequence of instruction and comfortable with the idea that they will be engaging in discussions and role-playing. Be aware that some youngsters, however, consider role-playing a very unpleasant experience; teachers will have to help these students work through this difficulty.

Preparation: Read Lessons in Advance

Read lessons completely prior to attempting to teach them. Some of the lessons require advance preparation of materials; for example, for a group with poor language skills, a teacher may need to prepare feedback and script cards to use during modeling and role-playing. Other lessons require the participation of a competent peer role model or another adult; still others require special props, or recommend a particular book or preparation of a comic strip or video.

Another reason for reading the lessons in advance is to determine whether they need to be modified to make them more age-appropriate or more relevant to the group's unique needs. For example, the lesson on keeping your desk in order (Lesson 5) is more likely to reflect the needs of students with intellectual disabilities and less likely to be appropriate for students with ASD, who typically like order. We include a lesson on recognizing and responding to teasing, name calling, and bullying in Volume 2 (Lesson 83), because these types of problems tend to be more intense at the middle-school level. However, a teacher who wants to address teasing with younger students can modify the lesson in a way that is relevant to a younger group. As long as all seven steps are followed when teaching the social skill lessons, teachers should feel free to alter the content of the lessons to address individual student needs and learning characteristics.

Instructional Procedures and Processes

Each lesson contains seven explicit steps and several embedded processes designed to enhance acquisition of social skills.

Step 1: Establish the Need

All of our direct instruction lessons begin with establishing the need for the skill. The purpose of this step is to enhance attention to the instruction by making the topic personally meaningful. Essentially, the teacher creates conditions or provokes thinking to make students aware of their need to acquire and employ a particular skill. Most lessons begin with questions, a story, a video, or a puppet skit that introduces the skill. Our field experiences revealed that stories were especially helpful, as many students with ASD or other developmental disabilities had difficulty drawing on memory or personal experience when discussing the focus skill. The discussion of personal experiences or the introductory story is designed to help students identify reasons why the skill is necessary and of value, by establishing the benefits of or consequences for knowing or not knowing the skill. For the most part, consequences should be elicited from students rather than provided by the teacher (although some students will need prompting to elicit consequences).

Step 2: Identify the Skill Components

After establishing the need for the skill, list the skill components, saying them aloud while writing them on posterboard, chalkboard, whiteboard, overhead projector, or displaying them electronically. Remember that for younger, nonreading students—as well as visual learners such as students with ASD—pictograms or other visual aids might be better than words. The process of providing students with ASD written and pictorial scripts has demonstrated utility for both initial instruction and generalization (Charlop & Milstein, 1989; Hundert & vanDelft, 2009; Kamps et al., 1992). Although skill components may be provided by the teacher or elicited from students, eliciting the steps from students is more likely to maintain their involvement.

After the skill components are identified, they need to be rehearsed. *Rote rehearsal* (e.g., unison reciting of the skill component, repeating a poem that presents the skill components, writing the skill steps on homework forms, daily review of the components) benefits young children, who may need cueing to elicit recall and recitation. For older children, a *verbal elaboration* strategy is more age appropriate and more successful than rote rehearsal. Verbal elaboration consists of teacher-led discussions covering each step of the skill. Discussion enables repeating a variety of aspects of the skill steps, pairs the skill with associative information, and makes it personally relevant to the students. Rehearsal of the skill components should occur over an extended period. One helpful procedure is to post the skill steps and review them occasionally to facilitate distributed practice. Another method is to directly query students on their recollection of the skill components.

Step 3: Model the Skill

Modeling helps maintain attention to the lesson. Both live and symbolic modeling are effective when teaching social skills. *Live modeling* consists of a teacher, another adult, or

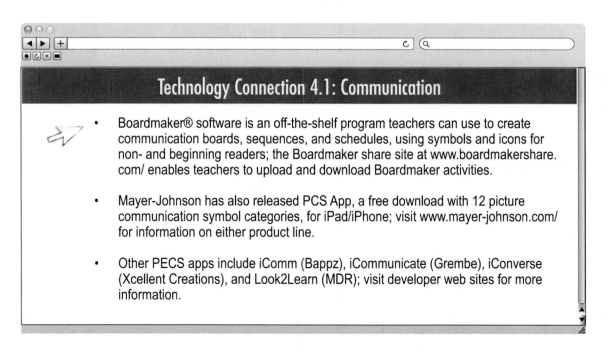

Technology Connection 4.1: Communication

- Boardmaker® software is an off-the-shelf program teachers can use to create communication boards, sequences, and schedules, using symbols and icons for non- and beginning readers; the Boardmaker share site at www.boardmakershare.com/ enables teachers to upload and download Boardmaker activities.

- Mayer-Johnson has also released PCS App, a free download with 12 picture communication symbol categories, for iPad/iPhone; visit www.mayer-johnson.com/ for information on either product line.

- Other PECS apps include iComm (Bappz), iCommunicate (Grembe), iConverse (Xcellent Creations), and Look2Learn (MDR); visit developer web sites for more information.

a competent peer performing the behavior. *Symbolic modeling* serves the same purpose, but uses videos, movies, or puppets to demonstrate the skill. Whereas students in the lower elementary school grades enjoy a puppet show, older children appreciate seeing their teacher and others they know perform. Modeling by competent peers (especially those with high status) also increases attention and motivation to learn social skills. As a reinforcement, teachers should ask students to summarize or discuss the skill steps they observe.

Due to their poor discrimination skills, students with ASD and intellectual disabilities need each of the skill components to be identified during the course of modeling the entire skill; both live and symbolic modeling should include *thinking aloud*. This can be done during symbolic modeling by stopping and narrating the scene being played out. For live modeling, the teacher or other competent model can demonstrate the think-aloud process. When using this procedure, the teacher is able to demonstrate the cognitive steps of many of the social skills, see Figure 4-1 which features a thinking aloud script to develop the skill on making invitations from Lesson 27.

Some lessons require modeling the skill more than one time. Each time the skill is modeled, change the context to demonstrate that the skill should be generalized to a variety of conditions or settings. (For example, the skill for responding appropriately to name-calling might be modeled for playground, home, classroom, and school bus settings; the person doing the name calling may be an adult, then a peer, then a sibling.)

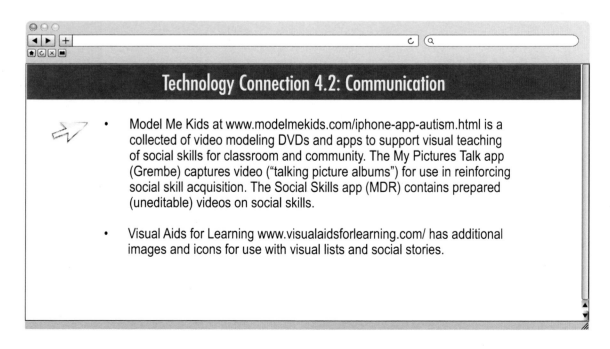

Technology Connection 4.2: Communication

- Model Me Kids at www.modelmekids.com/iphone-app-autism.html is a collected of video modeling DVDs and apps to support visual teaching of social skills for classroom and community. The My Pictures Talk app (Grembe) captures video ("talking picture albums") for use in reinforcing social skill acquisition. The Social Skills app (MDR) contains prepared (uneditable) videos on social skills.

- Visual Aids for Learning www.visualaidsforlearning.com/ has additional images and icons for use with visual lists and social stories.

Figure 4-1

Lesson 27: Asking Someone to Play With You

	Thinking aloud script	*Skill components modeled and narrated*
	 *Thinking aloud:* Gee, I don't have anything to do by myself. I think I'd like to go swimming. It would be nice to go with Bob Adams. I think I'll ask Bob. I think that I'll do it right now.	Choose what you want to do. Decide if you want someone else to join you. Decide whom you want to invite.
	 [Approaches Bob.]	Choose a time to invite the person.
	 Speaking: Hi Bob! Do you want to go swimming this afternoon? My mom can drive us.	Make the invitation.
	 Bob: Sorry, I can't right now.	
	 *Thinking aloud:* I don't get angry because Bob cannot go. I can ask someone else.	
	 Speaking: Ok, I'll try to find someone who's not busy.	If the person cannot join you, ask someone else.

Step 4: Role-Play

Role playing responds to the learning deficiencies of students with ASD and other developmental disabilities; students pay closer attention to the lesson when they take an active role, rehearse, or need to provide feedback. Feedback enhances student discrimination of specific skill components, helps to refine the skill to performance level, serves as a reinforcer, and helps students maintain the skill once acquired. When giving feedback assignments (either verbally or using feedback cards), the teacher simply tells the student to watch for a single specific skill component. (Feedback cards may be collected after each newly role-played situation and redistributed to give class members a new skill component to concentrate on while a fellow student performs.)

For some children, *prompting* is a very important aspect of role-playing: they need to be reminded of each step to perform the task correctly. After prompting a child to correct performance, the skill component or whole skill should be reinforced with praise or some other reward to assure that the correct behavior will occur again. However, when a child requires a great deal of prompting, the skill should be retaught at a later date and practiced extensively.

Role-playing also addresses generalization deficiencies. Creating a number of simulated and real-life (when possible) conditions provides students with a variety of circumstances under which the skill should be used. Each time a different student role-plays a skill, it should be in a unique circumstance. For example, in role-playing asking a friend to play, the first time it might be the target student role-playing with the teacher, then with an older student, and then with a sibling.

Step 5: Practice

For a new skill to be maintained and eventually generalized, it must be practiced. Children with ASD and intellectual disabilities need considerable practice in learning academic skills, and the same goes for learning social skills. There is a variety of ways to provide students with needed practice of social skills.

Whole-skill prompts. It's helpful to prompt skill performance as opportunities arise subsequent to initial instruction, with statements and cues to help the child initiate the sequence of the skill components. A typical prompt to an elementary school pupil would be something like "Show me how you are supposed to make eye contact," or "Tell me how to ask someone to play, and then you can go ask someone to play." The nature of the prompts, of course, should be tailored to suit the individual child.

Coaching. For children who are unable to execute a particular skill in total, teachers can offer coaching through the skill on a step-by-step basis. This procedure may be used in lieu of modeling to help involve a child in correctly role-playing the skill. *Coaching* simply means telling the student what to do and then providing feedback (see box, "Coaching").

Skill challenges. Skills may be practiced through skill challenges, where students must demonstrate use of a particular skill during a contrived social or classroom situation. For example, after initial instruction on the skill related to giving help, the teacher says: "Ann, I want you to ask Melinda to help you move this stack of books to the Media Center." Provide feedback to the students on how they performed their respective roles. Each student should be challenged individually at least once after a lesson has been taught.

> ## Coaching
>
> | Teacher: | We are going to practice the greeting skill today. First, John, I want you to look me right in the eye. |
> | Student: | (Makes eye contact) |
> | Teacher: | Good! Now I want you to smile and say "Hi, Mr. Jones." |
> | Student: | (Smiles) "Hi, Mr. Jones." |
> | Teacher: | Good, John—but you have to keep looking me in the eye. Let's try again. Look me in the eye, smile, and say "Hi, Mr. Jones." |
> | Student: | (Smiles and maintains eye contact) "Hi, Mr. Jones." |
> | Teacher: | That's right! Now, ask me a friendly question.... |

CHAPTER 4

Homework. The lessons in Chapter 5 generally call for informal homework (if any) for elementary-age children. Homework forms can be used when the skill is practiced outside the social skills setting; they constitute both a practice tool and an attempt to facilitate generalization and transfer. Writing the skill components constitutes an imposed rehearsal of the skill components; students also might be assigned to watch a video (if using video self-modeling or peer modeling) independently or practice the skill with siblings or parents. Figure 4-2 provides two sample homework forms for two different social skills lessons; a blank form is included in the Appendix, and the accompanying CD contains a Word template, which may be used with any of the social skill lessons. The accompanying CD also contains a Home-School Connection Form template (see the Appendix) that can be used to inform students' families about the skill being taught and how they can support this instruction. The student can use the Homework form as a self-monitoring tool at school and also in other settings.

Figure 4-2: Sample Homework Form #1

Homework Assignment for (Student name)		
Lesson 16: *Greeting Peers and Friends*	Date:	

The steps for this skill are:

1. *Make eye contact with your friend.*

2. *Smile at your friend.*

3. *Say "hi" or "hey" and your friend's name.*

4. *Ask them a question.*

5. *Listen to what they say in response.*

	Yes	No
I practiced this skill on [date]		
The friend I greeted was		
Did I follow all the steps?	Yes	No
1. *I made eye contact with my friend.*		
2. *I smiled at my friend.*		
3. *I greeted my friend and said his or her name.*		
4. *I asked my friend a question.*		
5. *I listened to what my friend said.*		
Do you think you did a good job practicing this skill?		

If you don't think you did a good job, what will you do differently next time?

Figure 4-2: Sample Homework Form #2

Homework Assignment for (Student name)		
Lesson 48: *Managing Emotions*	Date:	
The steps for this skill are: 1. *Recognize that what I wanted or tried to do didn't turn out the way I wanted.* 2. *Think of different reasons that things didn't turn out the way I wanted.* 3. *Don't get really mad, say bad things, or hit or throw things. [examples relevant to individual student]* 4. *Think of other things I could do to have the result I wanted.* 5. *Decide if I want to try again.* 6. *Try again or choose to try something else.*		
I practiced this skill on [date]		
I was frustrated because		
Did I follow all the steps?	Yes	No
1. *I recognized that what I wanted or tried to do didn't turn out the way I wanted.*		
2. *I thought of reasons that things didn't turn out the way I wanted.*		
3. *I didn't get really mad, say bad things, or hit or throw things.*		
4. *I thought of other things I could do to have the result I wanted.*		
5. *I decided if I want to try again.*		
6. *I tried again.*		
7. *I tried something else; I decided to:*		
Do you think you did a good job practicing this skill?		
If you don't think you did a good job, what will you do differently next time ?		

CHAPTER 4

Skill review sessions. Approximately once or twice a month, review previously taught social skills in a group session or with individual students. These sessions should review the reasons for using particular skills, the skill components, and modeling by one or two proficient group members.

Daily role-playing. Not all students require daily role-play; some students, though, need to role-play the skill several times to be able to refine it. Feedback during and after these practice sessions helps students shape skills to the correct performance.

"Skill of the week" (or month). Posting the skill components in the classroom helps emphasize a new skill being learned. At least once per day or session during the week, students should verbally rehearse the skill components. The skill of the week may need to be revisited several times after initial instruction.

Reteaching the lesson. The same lesson may be retaught (in an abbreviated form) at a later date. Reteaching normally occurs several weeks after first teaching the skill.

Reteaching at different levels. Some social skills need to be retaught as students become older. For example, a lesson on coping with teasing may be taught at the elementary level with a focus on name-calling; the skill later can be retaught with an emphasis on coping with the type of teasing that occurs on the bus or in a high school hallway.

Step 6: Generalization

Unless efforts are made to facilitate generalization, the instruction provided in the classroom is likely to go to waste. Teachers should be vigilant in their efforts to encourage generalization. Social skills that students demonstrate in a small group setting or classroom will not always generalize to other environments. Each social skills lesson contains at least two suggestions for promoting generalization; teachers can encourage students to generalize the social skills they've learned in a variety of ways.

Teaching the social skill lesson in a real-life situation—*en vivo instruction*—reduces some of the inevitable transfer problems when instruction is provided in small group settings. It increases motivation and makes better use of natural cues and consequences.

Generalization also can be supported in different environments by enlisting the support of other school personnel and the student's family. General education teachers, playground monitors, lunchroom monitors, and the school office staff can *prompt skill use* in different school settings, and parents can learn to use whole-skill prompting techniques to reinforce the social skills lesson at home. Similarly, general education class teachers, school administrators, and parents can *provide feedback* in different environments—if they are given precise information about the skill and its components. (The task analysis form template provided in the Appendix and on the accompanying CD can also be adapted for other observers to use as a feedback form.) This extended social skills team also can provide *reinforcement,* offering praise or other rewards to children for exercising the social skill. (Do not specify the type of reinforcement because children should become conditioned to the reinforcements that are likely to be delivered naturally by the people in their environment.)

Sometimes a skill is taught in simulation first and then retaught in the setting where it naturally occurs. For example, reteach the lesson on following cafeteria rules in the actual school cafeteria. For some students, *reteaching skills in the natural setting* may entail trips into the community to help facilitate generalization and transfer. For example, the skill on respecting the space of others might be reinforced by taking students to a community performance where they need to wait in line and sit in a group (at an appropriate distance from others in each case).

After teaching and practicing a skill with the whole group, *reteach or practice with a change in constellation*: Practice the skill with a different individual and a different size group. This may include teaching the same lesson in the general education classroom (rather than a small group), practicing with children from different classrooms, or changing the role-playing by including partners of different gender or age. Another change in constellation is to *instruct and practice the skill with a different trainer*: Ask other adults to teach, supervise, and give feedback on performance of a particular skill.

Ask students to *self-report* on their use of the skill. Students can also *self-monitor* their skill use, marking down on an index card each time they use a skill, or maintaining a more formal data collection form. Reward accurate reporting or monitoring of skill use with praise or other suitable *reinforcement.*

Some of the instructional aspects of our approach to helping students gain social skills—such as practice, developing verbal mediators, and training to a wide variety of examples—inherently address and support generalization. *Incorporating flexibility* also can support social skill mastery:

- **Teach and reinforce** choosing alternatives, praising or otherwise reinforcing students for considering and choosing alternative ways to solve social problems or engage in interactions.

- **Train** loosely: train without being precise about the social setting, problem, or condition.

- **Fade** teacher prompts and reinforcements to allow natural reinforcers to take their place.

Step 7: Evaluation

This last step is one of the most important, and it is the same for every lesson. After a period of time, it is necessary to determine, through observation and feedback from other school personnel, if the skills taught are being sustained and generalized. When skills are performed inadequately or fail to generalize, the teacher, counselor, or professional engaged in improving social skills acquisition should design individual interventions for selected students.

Both formative and summative assessment procedures are appropriate for use with individual students. *Evaluation* consists of observing students in a variety of settings where the skills will be needed and rating students according to the performance criteria. Most frequently, at the elementary school level this will be in general education classrooms and common areas such as cafeterias and playgrounds. To best assess social interaction skills, observe students—and ask other school staff to assist in observing them as well—in unstructured settings such as the playground, cafeteria, school hallway, and on field trips.

Supplemental Resources for Presenting Social Skills Lessons

The social skill lesson plans in Chapter 5 and in the accompanying volume recommend a variety of supplemental resources teachers can use in presenting the lessons, such as picture books or videos; cartoon and picture conversation strips; software or apps; and Internet games, worksheets, or quizzes. Cartoon and picture conversation strips, as well as videos (whether off-the-shelf, online, or created with the student), are especially appropriate for use with students with ASD. Research indicates that students with ASD respond better to pictures than to verbal or written information

(Kunda, M. & Goel, 2011), and this is borne out by self-reports by adults with autism (see Grandin, 2008).

Teachers can create comic and/or conversation strips using their own drawings, student photos or artwork, free clip art, copyright-free photographs, and so forth. Teachers can use Microsoft Word's AutoShapes (Object Palette) function, which includes thought and speech bubbles, to make short conversation strips (see Figure 4-3) incorporating these graphics; there are also several free and low-cost programs (software and online generators) to create comic strips and storybooks. The accompanying CD includes 44 line drawings that can be copied and pasted into comic strips, picture conversation strips, or other teaching materials.

CHAPTER 4

Progress Monitoring

As discussed earlier in this chapter, the social skills assessment form in the Appendix is both an evaluation tool for identifying which social skills students need to learn and a post intervention tool to establish mastery of the skill. This form and the task analysis form, also included in the Appendix, are likely to be sufficient for monitoring and determining the success of the social skills instruction for most students. However, learning a social skill to criterion and generalizing that skill may take several weeks or even years for some children with ASD and developmental disabilities. Some students require more intensive and long-term efforts to attain proficient levels on priority social skills—and in many cases, this may mean changing or adjusting strategies over the learning period.

The individual progress monitoring form template included in the Appendix (also on the accompanying CD) is designed to help instructional staff members monitor student progress with precision over an extended time period and in a variety of settings. The purpose of this form is to monitor performance of each skill step

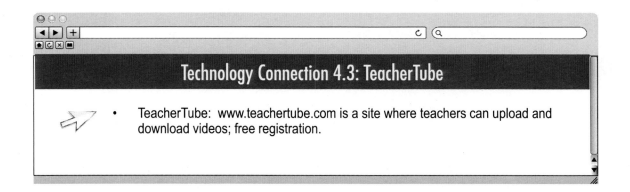

Technology Connection 4.3: TeacherTube

- TeacherTube: www.teachertube.com is a site where teachers can upload and download videos; free registration.

and to determine which require reinforcement, reteaching, or new strategies to strengthen performance. This tool also provides guidance for paraprofessionals and others working with the student to develop the targeted skill. Data collection when using the progress monitoring form may be as simple as recording a plus or minus sign, meaning the performance step occurred or it did not. A more precise data collection procedure would entail recording a prompting hierarchy (e.g., P = physical prompt, G = gestural prompt, V = verbal prompt, I = performed

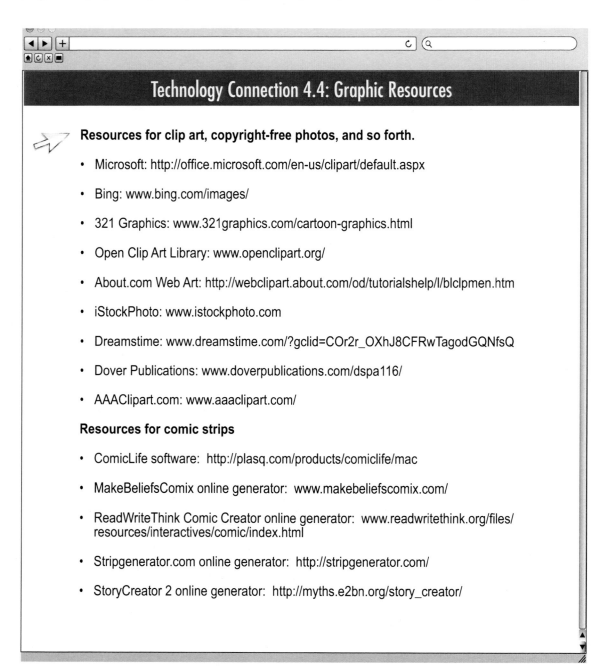

Technology Connection 4.4: Graphic Resources

Resources for clip art, copyright-free photos, and so forth.

- Microsoft: http://office.microsoft.com/en-us/clipart/default.aspx

- Bing: www.bing.com/images/

- 321 Graphics: www.321graphics.com/cartoon-graphics.html

- Open Clip Art Library: www.openclipart.org/

- About.com Web Art: http://webclipart.about.com/od/tutorialshelp/l/blclpmen.htm

- iStockPhoto: www.istockphoto.com

- Dreamstime: www.dreamstime.com/?gclid=COr2r_OXhJ8CFRwTagodGQNfsQ

- Dover Publications: www.doverpublications.com/dspa116/

- AAAClipart.com: www.aaaclipart.com/

Resources for comic strips

- ComicLife software: http://plasq.com/products/comiclife/mac

- MakeBeliefsComix online generator: www.makebeliefscomix.com/

- ReadWriteThink Comic Creator online generator: www.readwritethink.org/files/resources/interactives/comic/index.html

- Stripgenerator.com online generator: http://stripgenerator.com/

- StoryCreator 2 online generator: http://myths.e2bn.org/story_creator/

Figure 4-3

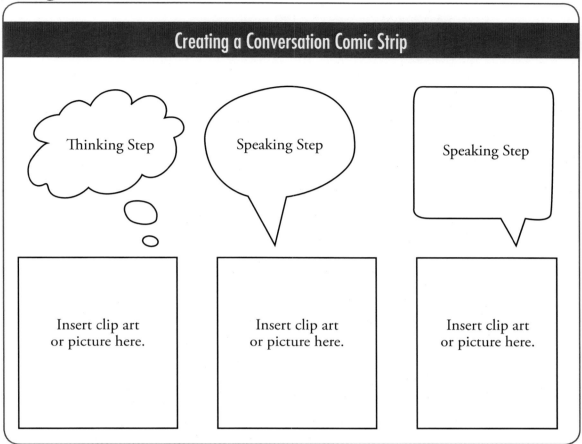

independently). Skill steps that are not at the independent level (i.e., without prompts) would require reteaching or additional practice trials to reach performance criterion.

Graphing trends allows teachers to monitor student progress and to make instructional decisions. Curriculum-based measurement techniques used to monitor academic progress are also useful for monitoring acquisition of nonacademic skills. The following steps are necessary for tracking student performance, whether in academic or social skills:

1.   Quantify skill performance.

2.   Establish baseline status.

3.   Create aim lines to identify acquisition targets.

4. Record trial dates.

5. Indicate/track changes in strategy and location.

6. Establish decision rules.

Figure 4-4 provides a sample trend graph for a student's social skills goal. On the graphing form, angled lines represent the aim line; the dark vertical lines represent changes in location and/or strategy. A blank trend graph form is included in the Appendix; the CD also includes a Word template of the form and an Excel file template that can be used to collect data and generate trend graphs.

Responding to Performance Deficits

Not all pupils will meet the performance criteria for each of the social skills introduced in structured learning lessons. In many cases, lessons will need to be repeated or followed by different strategies or interventions. In some cases, students may still exhibit performance deficits even after learning a skill adequately. *Performance deficits* exist when a student can perform a particular social skill but does not exercise the skill frequently enough; this will be highlighted by the summative assessment. A number of procedures can be used to ameliorate performance and self-control deficits: interdependent contingencies, token economy, behavioral contracts, social reinforcement, prompting and cueing, peer instruction, self-monitoring, and cognitive behavior modification. The Boys Town procedures (Black et al., 1984) described in Chapter 1 are powerful methods for responding to students with performance and self-control deficits.

Lesson 7: Requesting a Preferred Activity Using Talking-to-Self Dialogue

Thinking Step:

Student: "I finished my work. I wonder if we can do drawing now?"

Student answering self: "I can ask to do drawing if it looks like everyone else is almost done too."

Student: "It looks like a lot of kids are done. I'll raise my hand to ask the teacher."

Speaking Step:

Student [to teacher]: "Can we do drawing now?"

Thinking Step:

Student [when request is denied]: "Maybe I can do drawing later."

Student: "Good for me, I asked the right way. I'll give myself a check mark."

Figure 4-4

Sample Progress Trend Graph for Lesson 16: Greeting Peers and Friends

Student: Bryan Broeker	Grade: 5
	Teacher: Judith Martinez

Social skill goal:

Bryan will independently perform the skill of greeting peers in a variety of unstructured environments as measured on the skill task analysis form

Skill measures:

Bryan's performance will scored by observers based upon the six (6) steps in the skill. A score of 6 represents 100% correct performance.

Success criterion:

Success will be determined by 5 successive trials in each environment.

Target dates and location:

100% in classroom by Feb 15, 2009; 100% in hallways and cafeteria by April 1, 2009; 100% on the playground by June 5, 2009.

Comments:

Classroom training on the skill occurred 1/15 with intermittent prompting in classroom on follow-up. Skill monitored in halls and lunchroom without support. Bryan not successful in reaching criterion without support in unstructured setting. Parapro prompting and verbal praise added to hallway and lunchroom environments.

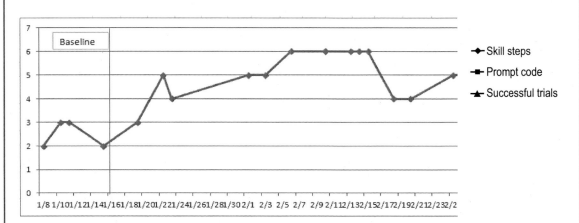

Note: Figure 4-4 looks slightly different than the templates provided on the CD. This figure represents an Excel template and has been formatted for inclusion in this book as an example.

Token economies can be used to reinforce appropriate behaviors. For example, in one primary classroom, dot stickers placed on the drawing of a butterfly were used as tokens to reward skills such as staying on task, listening, and completing work. When the butterfly was complete, the students earned a "lunch with the teacher." Because when all designated spots were covered there was a culminating activity, children were easily weaned from the reinforcement schedule. They had also mastered the target skills.

Behavioral contracts providing rewards for exhibiting appropriate social skills can be developed for students who compulsively act out or persist with some other socially unacceptable behavior. Changing criterion contracts, where small increments of change are expected each week, are very useful for developing social behaviors.

Peer-mediated instruction, as discussed in Chapter 3, is often used to help students learn academic skills and is very effective when used to improve social behaviors. Typically developing students, or students with disabilities who are proficient in the particular focus skill, can prompt, give feedback, and praise specified social behaviors.

Cognitive behavior modification can help students learn to talk to themselves *subvocally* (silently). The procedure involves having the student describe to himself the conditions or event, what the alternatives for behavior might be, and then reward himself with a subvocal statement (e.g., "good for me"). See box, "Talking-to-Self Dialogue," for an example of the process for a student who wants to request an activity.

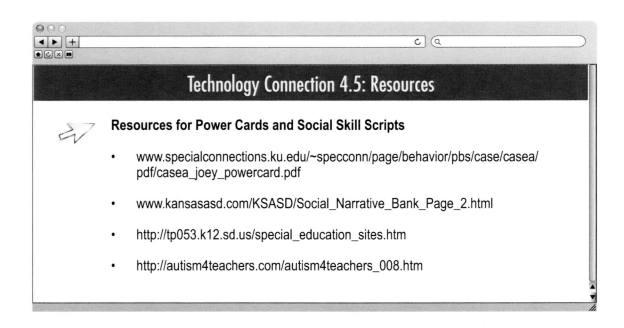

Technology Connection 4.5: Resources

Resources for Power Cards and Social Skill Scripts

- www.specialconnections.ku.edu/~specconn/page/behavior/pbs/case/casea/pdf/casea_joey_powercard.pdf

- www.kansasasd.com/KSASD/Social_Narrative_Bank_Page_2.html

- http://tp053.k12.sd.us/special_education_sites.htm

- http://autism4teachers.com/autism4teachers_008.htm

A system of *interdependent contingencies* may be used to reinforce individual social skills, while responding to students' differing social skill. After identifying individual social skill goals—whether reduction of obtrusive behaviors, or increasing interactions—the whole group becomes eligible for a reward each week. Each student has his or her own behavior and performance criterion. The more frequently a pupil reaches criterion, the more often a raffle ticket is added to a box. A ticket is pulled from the box once a week and the winner receives the prize. The intermittent nature of the reward tends to help maintain appropriate behaviors over long periods of time.

Home contingencies enable the student's family to provide reinforcement for appropriate behavior. For example, a student gets more TV or video game time or an outing with a friend when the teacher reports that the child performed some social skill correctly. Home contingencies have several advantages when trying to encourage improved social behavior:

- The skill is emphasized when the pupil is away from the stimulus control of the teacher.

- Families often are able to use more potent reinforcers to encourage appropriate behavior.

- The procedure helps create a dialogue between school and home.

Individual strategies for teaching social skills include social stories (Gray & Garand, 1993), pictorial scripts, cartoon conversations, power cards (Gagnon, 2001; Spencer et al., 2008), and behavior support plans; all are appropriate follow-up techniques for students who have not acquired specific skills through the direct instruction process.

Developing and Evaluating Positive Behavior Support Plans

Positive behavior support (PBS) plans are often used to provide interventions for students who lack appropriate social skills and for students who have behaviors that interfere with their social acceptance. When a social skill or behavior is missing from the repertoire of a student and that student has significant learning challenges, a PBS plan developed by a team of professionals may be warranted as an intervention.

What Is a Functional Behavior Assessment?

A functional behavioral assessment (FBA) looks beyond the behavior itself. The focus when conducting an FBA is on identifying significant, pupil-specific social, affective, cognitive, and/or environmental factors associated with the occurrence (and nonoccurrence) of specific behaviors. This broader perspective offers a better understanding of the function or purpose behind student behavior. Behavioral intervention plans based on an understanding of "why" a student misbehaves are extremely useful in addressing a wide range of problem behaviors.

(Center for Effective Collaboration and Practice, n.d., ¶2)

There are three basic strategies used to enhance positive behavior:

1. Teach a replacement behavior for the inappropriate one.

2. Teach a behavior that is incompatible with the inappropriate behavior.

3. Remove the events that reinforce and sustain the inappropriate behavior.

In developing a PBS plan (see the Appendix), the first step is to identify the missing or inappropriate social behavior by conducting an assessment of social skills that are needed at the student's developmental level. After identifying the target behavior(s), the student's educational team should conduct a functional behavior assessment (see box "What Is a Functional Behavior Assessment?") to determine antecedent and reinforcing events that sustain the unwanted behaviors.

A PBS plan should effectively collect in a single document the history of the student's behavior (including previous interventions), define the target behavior

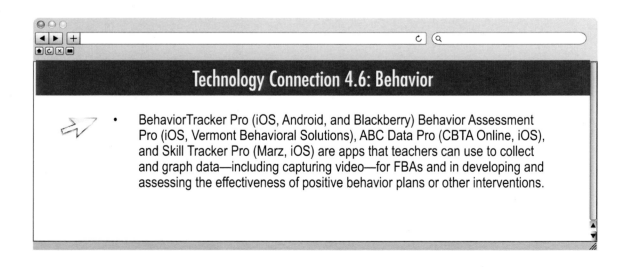

Technology Connection 4.6: Behavior

- BehaviorTracker Pro (iOS, Android, and Blackberry) Behavior Assessment Pro (iOS, Vermont Behavioral Solutions), ABC Data Pro (CBTA Online, iOS), and Skill Tracker Pro (Marz, iOS) are apps that teachers can use to collect and graph data—including capturing video—for FBAs and in developing and assessing the effectiveness of positive behavior plans or other interventions.

in observable terms, provide data and identify any communicative intent, and determine whether the behavior is a skill or performance deficit. The educational team then develops a hypothesis for improving the behavior and brainstorms possible solutions. In writing the PBS plan, the team needs to explicitly specify the actions and procedures designed to improve behavior, identifying replacement behaviors and reinforcements. The plan should include a method for collecting data and the criteria for determining success of the intervention. See the Appendix for a blank PBS plan template, which is also included on the accompanying CD; Table 4-4 provides a rubric for evaluating PBS plans.

Summary

Social skills instruction in group settings is effective when using direct instruction procedures. Although counseling techniques where students engage in discussions of how to exhibit socially acceptable behaviors may be successful in some cases, most students with ASD and intellectual disabilities need the power of modeling, practice, and effective strategies for facilitating generalization. Teaching social skills is a process requiring persistence and application of both group and individual strategies.

CHAPTER
4

Table 4-4. Rubric for Evaluating Positive Behavior Support Plans

An unacceptable plan...	A partially acceptable plan...	A basic plan...	A proficient plan...	An advanced plan...
Does not specify behavior in observable terms.	Defines behavior in observable terms.	Defines behavior in observable terms.	Defines behavior in observable terms.	Defines behavior in observable terms.
		Identifies previous interventions.	Identifies previous interventions.	Identifies previous interventions.
		Provides evidence that data has been reviewed.	Provides evidence that data has been reviewed.	Provides evidence that data has been reviewed.
			Identifies the communicative intent of the behavior.	Identifies the communicative intent of the behavior.
			Presents evidence of brainstorming a solution.	Presents evidence of brainstorming a solution.
				Identifies target behavior from functional assessment.
				Presents interview and observational data.
				States whether behavior is a skill or performance deficit.
				Presents a hypothesis for what may improve behavior.

Table 4-4. Rubric for Evaluating Positive Behavior Support Plans (Continued)

An unacceptable plan...	A partially acceptable plan...	A basic plan...	A proficient plan...	An advanced plan...
Uses only punishment procedures to improve behavior..	Includes a behavioral goal.	Includes a behavioral goal.	Includes a behavioral goal.	Includes a behavioral goal.
		Specifies actions and procedures designed to improve behavior.	Specifies actions and procedures designed to improve behavior.	Specifies actions and procedures designed to improve behavior.
			Identifies replacement behaviors.	Identifies replacement behaviors.
			Specifies procedures for reducing inappropriate behavior (if necessary).	Specifies procedures for reducing inappropriate behavior (if necessary).
				Explicitly specifies actions and procedures designed to improve behavior.
				Presents a hypothesis for what may improve behavior.

CHAPTER
4

Table 4-4. Rubric for Evaluating Positive Behavior Support Plans

An unacceptable plan...	A partially acceptable plan...	A basic plan...	A proficient plan...	An advanced plan...
Does not specify responsibilities for actions.	Specifies reinforcements.	Specifies reinforcements.	Specifies reinforcements.	Specifies reinforcements.
	Establishes criteria for determining success.	Establishes criteria for determining success.	Establishes criteria for determining success.	Establishes criteria for determining success.
	Specifies staff responsibilities.	Specifies staff responsibilities.	Specifies staff responsibilities.	Specifies staff responsibilities.
		Identifies a data collection procedure and criteria for determining success.	Identifies a data collection procedure and criteria for determining success.	Identifies a data collection procedure and criteria for determining success.
		Establishes review dates.	Establishes target start and completion dates as well as review dates.	Establishes target start and completion dates as well as review dates.
			Specifies Evaluation Plan.	Specifies Evaluation Plan.
				Assigns staff specific responsibilities.
				Graphs baseline data and establishes aim line.

Chapter 5
Social Skills Lesson Plans for Students in Elementary School

LESSON 1
Classroom Rules: Paying Attention to the Teacher, Getting the Teacher's Attention, Asking Questions

Objective: Student will master basic classroom behaviors for attending to the teacher, appropriately gaining attention, and asking questions.

Performance Criteria

These skills will be *performed adequately* when the student:

1. Maintains upright sitting posture facing in the direction of the teacher.
2. Watches teacher during instruction (i.e., when teacher is giving directions or demonstrating); moves head to follow teacher with eyes as she/he moves/points.
3. Raises hand and waits to be called upon; refrains from obtrusive motor or vocal behavior to gain teacher attention; refrains from speaking until called upon.
4. When permitted to be out of seat, to obtain attention stands in spot where visible or uses a single light tap on the shoulder if not visible, combined with saying teacher's name.
5. Speaks when called upon or acknowledged.
6. Makes request for help, information, or permission in appropriate tone and volume, using appropriate interrogative when asking a question (*who, what, when, where, how, can, would*).

Materials Required

Dolls, puppets, or stuffed animals to represent "teacher" and "students"
Materials to create poster of classroom rules (text + icons)—may be developed with students as part of lesson; may need to duplicate/make smaller version (icons only) for individual student desks

Other Preparation

Prepare competent peers to participate in the modeling and role-playing portions of the lesson.
Video modeling may be appropriate for role-playing.

Special Considerations

Lack of attention during instruction may mean that the subject matter is beyond a student's comprehension.

Use positive reinforcers (e.g., star chart with special/favorite activity reward) for students struggling with this skill.

Some students may need coaching through the role-playing process.

Some students may require encouragement/support/prompting to ask questions.

Forms and Supplementary Materials (see CD)

Student Self-Monitoring Form (Homework Form)

Staff Feedback Form (Task Analysis Form)

Technology Resources

Software: Boardmaker/Writing With Symbols (both Mayer-Johnson); School Rules! software (Social Skill Builder)

iPad/iPhone apps: Social Skills (MDR); First Then Visual Schedule (Good Karma)

Related Lessons

Lesson 10: Being Patient: Learning How to Wait

Lesson 12: Appropriate Classroom Participation

Lesson 72, Volume 2: Recognizing and Using Tone of Voice and Vocal Inflection

PROCEDURES 7 STEPS

Step 1 Establish the Need

a. Introduce the topic of "classroom rules" for behavior at school.

b. Using puppets, dolls, or stuffed animals, act out a classroom scene where students are out of their seats, talking at the same time, not waiting to be called on, and so forth (illustrate frustration of teacher and students.)

c. Using puppets, dolls, or stuffed animals, act out a classroom where students take turns asking questions, wait to be called on, speak clearly, and so forth.

d. Ask students to identify consequences of attending to the teacher. Elicit that *students will learn more, teachers will be happy,* and *parents will be happy.*

Step 2 Identify Skill Components

a. Elicit through discussion or provide students with the following rules:

1) Sit up straight.

    2) Listen carefully and look where the teacher points and where the teacher moves.

    3) Look to see if the teacher can see you; if so, raise your hand.

    4) Wait to be called on.

    5) Remain quiet while waiting; no wiggling or making noise.

    6) If the teacher can't see you, put your hand down.

    7) When called on, tell the teacher what you need/ask your question.

  b. Write steps on board, overhead, or chart paper. Develop poster (with text and icons).

  c. To reinforce attention element, classroom teachers might also use a prompt-and-response rhyme: Teacher: "1, 2, 3 eyes on me!" Students: "1, 2 eyes on you!"

  d. Review the steps with students using *chaining* to help students remember the sequence (i.e., Say Rule 1 in unison, then Rule 1 and Rule 2, then Rules 1, 2, and 3, etc.).

  e. Have students restate or paraphrase the steps.

Step 3 Model the Skill

  a. Appoint a student (competent peer) to act as the teacher. The student's job will be to tell the class what he or she is wearing and to indicate where three other classmates sit in the classroom.

  b. Before the student begins to speak, role-play using thinking aloud to point out that you are sitting straight, facing the speaker, and looking at him/her. Narrate how you are attending to the speaker and moving your head to follow the speaker and to look where the speaker points.

  c. Repeat the modeling process for gaining teacher attention; with a competent peer acting as "teacher," narrate the rules for gaining attention using thinking aloud:

    1) "Now I'm looking to see if the teacher can see me."

    2) "The teacher can see me so now I am raising my hand."

  d. Model the entire process without using thinking aloud and ask the class to evaluate how you did. Elicit from them each of the skill components that they observed. Modeling may have to be repeated until students are able to articulate each of the skill components.

(Use the same procedure when working on the sub-skill gaining teacher attention when permitted to be out of seat. Rules can be generated from the task analysis.)

CHAPTER 5

Step 4 Role-Play

    a. Tell the students that each of them will have to demonstrate the procedure twice. First, they will appropriately get the teacher's attention; second, they appropriately get attention and tell which rule(s) they are following. Each student in the class will be given an opportunity to demonstrate. Have a competent peer perform first.

    b. Give students feedback and praise.

    c. Have students evaluate their own performance and provide feedback to each other.

Step 5 Practice

    a. For four or five days subsequent to the lesson, begin class with the unison repetition of the steps for following classroom rules.

    b. During instruction, provide feedback and reinforcement to students for successfully demonstrating the skill.

    c. Randomly and periodically ask individual students to demonstrate the skill for the class.

    d. Use "show me" challenges periodically (e.g., "Sherrice, show me how ask for help or information.").

    e. Give students an assignment to test themselves on following the rules when in a general education class or "special" (e.g., Art, Music, PE). Have them report on how they did.

    f. Continue to intermittently provide feedback and reinforcement.

Step 6 Generalization

    a. Ask general education/specials teachers to teach an abbreviated form of this lesson in their classes.

    b. Provide other staff/teachers with a list of the rules and ask them to reinforce and to provide praise for appropriately gaining teacher attention. (If lists are posted on student desks, the teacher or aide can mark a + or – to indicate how well a student is following the rules.)

    c. Review the rules about once a month, fading to every 2 months.

    d. Have students self-evaluate and report on how well they have been doing on mastering the skill.

    e. Have students use self- and peer-monitoring forms (adapt Homework form for this use).

    f. Ask students to report on how well they attended in other settings/classes

    g. Ask other teachers/staff to complete feedback forms (adapt Task Analysis form);

reteach skill for students who receive unfavorable ratings. Reinforce students for attending and gaining attention successfully and restate the procedures.

Step 7 Evaluation

After a period of time it is necessary to determine if the skills taught are being sustained and generalized. The following practices are used to determine long-term success of instruction.

a. Periodically observe the students in general education settings and rate their performance according to the performance criteria listed at the beginning of the lesson.

b. Ask general education teacher(s)/other support staff to rate students according to the performance criteria.

c. Collect data using progress-monitoring strategies.

d. Design individual interventions for students not benefiting from small-group interventions (i.e., students who perform the skill inadequately or fail to generalize the skill to other settings).

CHAPTER
5

LESSON 2
Responding to Questions From a Teacher or Other Adult

Objective
Student will respond to a question from a teacher or other adult.

Performance Criteria
This skill will be *performed adequately* when the student:
1. Attends to the question.
2. Makes eye contact with the adult.
3. Asks that question be restated, if necessary.
4. Responds to question with appropriate tone and volume (even if he or she does not know the answer).
5. Attempts to maintain eye contact/look toward the other person throughout the process.

Materials Required
Dolls, puppets, or stuffed animals to use as props/modeling

Other Preparation
Video modeling is appropriate for both modeling and role-playing steps of this lesson.

Special Considerations
Many students with ASD require extra time to consider and formulate a response to a question; avoid repeated prompting, which may distract the student.
Many students with ASD have difficulty making and maintaining eye contact; reinforce and reward student success.

Forms and Supplementary Materials (see CD)
Student Self-Monitoring Form (Homework Form)

Technology Resources
iPad/iPhone apps: Look in My Eyes Car Mechanic/Undersea/DinosaurRestaurant/Eye Contact-Toybox (FizzBrain)

Related Lessons
    Lesson 3: Active Listening in the Classroom
    Lesson 15: Greeting Teachers and Adults
    Lesson 52, Volume 2: Interacting With School and Public Authorities

PROCEDURES 7 STEPS

Step 1 Establish the Need
    a. Ask students to identify why it is important to listen and answer questions from the teacher or other adults. Elicit that it *helps them learn*, *makes people happy*, and *shows what they know*.
    b. If students have difficulty comprehending or articulating the value of the skill, use puppets or stuffed animals to dramatize a situation where a student fails to listen and answer questions. Have students identify the consequences for not listening and answering.

Step 2 Identify Skill Components
    a. Elicit through discussion or provide students with the following rules:
        1) I respond when the teacher says my name.
        2) I keep my eyes on the teacher.
        3) I ask for the question again if I cannot hear or don't understand.
        4) I answer or say I don't know.
    b. Post the rules on chalkboard, whiteboard, posterboard, or chart paper for later review.

Step 3 Model the Skill
    a. Using puppets or dolls, demonstrate how to respond to a teacher's question. Narrate the skill component using the thinking aloud procedure.
    b. Have a competent peer model the skill and thinking aloud.
    c. Demonstrate responding to questions which require long and short responses and demonstrate responding when the answer is not known.
    d. Ask students to identify all of the skill components that they observed.

Step 4 Role-Play
    a. First have a competent peer model the skill again.
    b. Ask the questions and have pupils narrate what they are going or what they

must do before the question is answered.

   c. Provide feedback to students on their skill performance and ask them to provide feedback to each other.

Step 5 Practice

   a. Practice opportunities are likely to occur daily. On occasion, the rules for answering questions should be repeated.

   b. Use a relevant picture book (e.g., *Where the Wild Things Are* by Maurice Sendak (1988)) and have students practice maintaining eye contact (e.g., some students are Max, some are monsters).

Step 6 Generalization

   a. Have students use a self-monitoring form (adapt Homework form) to record when they answer questions in the general education classroom or "specials" (PE, Art, Music, library). Reward them for answering questions in these other settings.

   b. Inform classroom teachers/support staff of the skill being taught and request that they prompt the behavior in other settings.

   c. Monitor student performance; prompt and reinforce performance as warranted.

Step 7 Evaluation

After a period of time it is necessary to determine if the skills taught are being sustained and generalized. The following practices are used to determine long-term success of instruction.

   a. Periodically observe the students in general education settings and rate their performance according to the performance criteria listed at the beginning of the lesson.

   b. Ask general education teacher(s)/other support staff to rate students according to the performance criteria.

   c. Collect data using progress-monitoring strategies.

   d. Design individual interventions for students not benefiting from small-group interventions (i.e., students who perform the skill inadequately or fail to generalize the skill to other settings).

CHAPTER 5

LESSON 3
Active Listening in the Classroom

Objective
Students will follow verbal directions when given by a teacher or school staff member.

Performance Criteria
This skill will be *performed adequately* when the student:
1. Faces and looks at teacher when directions are being given.
2. Waits until directions are complete before beginning task.
3. Repeats directions to self.
4. Follows directions immediately.
5. Asks to have forgotten directions repeated.
6. Completes assignment or task per directions.

Materials Required
Book on the theme, such as *My Mouth Is a Volcano* by Julia Cook and Carrie Hartman (2006); *My Mouth Is a Volcano Activity and Idea Book* by Julia Cook and Carrie Hartman (2009).

Other Preparation
For additional resources, see *Grid and Graph it: Graphing Activities for Listening and Following Directions* by Will C. Howell and Pattie Silver (2002).

Special Considerations
Some students with ASD appear not to be listening/paying attention when they are. Some students may benefit from Theraputty or other materials to keep hands occupied and enhance cooperation.

Forms and Supplementary Materials (see CD)
Home-School Connection form

Technology Resources
Software: Boardmaker/Writing With Symbols software (both Mayer-Johnson)
Internet: Boardmaker share site has several "following directions" visuals at www. boardmakershare.com/Activities/Search/?SearchText=following%20directions&FileSearchCategoryID=-1

Free Language Stuff (http://freelanguagestuff.com/tag/following-directions/) has worksheets for pairs to use; one person reads directions and the other completes the task

Find Our House game (http://fog.ccsf.cc.ca.us/~lfried/activity/houses.html); student must listen to information about the house and select the one described

Related Lessons
Lesson 12: Appropriate Classroom Participation
Lesson 18: Active Listening to Peers
Lesson 63, Volume 2: Maintaining a Conversation: Active Listening and Joint Attention

PROCEDURES 7 STEPS

Step 1 Establish the Need
a. Introduce the concept of active listening to directions by reading a themed book to the class.
b. Discuss the book, highlighting the consequences of not following verbal directions.
c. Ask students to identify other situations where it's important to follow directions.
d. Elicit from students that when in school, it's important to follow directions because *it helps everyone in the class to learn, everyone can get their work done.*

Step 2 Identify Skill Components
a. Write the following rules for following directions on the board; have the students copy them or distribute small reproductions for student desks.
    1) Look at the person giving directions.
    2) Wait until you hear all of the directions.
    3) If you forget, ask to have the direction repeated.
    4) Say the direction back to the person.
    5) Follow all the directions right away.
b. Cover the rules at least twice and discuss examples for each component.

Step 3 Model the Skill
a. Choose the best reader in the group and have them read directions for a task to you.
b. While following the directions, use the thinking aloud procedure to narrate

execution of the skill components.

c. Discuss the modeled situation and have students identify how you followed the rules.

d. Model the skill again, following a new/different set of directions but leave out a skill component. Ask students to identify what was left out.

e. Have a competent peer model the skill with a third set of directions.

Step 4 Role-Play

a. Give each student a different two-step direction and have them thinking aloud as they role-play the skill. Make sure that the directions represent a functional activity.

b. Coach students to repeat the directions back to you. Get them accustomed to making statements, such as, "Ok, just to make sure I understand, you want me to [repeats direction]."

c. Give each student feedback and ask them to evaluate their own performance.

Step 5 Practice

a. During the week following introduction of the lesson, hold two or three sessions focusing on following directions. Give feedback and praise to students.

b. Take advantage of naturally occurring events to reinforce students for following verbal directions.

c. Send students on errands outside the classroom. Give feedback and praise for skill performance.

d. Periodically repeat directions/rules following practice.

Step 6 Generalization

a. Send information home with students explaining the lesson on following rules/active listening. Ask families to reinforce by giving students directions to follow for a chore at home; ask them to reinforce use of the specific steps.

b. Solicit the assistance of other school staff members to give verbal directions and provide feedback. (For example, give some written directions to the school secretary; send students to her one at a time and have her relay the directions to them.)

c. Ask students to report on use of the skill. Praise students for self-reporting.

d. Request that general education teachers and "specials" teachers (PE, Art, Music) prompt and praise direction following.

Step 7 Evaluation

After a period of time it is necessary to determine if the skills taught are being sustained and generalized. The following practices are used to determine long-term success of instruction.

a. Periodically observe the students in general education settings and rate their performance according to the performance criteria listed at the beginning of the lesson.

b. Ask general education teacher(s)/other support staff to rate students according to the performance criteria.

c. Collect data using progress-monitoring strategies.

d. Design individual interventions for students not benefiting from small-group interventions (i.e., students who perform the skill inadequately or fail to generalize the skill to other settings).

LESSON 4
Classroom Rules: Sitting in Your Own Space

Objective
Student will maintain appropriate distance from others during classroom activities.

Performance Criteria
This skill will be *performed adequately* when the student:
1. Maintains an appropriate distance from other students when sitting in a group (e.g., circle on floor; sitting around a table).
2. Maintains space of an arm's length when working face-to-face with a partner or group of peers.
3. Maintains appropriate distance from others when walking in line.
4. Is able to express when he or she needs more personal space.

Materials Required
Book on the theme, such as such as *Personal Space Camp* by Julia Cook (2007); *Personal Space Camp Activity and Idea Book* (2010) by Julia Cook and Carrie Hartman.

Other Preparation
Materials/software/app to support creating social story.

Special Considerations
Although some students with ASD and other developmental disabilities dislike being too close to others and will gravitate to the outskirts of a group or an area apart from others, other students with ASD have difficulty understanding when they get too close or violate another's personal space. This lesson should be adapted to suit the student's particular challenges.

Forms and Supplementary Materials (see CD)
Home-School Connection form

Technology Resources
iPad/iPhone app: Stories2Learn (MDR) or Pictello (AssistiveWare) for creating social stories
Internet: Boardmaker "share" site has a sample social story relating to this topic at www.boardmakershare.com/Activity/358702/personal-space-booklet

CHAPTER 5

Related Lessons

Lesson 8: Hallway Etiquette: Staying in Line, Entering a Room/Area
Lesson 16: Greeting Peers and Friends
Lesson 39: Avoiding Inappropriate Contact
Lesson 51, Volume 2: Hallway Etiquiette: Interactions With Others

PROCEDURES 7 STEPS

Step 1 Establish the Need

a. Introduce the topic by reading a themed book.
b. Through group discussion, elicit from students what amount of space makes them feel comfortable. "Do you like to have some space around you when you are around people you don't know too well?" "If someone is standing far away from you, can you have a conversation with them?" Elicit that *standing too close can make people nervous*; *standing too far away makes people think you don't like them.*
c. Ask students to list times when they don't have a choice how close or far to be from another person. Elicit such times as *riding a crowded bus, sitting next to one another in the cafeteria,* and so forth.
d. Point out the need for making any distinctions in determining the space that should be respected.

Step 2 Identify Skill Components

a. Engage students in a game or group activity illustrating/practicing different "spaces": use dolls, cars, or other toys and have students demonstrate when space is appropriate to the condition (e.g., working together at desks vs. standing in line).
b. Instruct how to visualize maintaining an appropriate distance from each other: when standing, have students extend their arms and turn around; explain that this imaginary circle is their personal space. Use string to create slightly overlapping circles for group circle time and have students sit in them.
c. Provide students with guidelines for maintaining appropriate distance. These are helpful for students who do not discriminate the social cues for culturally appropriate space allowance. Examples:
   1) When talking to a person face-to-face, stay at least one arm's-length away.
   2) When in a group or a circle and next to someone, try to keep the distance that is the same as from your shoulder to your elbow.

Step 3 Model the Skill

a. Model the skill under the different conditions (whole class, in line, working with a partner); thinking aloud to illustrate visualization of being too close, too far, or the right distance from another person. Demonstrate the arm's length and shoulder-to-elbow length guideline.

b. Show students pictures of groups of people and ask "are they too close? Too far? Or just right?" Reinforce correct responses.

c. Have students model the skill and encourage feedback on each other's performance.

Step 4 Role-Play

a. Create a social story with students: take pictures of them modeling the skill correctly and elicit the steps as text.

b. Use video modeling with pairs of students in differing conditions.

Step 5 Practice

a. Assign students "homework": share the social story with their families or share the video at home (send information using the Home-School Connection form).

b. At different times and under different conditions the week after introducing the skill, ask students to thinking aloud the skill elements.

c. At different times the week after introducing the skill, ask students "am I too close? Too far? Or just right?"

Step 6 Generalization

a. Ask general education teachers/other staff to monitor/reinforce; it may be helpful to provide an agreed-upon cue (e.g., "check your space")

b. Ask other staff to observe and report on student behaviors in other settings (e.g., hallway, cafeteria line)

Step 7 Evaluation

After a period of time it is necessary to determine if the skills taught are being sustained and generalized. The following practices are used to determine long-term success of instruction.

a. Periodically observe the students in general education settings and rate their performance according to the performance criteria listed at the beginning of the lesson.

b. Ask general education teacher(s)/other support staff to rate students according to the performance criteria.

CHAPTER 5

   c. Collect data using progress-monitoring strategies.

   d. Design individual interventions for students not benefiting from small-group interventions (i.e., students who perform the skill inadequately or fail to generalize the skill to other settings).

LESSON 5
Keeping Your Desk in Order

Objective

Students will maintain an orderly desk and be able to find personal belongings and school materials.

Performance Criteria

This skill will be *performed adequately* when the student:
1. Keeps papers and books stacked neatly in appropriate compartment (this may be inside desk or on rack under desk chair).
   a. Books are stacked so they don't fall over.
   b. Papers are placed in folders or notebooks to prevent them from becoming tattered or lost.
2. Keeps pens and pencils inside desk or other appropriate container (e.g., school box).
3. Keeps top of desk clear to work on.
4. Picks up dropped papers, books, pencils, or other materials.
5. Keeps floor around desk clear of debris.
6. Stores outerwear garments somewhere other than in or on desk.

Materials Required

Student desks; school box/folders; pens, pencils, papers, and schoolbooks; stuffed animal or doll
Whiteboard/chalkboard/overhead projector/posterboard/chart paper
Digital or Polaroid camera

Other Preparation

Need to set up "messy" and "neat" desk before presenting lesson.

Special Considerations

Some students with ASD and other developmental disabilities have difficulty organizing materials and may benefit from labeled or fixed containers for different items, or from a picture of where everything should go, on the desk itself.

Forms and Supplementary Materials (see CD)

None for this lesson.

Technology Resources
None for this lesson.

Related Lessons
Lesson 17: Using Classroom Materials

PROCEDURES 7 STEPS

Step 1 Establish the Need
   a. Present to students the two sample student desks, one messy and one neat.
   b. Using a stuffed animal or doll or puppet, identify the messy desk as belonging to "Messy Bear" (or name of doll).
   c. As "teacher," instruct the character to get something from the desk. Pantomine or use thinking aloud procedure about the character trying to find the item and being frustrated and unable to comply.
   d. Ask students what happens to personal belongings in desks like Messy Bear's. Elicit that *things like pencils get lost* and *papers get torn.*
   e. Introduce the neat desk and discuss with the class how to make a messy desk a neat desk.

Step 2 Identify Skill Components
   a. Tell students that there are rules to follow for keeping their desks straight. Write the following rules on the board/overhead (or use picture icons for nonreaders):
       1) Keep books stacked straight.
       2) Keep papers in a folder.
       3) Keep pencils in one spot.
       4) Pick up things dropped.
       5) Keep the desktop clear.
   b. Discuss each of the skill components as they relate to classroom desks and procedures (e.g., if school boxes are used, discuss what materials belong in a school box).
   c. Orally rehearse the skill steps in unison at least twice.

Step 3 Model the Skill
   a. Using the messy desk, show students exactly where to put each item, using the thinking aloud procedure. Be specific.
   b. Ask students if you followed all the rules.
   c. Take a picture of the desk when everything is in order.

Step 4 Role-Play

    a. Tell students that each of them has to show how well they can follow the rules. Give class a couple of minutes to straighten desks.

    b. Have students change seats and evaluate how well the rules have been followed. Repeat the rules one at a time to have students check for each skill component, and compare their straightened desks to the picture of the "neat desk."

    c. Send students back to their own desks and provide feedback on their performance.

    d. At the end of the school day, ask students to make their desks look like the "neat desk" picture.

Step 5 Practice

    a. For the week following the introduction of the lesson, review the rules for a neat desk at least once daily.

    b. Have students take turns turning a messy desk into a neat desk.

    c. Establish *skill challenges* by asking students to evaluate how well they are following the rules for keeping a neat desk.

    d. Make a point of praising students who keep neat desks.

Step 6 Generalization

    a. Use occasional praise to reinforce students for keeping neat desks.

    b. Ask general education classroom teachers and other staff to intermittently reinforce students for keeping their desks neat.

    c. Ask students to report on how well they have kept their desks straight.

    d. Have students rate themselves on a card with a picture of a neat desk.

Step 7 Evaluation

After a period of time it is necessary to determine if the skills taught are being sustained and generalized. The following practices are used to determine long-term success of instruction.

    a. Periodically observe the students in general education settings and rate their performance according to the performance criteria listed at the beginning of the lesson.

    b. Ask general education teacher(s)/other support staff to rate students according to the performance criteria.

    c. Collect data using progress-monitoring strategies.

    d. Design individual interventions for students not benefiting from small-group interventions (i.e., students who perform the skill inadequately or fail to generalize the skill to other settings).

CHAPTER
5

LESSON 6
Saying "Please" and "Thank You"

Objective

Students will say "please" prior to making a request and "thank you" after their request is answered.

Performance Criteria

This skill will be *performed adequately* when the student:

1. Comes within range of the person with whom they need to speak and faces toward them.
2. Prefaces or ends request with "please."
3. Listens for response.
4. Says "thank you" when request is granted or denied.

Materials Required

Book on the theme, such as *Richard Scarry's Please and Thank You Book* by Richard Scarry (1973), *Say "Please": A Book About Manners* by Catherine Lukas (2006), or *Time to Say Please* by Mo Williems (2005)

Materials to create poster of classroom rules (text + icons)

Dolls, stuffed animals, or puppets to model skill (optional)

Tokens, treats, school materials, and so forth, for role-playing step

Other Preparation

Select competent peers to demonstrate the skill during the modeling step.

Special Considerations

Most children have been exposed to this skill at home. The purpose of this lesson is to help generalize the skill to school.

Forms and Supplementary Materials (see CD)

None for this lesson.

Technology Resources

Software: Boardmaker/Writing With Symbols (both Mayer-Johnson)

Related Lessons

Lesson 7: Requesting a Preferred Activity

Lesson 17: Using Classroom Materials: Sharing, Taking Care of Supplies, and Requesting Materials From Others

PROCEDURES 7 STEPS

Step 1 Establish the Need

a. Read a story with the theme of manners/please-and-thank you; discuss the story.

b. Ask children what they say at home when they ask for something to eat or something else they want. Elicit that *they should say "please."*

c. Ask children what they should say when someone gives them something. Elicit *"thank you."*

d. Ask students to identify times and situations where they should say "please" and "thank you."

Step 2 Identify Skill Components

a. Tell students that you will be giving them a chance to show how good they are at saying "please" and "thank you," but first you will show them the very best way.

b. Illustrate the process using dolls, puppets, or stuffed animals (optional).

c. Create a poster for the classroom (text + icons for younger nonreading students):
   1) Come near the person you want to talk to and face them.
   2) Say "please."
   3) Listen to the answer.
   4) Say "thank you."

Step 3 Model the Skill

a. Have a competent peer model saying "please" and "thank you," requesting to be given something and requesting permission to do something.

b. Ask students to either identify all the steps performed or identify any missing components.

Step 4 Role-Play

a. Have available items students may ask for (e.g., treats, small toys, school materials, or tokens such as stars or smiley faces).

b. Pair student(s) with competent peer(s).

c. Have each student make a request and receive something. Praise correct performance of the skill.

d. Have each student make a request for permission to do something using "please" and "thank you."

Step 5 Practice

a. During the week following introduction of the lesson, have students practice the skill whenever school materials are passed out or when they need to request permission to do something.

b. Provide students feedback and praise on their performance.

Step 6 Generalization

a. Solicit the cooperation of other school staff members and set up situations where students will be required to make a request. Have the cooperating person prompt and praise students for performing the skill. (The school secretary, librarian, custodian, cafeteria, specials teachers, etc. may be able to fill this cooperative role.)

b. Request that general education teachers prompt "pleases" and "thank yous"; share the poster with other teachers for posting throughout the school..

c. Gradually fade prompts and reinforcements.

Step 7 Evaluation

After a period of time it is necessary to determine if the skills taught are being sustained and generalized. The following practices are used to determine long-term success of instruction.

a. Periodically observe the students in general education settings and rate their performance according to the performance criteria listed at the beginning of the lesson.

b. Ask general education teacher(s)/other support staff to rate students according to the performance criteria.

c. Collect data using progress-monitoring strategies.

d. Design individual interventions for students not benefiting from small-group interventions (i.e., students who perform the skill inadequately or fail to generalize the skill to other settings).

LESSON 7
Requesting a Preferred Activity

Objective
Students will request a preferred activity using voice or AAC device.

Performance Criteria
This skill will be *performed adequately* when the student:
1. Gains an adult's attention by raising hand or approaching.
2. Makes request using voice or AAC device.
3. Uses proper etiquette (i.e., please and thank you).
4. Does not object if request is denied.

Materials Required
AAC (Augmentative and Alternative Communication) device for nonspeaking students.

Other Preparation
May need to assist student in learning to use AAC device.

Special Considerations
None for this lesson.

Forms and Supplementary Materials (see CD)
None for this lesson.

Technology Resources
AAC device
iPad/iPhone/android apps: There are currently over 100 apps designed to support communication for students who are nonverbal or have communication difficulties. Among the best known are Proloquo2go (AssistiveWare), iComm (Bappz), Look2Learn (MDR), Tap to Talk (Assistyx), and iConverse (Xcellent Creations); AppsforAAC web site has an extensive list http://appsforaac.net/applist

Related Lessons

Lesson 6: Saying "Please" and "Thank You"
Lesson 10: Being Patient: Learning How to Wait
Lesson 27: Asking Someone to Play With You
Lesson 48: Managing Emotions: Dealing With Frustration

PROCEDURES 7 STEPS

Step 1 Establish the Need

a. Perform a skit (using puppets or dolls) where a character has an option or choice but does not voice this; elicit that the character is *disappointed* or *frustrated*.

b. Illustrate that the teacher or leader did not know what the character wanted to do.

c. Play-act the character requesting and receiving a preferred activity; elicit that the character is *happy they get to do something they like to do*.

d. Play-act the character requesting a preferred activity, but at an inappropriate time. Illustrate appropriate response and acceptance of delayed gratification.

Step 2 Identify Skill Components

a. With students, identify the skill components from the skit:
   1) I decide what I want to do.
   2) I decide if what I want to do is appropriate.
   3) If it's appropriate, I raise my hand or approach.
   4) I ask for what I want politely.
   5) I'm ok if the answer is no. Maybe I can do it later.
   6) If the answer is yes, I can do what I wanted to do!

b. Demonstrate a talking-to-self dialogue (see Chapter 4) for accepting denial of a request.

Step 3 Model the Skill

a. Model the skill correctly using the same puppets or dolls from the introduction of the lesson. Use the thinking aloud procedure to repeat/reinforce the steps of the skill.

b. Model the skill correctly and have students identify the elements of the skill.

c. Model the skill incorrectly and ask students to identify missing elements.

d. Have a competent peer model the skill with teacher or another adult.

Step 4 Role-Play

a. Have students practice the skill individually and provide feedback/reinforcement.

b. Have students practice the skill in pairs, with one student playing "teacher."

Step 5 Practice

a. Announce that there is some free time in class. Purposely suggest a nonpreferred activity. If necessary, encourage students to ask for an activity they would rather do.

b. During the week following introduction of the skill, incorporate opportunities for students to exercise and express choice among various options.

Step 6 Generalization

a. Solicit the cooperation of other school staff members and set up situations (e.g., "specials" classes such as PE; recess, lunch) where students have an opportunity to make a request. Have the cooperating person prompt and praise students for performing the skill.

b. Gradually fade prompts and reinforcements.

Step 7 Evaluation

After a period of time it is necessary to determine if the skills taught are being sustained and generalized. The following practices are used to determine long-term success of instruction.

a. Periodically observe the students in general education settings and rate their performance according to the performance criteria listed at the beginning of the lesson.

b. Ask general education teacher(s)/other support staff to rate students according to the performance criteria.

c. Collect data using progress-monitoring strategies.

d. Design individual interventions for students not benefiting from small-group interventions (i.e., students who perform the skill inadequately or fail to generalize the skill to other settings).

LESSON 8
Hallway Etiquette: Staying in Line, Entering a Room/Area

Objective
Students will walk in an orderly manner in school hallways and entry areas.

Performance Criteria
This skill will be *performed adequately* when the student:
1. Stands straight with hands at side.
2. Keeps an appropriate distance from preceding student.
3. Walks quietly through hallways and entry areas.

Materials Required
Book on the theme, such as *The Quiet Book* by Deborah Underwood (2010).
Toy cars, masking tape
Posterboard/sign materials

Other Preparation
Tape off long strips on classroom floor to serve as "road" and "hallway."
Prepare SHOW poster and chart of steps with pictures and words.

Special Considerations
None for this lesson.

Forms and Supplementary Materials (see CD)
None for this lesson.

Technology Resources
None for this lesson.

Related Lessons
Lesson 10: Being Patient: Learning How to Wait
Lesson 51: Hallway Etiquette: Interactions With Others

CHAPTER 5

PROCEDURES 7 STEPS

Step 1 Establish the Need

a. Introduce the topic by reading a themed book.

b. Ask students to identify times during the school day when it's important to be quiet; elicit *in the hallway*.

c. Elicit that it's important to be quiet and orderly in the hallway because

1) It can be difficult for other people (in classrooms, at work) to concentrate if people in the hallway are noisy

2) They might hurt people if they are running or not paying attention where they are going.

Step 2 Identify Skill Components

a. Tell the students you are going to SHOW them the best way to walk in the hallway. Post a sign that says SHOW.

b. Delineate the steps of the skill:

1) S – Stand straight.

2) H – Hands to your side.

3) O – One in front of the other.

4) W – Walk quietly.

c. Post a second poster with the steps spelled out and images/pictures illustrating the steps.

Step 3 Model the Skill

a. In the "hallway" area of the classroom (taped lines), have students line up and repeat the skill steps.

b. Model the skill as a class.

c. Model the skill without speaking; use Stop and Go signs to direct students.

Step 4 Role-Play

a. Distribute toy cars to students. Ask them to line their cars up on the "road" (taped lines).

b. Provide feedback on appropriate distance.

c. Have students "drive" cars, with the instruction that they have to stay in a line, and may not pass. They have to be patient drivers. (Optional: Show what happens if one car goes too fast and crashes into the car ahead.)

Step 5 Practice
   a. Rehearse the skill steps when preparing to walk through school hallways.
   b. Use the Stop and Go signs in the hallway to reinforce.

Step 6 Generalization
   a. Share the SHOW mnemonic with other instructional staff (i.e., general education teachers, "specials" teachers, librarian) and ask them to post the steps in their rooms and reinforce when students enter/leave these areas.
   b. Gradually fade use of Stop and Go signs.

Step 7 Evaluation
   After a period of time it is necessary to determine if the skills taught are being sustained and generalized. The following practices are used to determine long-term success of instruction.
   a. Periodically observe the students in general education settings and rate their performance according to the performance criteria listed at the beginning of the lesson.
   b. Ask general education teacher(s)/other support staff to rate students according to the performance criteria.
   c. Collect data using progress-monitoring strategies.
   d. Design individual interventions for students not benefiting from small-group interventions (i.e., students who perform the skill inadequately or fail to generalize the skill to other settings).

CHAPTER
5

LESSON 9
Riding the School Bus

Objective
Students will follow school bus riding rules.

Performance Criteria
This skill will be *performed adequately* when the student:
1. Greets bus driver.
2. Chooses a vacant seat.
3. Remains seated.
4. Keep hands, arms, and legs inside the seat area.
5. Keeps track of personal belongings.
6. Uses a quiet voice.
7. Refrains from interfering with other bus riders.
8. Stays seated until the bus stops.
9. Exits bus at appropriate stopping place.

Materials Required
Chairs, chalkboard/whiteboard

Other Preparation
Need to develop comic strips (see Chapter 4) before presenting lesson; one strip should present inappropriate bus behavior, the other appropriate behavior. (Alternatively, may compile pictures/drawings illustrating inappropriate bus behavior and/or use dolls or puppets to demonstrate.)

Special Considerations
Students with ASD and other developmental disabilities may have difficulty riding in an unfamiliar vehicle.

Forms and Supplementary Materials (see CD)
None for this lesson.

Technology Resources
Software/apps: Comic Life software and app (Plasq.com); Strip Designer app (www.mexircus.com/Strip_Designer/index.html)

Internet: Makebeliefscomix (www.makebeliefscomix.com/), ReadWriteThink Comic Creator (www.readwritethink.org/files/resources/interactives/comic/), StripGenerator (http://stripgenerator.com/), StoryCreator 2 (http://myths.e2bn. org/create/tool527-story-creator-2.html)

Related Lessons
None for this lesson.

PROCEDURES 7 STEPS

Step 1 Establish the Need
    a. Introduce the topic:
        1) Present the comic strip "Riding the Bus" to the class; ask students to identify what the students in the comic strip are doing wrong. OR
        2) Present pictures/drawings illustrating inappropriate behaviors / use dolls/ puppets to demonstrate. Ask students to identify what the "students" are doing wrong.
    b. Present the comic strip showing appropriate bus-riding behavior. Ask the children to identify the rules for riding on the school bus that they see in the pictures. Elicit that they should stay seated, not bother other children, and talk quietly.
    c. Ask students what might happen if children were allowed to walk around while the bus was moving. Elicit that they might fall and be hurt.
    d. Ask students what might happen if they got in a fight on the bus. Elicit that they could distract the bus driver and cause an accident and they may be denied their bus riding privileges.

Step 2 Identify Skill Components
    a. Tell students that the bus drivers like to have children on their bus who:
        1) Smile or say hello.
        2) Find an empty seat.
        3) Talk quietly.
        4) Stay in their seat.
        5) Get off at the right stop.
    b. Rehearse the five things bus drivers like in unison.
    c. Rewrite the comic strip so that the characters are behaving appropriately.
    d. Give each student a copy of the comic strip.

Step 3 Model the Skill
a. On a parked school bus, model the skill using the thinking aloud procedure to point out the skill components. OR
b. Set up some chairs in the classroom to simulate a school bus and model the skill using the thinking aloud procedure to point out the skill components.

Step 4 Role-Play
a. Have students role play the skill in groups.
b. Give students feedback on their performance.
c. Have each student evaluate his or her performance.

Step 5 Practice
a. Repeat the role-playing two or three times during the week following the introductory lesson in the classroom.
b. Arrange to practice the skill on a stationary school bus.
c. Review the skill components daily for a week. Have students state bus riding rules in unison.
d. Provide students with cards listing the rules.

Step 6 Generalization
a. Provide school bus drivers with the list of bus-riding rules and ask them to reinforce and to occasionally praise students for following the rules.
b. Follow up with bus drivers on student behavior. Praise or reward students for good bus-riding behavior.
c. Ask students to report on their own bus-riding behavior. Praise students for self-reporting.

Step 7 Evaluation
After a period of time it is necessary to determine if the skills taught are being sustained and generalized. The following practices are used to determine long-term success of instruction.
a. Periodically observe the students in general education settings and rate their performance according to the performance criteria listed at the beginning of the lesson.
b. Ask general education teacher(s)/other support staff to rate students according to the performance criteria.
c. Collect data using progress-monitoring strategies.
d. Design individual interventions for students not benefiting from small-group

interventions (i.e., students who perform the skill inadequately or fail to generalize the skill to other settings).

LESSON 10
Being Patient: Learning How to Wait

Objective
Students will be able to wait in different situations and circumstances.

Performance Criteria
This skill will be *performed adequately* when the student:
1. Demonstrates waiting to be called on: hand raised, not talking or blurting out answer.
2. Demonstrates waiting while seated: does not talk or walk around.
3. Demonstrates waiting in line: stays in place, keeping appropriate distance from others and hands and feet to self.

Materials Required
Book on the theme, such as *My Mouth Is a Volcano* (2006) by Julia Cook; *My Mouth Is a Volcano Activity and Idea Book* (2009) by Julia Cook and Carrie Hartman.

Other Preparation
Prepare a competent peer to assist in modeling the skill.
Video modeling may be helpful to support role-playing and practice steps.

Special Considerations
Some students may need the added support of a timer or visual aid.

Forms and Supplementary Materials (see CD)
None for this lesson.

Technology Resources
Internet: SpeakingofSpeech.com has several prepared social stories on the theme at www.speakingofspeech.com/Social_Skills_Pragmatics.html
iPad/iPhone apps: Time Timer (Time Timer LLC); First Then Visual Schedule (Good Karma); iPrompt (Handhold Adaptive)

Related Lessons

Lesson 8: Hallway Etiquette: Staying in Line, Entering a Room/Area
Lesson 41: Playing Games With Peers: Following the Rules and What to Do When Someone Cheats

PROCEDURES 7 STEPS

Step 1 Establish the Need

a. Read a book on the theme to introduce the lesson.
b. Lead a class discussion. Ask students a series of questions to establish why it is important to learn to wait to be called on, why it is important not to blurt out answers, why waiting in line is necessary, and why it is important to stay in place during class.
c. Elicit from the students that the *teacher may have to help other students*, that *they should be polite and not answer questions that are asked of others*, and that *they should not disrupt class by wandering away from their seats*.
d. Elicit through questions and prompts that learning is diminished when students blurt out, fail to wait to have questions answered, or get out of seats.

Step 2 Identify Skill Components

a. List on overhead, whiteboard, or chalkboard the steps of the skill:
   1) Wait to answer class questions: Raise your hand (or use other appropriate procedure to be called upon, e.g., raise a flag on their desk).
   2) Do not blurt out answers or statements until called upon.
   3) Stay in your in seat.
   4) Stay in line until you enter a different space.
b. Have students make posters with pictures or icons illustrating the skill steps.

Step 3 Model the Skill

a. Using puppets or stuffed animals, model the skill of hand raising and waiting to be called upon. (Alternatively, may model with another school staff member playing the role of "teacher.")
b. Using the thinking aloud procedure, model hand-raising when the teacher is looking and lowering hand when the teacher is not looking.
c. Have a competent peer model the skill of waiting and hand raising.
d. Using the thinking aloud procedure, model staying in one's seat and staying in line.

Step 4 Role-Play

a. Have students demonstrate waiting to be called upon and refraining from blurting out.

b. Ask students to use the thinking aloud procedure to describe why they are staying in their seats or staying in line.

c. Provide feedback and coaching on how the students demonstrate the desired behaviors.

Step 5 Practice

a. Play a waiting game (e.g., Red Light, Green Light)

b. Ask the group questions and avoid calling on some students. Provide verbal or other forms of reinforcement to students for correct performance.

c. Use the "show me" cue to have students remain seated or appropriately proceed with a line.

CHAPTER 5

Step 6 Generalization

a. In the hallways or settings outside the school, use the "show me" me cue to elicit proper waiting while in line.

b. Inform general education teachers that your groups is working on appropriate waiting behavior. Have the general educators report back on student performance.

c. Ask general education and specials teachers to praise appropriate behavior and correct inappropriate behavior.

Step 7 Evaluation

After a period of time it is necessary to determine if the skills taught are being sustained and generalized. The following practices are used to determine long-term success of instruction.

a. Periodically observe the students in general education settings and rate their performance according to the performance criteria listed at the beginning of the lesson.

b. Ask general education teacher(s)/other support staff to rate students according to the performance criteria.

c. Collect data using progress-monitoring strategies.

d. Design individual interventions for students not benefiting from small-group interventions (i.e., students who perform the skill inadequately or fail to generalize the skill to other settings).

LESSON 11
Using the Restroom

Objective
Students will use the school restroom appropriately.

Performance Criteria
This skill will be *performed adequately* when the student:
1. Asks to use rest room only when needed.
2. Proceeds directly to the gender-appropriate rest room.
3. Selects and uses appropriate restroom fixture as determined by personal need.
4. Refrains from playing in the restroom.
5. Does not peek in other stalls.
6. Does not sit on the restroom floor.
7. Flushes toilet or urinal (if possible).
8. Washes and dries hands after using.
9. Deposits paper towels in appropriate trash container.
10. Refrains from spending more time in rest room than necessary.

Materials Required
Feltboard/poster that can accommodate removable Velcro items, or whiteboard
Dolls/puppets

Other Preparation
None for this lesson.

Special Considerations
Video modeling may be appropriate for modeling and role-playing some elements of the target skill (e.g., asking for permission, walking to restroom, washing and drying hands).

Forms and Supplementary Materials (see CD)
None for this lesson.

CHAPTER 5

Technology Resources
None for this lesson.

Related Lessons
Lesson 34: Recognizing and Expressing Bodily Needs
Lesson 43: Hygienic Behavior: Handwashing, Personal Grooming, and Cleanliness

PROCEDURES 7 STEPS

Step 1 Establish the Need

a. Describe for the students inappropriate restroom behavior (dawdling on the way to restroom, playing with water in the sink, throwing paper on the floor).

b. Ask students what the consequence of this behavior might be. Elicit *breaks school rules*; *school personnel will be unhappy*; *other students won't want to use the restroom.*

c. Ask students what is appropriate when using the restroom; elicit *go straight there, keep restroom neat and clean,* and *come right back.*

Step 2 Identify Skill Components

a. Tell class that there are some rules to follow when using the school rest room. Read and show the students the following phrases and have them place them in the proper category, "Do" or "Don't." (This can be done on feltboard, on a poster that accommodates Velcro strips, or on an interactive whiteboard; it can also be written on a chalkboard or overhead.)

Do	Don't
Ask permission to use the rest room.	Stop and talk.
Go straight to the rest room.	Play in the sink.
Use the toilet properly.	Fool around with friends.
Flush.	Throw papers on the floor.
Wash hands.	Stay too long.
Come right back to class	

b. Review the rules and have the class repeat them in unison several times.

Step 3 Model the Skill

a. Use dolls or puppets to model certain elements (e.g., ask for permission, walk to restroom, wash hands).

b. Ask class to name the rules they saw being followed.

Step 4 Role-Play

a. Have students role-play the rules governing using the restroom.

b. Provide feedback to each student and ask classmates to provide feedback.

c. Have students evaluate their own performance.

Step 5 Practice

a. Review the rules and have the class repeat them in unison once each day during the week following introduction of the lesson.

b. Take advantage of real need situations to review the rules and give feedback to students for using the skill.

Step 6 Generalization

a. Solicit the assistance of same-gender school staff to accompany students to the restroom and reteach or reinforce skill elements as needed.

b. Ask school officials to occasionally monitor and provide feedback to students on their restroom use behavior.

c. Before class field trips, rehearse the rules; after, provide feedback and praise to students for appropriate use of public restrooms.

d. Use reminders and reinforcers for handwashing.

e. Gradually fade use of prompts and reinforcements.

Step 7 Evaluation

After a period of time it is necessary to determine if the skills taught are being sustained and generalized. The following practices are used to determine long-term success of instruction.

a. Periodically observe the students in general education settings and rate their performance according to the performance criteria listed at the beginning of the lesson.

b. Ask general education teacher(s)/other support staff to rate students according to the performance criteria.

c. Collect data using progress-monitoring strategies.

d. Design individual interventions for students not benefiting from small-group interventions (i.e., students who perform the skill inadequately or fail to generalize the skill to other settings).

LESSON 12
Appropriate Classroom Participation

Objective

Students will actively participate in classroom activities.

Performance Criteria

This skill will be *performed adequately* when the student:
1. Answers questions posed by the teacher or other school staff member.
2. Raises hand to make a comment or volunteer to respond.
3. Makes appropriate comments and responds appropriately.
4. Follows directions in games and activities.
5. Joins in and participates with group activities.

Materials Required

Video clips of student participating and working in an elementary classroom. Chart paper, markers

Other Preparation

Prepare competent peers to assist in modeling and role-playing steps.
Prepare mini lessons on age-appropriate topics for use when teaching social behaviors.

Special Considerations

Video modeling is recommended for the modeling and practice steps.

Forms and Supplementary Materials (see CD)

None for this lesson.

Technology Resources

My School Day Enhanced CD (Social Skill Builder) contains scenarios to demonstrate behaviors such as listening, compromising, following directions, cooperating, and rules.
Social Skills (S2L; MDR) app has 12 prepared social stories including joint attention, structured game play, and classroom rules, which can be adapted to include photos of target students.

CHAPTER
5

Related Lessons

Lesson 1: Classroom Rules

Lesson 2: Responding to Questions From a Teacher or Other Adult

Lesson 3: Active Listening in the Classroom

PROCEDURES 7 STEPS

Step 1 Establish the Need

a. Show video clips of students attending in class and working on cooperative activities. Following the video clips, ask students to identify what the students were doing that makes them good learners. Elicit that they were looking at the teacher, everyone participated in the cooperative tasks, no one blurted out answers, and everyone talked only about the content of the lessons.

b. Ask students to identify what consequences may occur when students do not engage in the good learning behaviors. Elicit that they will not learn, they will disrupt other students' learning.

Step 2 Identify Skill Components

a. Review classroom and school building rules as they are related to these skills.

b. Use a T-chart with the class to develop lists of appropriate participation and inappropriate participation (i.e., Do's and Don'ts). Elicit the following appropriate behaviors:

   1) Answer questions from the teacher

   2) Ask questions or makes comments only about the lesson.

   3) Join cooperative groups and participate.

   4) Follow directions.

Step 3 Model the Skill

a. Have competent peers model the skill; use the thinking aloud procedure to delineate the skill steps.

b. Have competent peers model the skill without thinking aloud. Ask students to identify the skill steps.

c. Have competent peers model the skill but make a mistake (e.g., makes a comment that isn't relevant to the discussion). Ask students to identify the error.

Step 4 Role-Play

a. Divide the social skills group into actors and observers. Then teach a mini lesson on an age-appropriate topic. Provide the observers with feedback cards on the appropriate participation components and have them provide feedback to the actors. Switch the roles of participants and repeat the process.

b. Arrange a cooperative learning activity or a game and have students participate. Include competent peers in the activity. Provide feedback on performance of students including reinforcing positive behaviors and correcting inappropriate behaviors.

c. Have student self-evaluate after each of the activities.

Step 5 Practice

a. Pair a target student with two supportive peers to play games. Rotate though the pairs providing feedback on their participation.

b. Have students evaluate video clips of students participating in classroom instruction and group activities.

c. Provide support and feedback to students while they are included in general education or "specials" classes. Have students evaluate their performance in these settings.

Step 6 Generalization

a. Arrange with general education or "specials" teacher to ask target student a question in class. Practice and prepare the student ahead of time.

b. Have other staff members teach mini lessons and arrange group learning tasks. Have these other staff members also provide students with feedback on their performance.

Step 7 Evaluation

After a period of time it is necessary to determine if the skills taught are being sustained and generalized. The following practices are used to determine long-term success of instruction.

a. Periodically observe the students in general education settings and rate their performance according to the performance criteria listed at the beginning of the lesson.

b. Ask general education teacher(s)/other support staff to rate students according to the performance criteria.

c. Collect data using progress-monitoring strategies.

d. Design individual interventions for students not benefiting from small-group interventions (i.e., students who perform the skill inadequately or fail to generalize the skill to other settings).

LESSON 13
Cafeteria Rules: Going Through the Lunch Line and Sitting With Peers

Objective

Students will follow lunchroom rules and standard procedures.

Performance Criteria

This skill will be *performed adequately* when the student:

1. Takes place in lunch line.
2. Chooses milk/drink and takes food tray from serving line.
3. Puts appropriate utensils on tray.
4. Carries tray to specified table; selects table and seat.
5. Keeps hands on own tray.
6. Assists in cleaning up.

Materials Required

Materials to create list of cafeteria rules; may want to use text + icons
Puppets or dolls, and small or toy furniture to simulate a lunchroom
Borrowed lunch tray and utensils from cafeteria

Other Preparation

None for this lesson.

Special Considerations

Many students with ASD have sensory-dietary issues; may need to address how student should respond if he/she doesn't like the food that is offered. Similarly, need to model/role-play for students who bring their lunch from home.

Forms and Supplementary Materials (see CD)

None for this lesson.

Technology Resources

Software: Boardmaker Writing/With Symbols (both Mayer-Johnson)

Related Lessons

Lesson 14: Cafeteria Rules: Table Manners and Having a Conversation

PROCEDURES 7 STEPS

Step 1 Establish the Need

   a. Begin a class discussion with questions related to the need for following cafeteria rules (e.g., lunch ticket or student number). Ask if they know the rules. Elicit or provide the rules that are used in your school building.

   b. Ask students why it is important to follow the rules. Elicit that *they are important for keeping the cafeteria quiet and clean*, and to *give others a chance to have a peaceful lunch*.

Step 2 Identify Skill Components

   a. Using the list of items generated by the class, include the following skill components (incorporate any school-specific procedures).

      1) Take your place in line.

      2) Be careful carrying your tray.

      3) Sit down when you eat.

      4) Don't touch anyone else's food.

      5) Clean up when you're finished.

   b. Post the list of rules in the classroom, near the door for review when leaving for lunch.

   c. Rehearse the steps in unison.

Step 3 Model the Skill

   a. Using hand puppets or dolls, model the skill correctly. Narrate the actions.

   b. Model the skill live, in the cafeteria, and use the thinking aloud procedure to narrate the skill components.

   c. Have a competent peer participate in modeling the skill in the cafeteria; ask students to tell the peer model what to do.

Step 4 Role-Play

   a. Using the materials borrowed from the school cafeteria, have students role-play the skill. If possible, the role-play should be conducted in the cafeteria.

   b. Provide feedback to students and make sure each student performs the skill correctly at least once.

   c. Give feedback assignments and have class members provide feedback.

   d. Have students evaluate their own performance.

Step 5 Practice

a. Using the borrowed materials, repeat the modeling and role-playing steps on another day. Coach students to correct performance.
b. Give feedback and prompt students to correct performance.
c. Praise or otherwise reward correct performance.

Step 6 Generalization

a. Take class to the cafeteria at lunch time and repeat the modeling and role-playing steps.
b. Solicit the assistance of cafeteria workers to occasionally provide feedback to students on their lunchroom behavior.
c. Occasionally, observe students in lunchroom and provide feedback on their behavior.
d. Ask lunchroom monitors to report on the students' behavior. Reward students for good reports.
e. To generalize skills to other settings, go on a field trip
    1) To another school where students can eat lunch; provide feedback to students on performance.
    2) To a fast-food restaurant; provide feedback to students on performance.
f. Gradually thin prompts and reinforcements.
g. Ask cafeteria workers to praise students for doing a good job.

Step 7 Evaluation

After a period of time it is necessary to determine if the skills taught are being sustained and generalized. The following practices are used to determine long-term success of instruction.

a. Periodically observe the students in general education settings and rate their performance according to the performance criteria listed at the beginning of the lesson.
b. Ask general education teacher(s)/other support staff to rate students according to the performance criteria.
c. Collect data using progress-monitoring strategies.
d. Design individual interventions for students not benefiting from small-group interventions (i.e., students who perform the skill inadequately or fail to generalize the skill to other settings).

CHAPTER
5

LESSON 14
Cafeteria Rules: Table Manners and Having a Conversation

Objective
Students will demonstrate appropriate table manners in the school cafeteria.

Performance Criteria
This skill will be *performed adequately* when the student:
1. Takes seat at table.
2. Puts napkin in lap.
3. Uses eating utensils for intended use, cutting food as needed.
4. Chews with mouth closed.
5. Avoids talking with mouth full.
6. Uses straw appropriately.
7. Sits upright while eating.
8. Does not eat food dropped on the floor.
9. Uses napkin to wipe mouth and chin.

Materials Required
Book on the theme, such as *Emily's Everyday Manners* by Peggy Post (2006), *Excuse Me! A Little Book of Manners* by Karen Katz (2002), or *How Do Dinosaurs Eat Their Food?* by Jane Yolan (2005)
Eating utensils, dishes and napkins from cafeteria; food which requires cutting

Other Preparation
Create smiley-face charts/Good Manners certificates

Special Considerations
Preliminary instruction on how to cut food with a knife will be necessary for some children.

Forms and Supplementary Materials (see CD)
Home-School Connection form

Technology Resources
Internet: There are several videos featuring "bad table manners" on Youtube.com, including some from television episodes and cartoons, which can be used in Step 1;

web streaming sites for teachers may also have relevant footage.
Internet: Award certificate makers at http://www.teach-nology.com/web_tools/
certificates/ and http://www.senteacher.org/Worksheet/3/Certificates.xhtml

Related Lessons
Lesson 13: Cafeteria Rules: Going Through the Lunch Line and Sitting With Peers

PROCEDURES 7 STEPS

Step 1 Establish the Need
a. To introduce the topic,
    1) Read a themed book to the class and discuss. OR
    2) Show the class a video clip of bad table manners. Ask them to identify both the offensive behavior and other diners' reaction to eating with someone with bad table manners.
b. Ask students why it is important to have good table manners. Elicit that *people with good table manners are cleaner* and *most people are happier to eat with someone with good manners.*

Step 2 Identify Skill Components
a. Ask students to identify some good table manners. Elicit:
    1) Sit at the table in your chair.
    2) Use a napkin to wipe your face and hands.
    3) Cut or bite off small pieces of food.
    4) Chew with your mouth closed.
    5) Don't talk with mouth full.
    6) Don't make noises with a straw.
    7) Don't eat dropped food.
b. Reinforce the listed skills through question and response:
    1) How do you sit?
    2) What do we do with a napkin?
    3) How do we cut our food?
    4) What must we not do when our mouths our full?
    5) Do we ever eat dropped food?
    6) How is our mouth supposed to be when we chew?

Step 3 Model the Skill

a. Using the borrowed dishes and utensils, model the skill, making sure that food is cut into small pieces before eating. Using the thinking aloud procedure, narrate what you are modeling.

b. Ask the students to identify which good manners you used.

c. Repeat the modeling situation and make some errors. Ask students to cite the errors.

d. Model the skill correctly the third time.

Step 4 Role-Play

a. Distribute the utensils, dishes, and food to half of the students. Reverse the roles after the first group is completed.

b. Repeat all of the manners previously listed and direct students carry them out.

c. Prompt students to correct performance and provide feedback and praise.

d. Ask students to evaluate their own performance and the performance of other students.

e. For students who meet all of the criteria, send home smiley-face or Good Manners certificates for having good table manners.

Step 5 Practice

a. Plan to have a treat sometime during the week. Take the class to the cafeteria, repeat all of the manners, and have all of the students practice the skill. Provide feedback and praise for correct performance of the skills.

b. Prior to going to lunch each day during the week of the lesson, repeat the list of the manners and the rehearsal questions.

c. For students who have difficulty reaching criterion, repeat modeling and role-playing steps in groups.

Step 6 Generalization

a. Occasionally, visit cafeteria and provide students with feedback on their eating behavior.

b. Solicit cooperation from cafeteria monitors/staff to occasionally prompt and provide feedback to students on their table manners.

c. Have typical peers serve as "Manner Monitors," whose job is to remind others to follow good table manners (monitors the entire class).

d. Use the Home-School Connection form to let families know which manners you are working on. Request parents to prompt their children to use good manners (e.g., "Show us the good manners you are using in school.").

Step 7 Evaluation

After a period of time it is necessary to determine if the skills taught are being sustained and generalized. The following practices are used to determine long-term success of instruction.

a. Periodically observe the students in general education settings and rate their performance according to the performance criteria listed at the beginning of the lesson.

b. Ask general education teacher(s)/other support staff to rate students according to the performance criteria.

c. Collect data using progress-monitoring strategies.

d. Design individual interventions for students not benefiting from small-group interventions (i.e., students who perform the skill inadequately or fail to generalize the skill to other settings).

LESSON 15
Greeting Teachers and Other Adults

Objective

Students will greet teachers by making eye contact, smiling, and responding verbally to a greeting.

Performance Criteria

This skill will be *performed adequately* when the student:

1. Makes eye contact.
2. Smiles at greeter.
3. Says "hi" with the name of the teacher/adult (e.g., "Hi, Mr. Thompson."); if nonverbal, waves.
4. Shakes hands if greeter extends hand.
5. Responds to greeter's question. (Question: e.g., "What's new?" Response: e.g., "I went on a trip over the weekend.").
6. Asks return cordial question after response (e.g., "What have you been doing?").
7. Responds to greeter's conversation question with appropriate on-the-topic response (e.g., "Yes, I'll be at the assembly.").
8. Takes leave with short leave statement (e.g., "See you later.").

Materials Required

Chalkboard/whiteboard/posterboard; pictures/photographs illustrating component steps

Other Preparation

A conversation comic strip (see Chapter 4) is helpful for introducing this skill; need to prepare before presenting lesson.

Video modeling is recommended for the modeling and role-playing steps.

Support from other school staff members is required for modeling, role-playing, and practice steps. For modeling and role-playing, the supporting staff members should be familiar to/have interacted with the student(s).

Special Considerations

Nonverbal students may use PECS to communicate.

Many students with ASD and other developmental disabilities may require extra time to consider and formulate a response to a question; avoid repeated prompting, which may distract the student.

Many students with ASD have difficulty making and maintaining eye contact; reinforce and reward student success.

Forms and Supplementary Materials (see CD)
Home-School Connection Form

Technology Resources
iPad/iPhone app: Social Skills (MDR)

Software/apps: Comic Life software and app (Plasq.com); Strip Designer app (www.mexircus.com/Strip_Designer/index.html)

Internet: Makebeliefscomix (www.makebeliefscomix.com/), ReadWriteThink Comic Creator (www.readwritethink.org/files/resources/interactives/comic/), StripGenerator (http://stripgenerator.com/), StoryCreator 2 (http://myths.e2bn.org/create/tool527-story-creator-2.html)

Related Lessons
Lesson 2: Responding to Questions From a Teacher or Other Adult

Lesson 52, Volume 2: Interacting With School and Public Authorities

PROCEDURES 7 STEPS

Step 1 Establish the Need
a. Introduce the topic:
    1) Present the comic strip to the class; ask them to identify problems the characters are having in greeting. OR
    2) Enact a greeting with another staff member displaying inappropriate behavior (e.g., stand far away from the person, speak in a low voice, turn away). Ask students to identify components.
b. Ask students why it is important to greet adults in a certain way. Elicit *they will be treated better*, it will *make others happy, they will be better liked.*

Step 2 Identify Skill Components
a. Tell the students that you have some helpful hints on how to meet adults. List the rules on the board or poster board; attaching pictures will help nonreaders and visual learners.

1) Look the person in the eye and smile.
2) Say "How do you do?" or answer "I am fine. Thank you."
3) If offered, shake hands firmly.
4) Squeeze the hand but not too hard.

   b. Rehearse the steps through unison reading of the steps.

   c. Discuss alternatives to saying "How do you do?" and answering similar greetings with "I am fine."

Step 3 Model the Skill

   a. Model the whole skill with another staff member, using the thinking aloud procedure to narrate skill components.

   b. Model the skill without using the thinking aloud procedure.

Step 4 Role-Play

   a. Teach students to shake hands firmly. Have each student shake your hand and then prompt them to correct performance of this skill step.

   b. Have students role-play greeting you, including a handshake.

   c. Have students role-play greeting another staff member. (The staff member should ask them random greeting questions.)

   d. Provide students with feedback; ask them to evaluate their own performance and the performance of other students.

Step 5 Practice

   a. On a day subsequent to the initial lesson, have students practice the skill with another staff member (preferably the opposite sex from the teacher). Have the staff person give feedback and praise.

   b. Challenge students one by one during the course of the week when the skill is emphasized. Provide feedback and praise.

   c. Review the skill components and have the skill modeled at a skill review session.

Step 6 Generalization

   a. Ask students' families for help practicing the skill outside the classroom, in different types of social gatherings. Ask them to reinforce the four skill components.

   b. When using the skill outside the classroom, practice it in different sized groups.

CHAPTER 5

Step 7 Evaluation

After a period of time it is necessary to determine if the skills taught are being sustained and generalized. The following practices are used to determine long-term success of instruction.

a. Periodically observe the students in general education settings and rate their performance according to the performance criteria listed at the beginning of the lesson.

b. Ask general education teacher(s)/other support staff to rate students according to the performance criteria.

c. Collect data using progress-monitoring strategies.

d. Design individual interventions for students not benefiting from small-group interventions (i.e., students who perform the skill inadequately or fail to generalize the skill to other settings).

LESSON 16
Greeting Peers and Friends

Objective

Students will greet peers by making eye contact, smiling, and making a verbal greeting.

Performance Criteria

This skill will be *performed adequately* when the student:
1. Makes eye contact with peer.
2. Smiles at peer.
3. Begins with conventional short verbal greeting using the peer's name.
4. Follows short greeting with question if no conversation is desired (e.g., "How are things going today?", "What do you think about this weather?", "What have you been up to?").
5. Waits for response.
6. If a conversation is desired, follows short greeting with a statement or question which covers a specific discussible topic (e.g., "Are you going to cub scouts after school?").

Materials Required

Chalkboard/whiteboard; icons/pictures illustrating components

Other Preparation

Prepare the conversation comic strip (see Chapter 4) prior to beginning the lesson. Video modeling is recommended for the modeling and role-playing steps. Prepare competent peers to support modeling, role-playing, and practicing the skill.

A social story may support student mastery of the skill.

Special Considerations

Nonverbal students may use PECS to communicate.

Many students with ASD require extra time to consider and formulate a response to a question; peer models should avoid repeated prompting, which may distract the student.

Many students with ASD have difficulty making and maintaining eye contact; reinforce and reward student success.

The Circle of Friends peer support approach (see Chapter 3) may support generalization of the skill.

Forms and Supplementary Materials (see CD)
Home-School Connection form
Conversation Strip Template

Technology Resources
iPad/iPhone app: Conversation Builder (Mobile Education Store)
iPad/iPhone app: Smile at Me (MDR)
Software/apps: Comic Life software and app (Plasq.com); Strip Designer app (www.mexircus.com/Strip_Designer/index.html)
Internet: Makebeliefscomix (www.makebeliefscomix.com/), ReadWriteThink Comic Creator (www.readwritethink.org/files/resources/interactives/comic/), StripGenerator (http://stripgenerator.com/), StoryCreator 2 (http://myths.e2bn.org/create/tool527-story-creator-2.html)

Related Lessons
Lesson 27: Asking Someone to Play With You
Lesson 45: Asking a Peer for Help
Lesson 51, Volume 2: Hallway Etiquette
Lesson 62, Volume 2: Initiating a Conversation

PROCEDURES 7 STEPS

Step 1 Establish the Need
a. Introduce the topic: Tell students that most people like it when you look at them when they speak to you, and when you smile at them when they say hello. Identify these behaviors as *skills that are important for making and keeping friends.*
b. To initiate a class discussion,
  1) Present the comic strip to the class; ask them to identify problems the characters are having in greeting. OR
  2) Enact a greeting with another staff member, but do not greet appropriately (e.g., stand far away from the person, speak in a low voice, turn away). Ask students to identify components. OR
  3) Have competent peers enact a greeting, but not appropriately; ask students to identify components.

Step 2 Identify Skill Components
a. Through discussion, elicit a sequence of behaviors for initiating and responding to a greeting.

b. Write the list on chalkboard, whiteboard, or feltboard; add icons/pictures for components. The list should contain (words in **bold** may be represented by a picture or icon):
1) Look the greeter in the **eyes**.
2) **Smile.**
3) Make a short **greeting**, including the peer's name.
c. Have the class repeat the sequences, in unison and individually.

Step 3 Model the Skill

a. Select two general education classroom peers with good social skills to model appropriate greetings. Narrate the performance.
b. Have the peer models perform the skills without narrating; ask students to identify the skill components.

Step 4 Role-Play

a. Pair target students with competent peers and have them role-play a greeting. Ask students to self-evaluate and to evaluate each other.
b. Have "teams" of students watch each other role-play greeting, and identify the steps and evaluate. Each student should role-play initiating and responding to a greeting at least twice.
c. Monitor teams and provide feedback.

Step 5 Practice

a. Provide students with a homework assignment. Direct them to greet at least two friends at another time of the school day or after school. On the next day, have students report on who and how they made greetings.
b. On an irregular basis, repeat the homework and self-reporting assignment.
c. Reinforce students who make appropriate greetings with statements such as "John, I like the way you look at a person when you say hello" and "That's a pleasant way to say goodbye to someone."

Step 6 Generalization

a. Ask the competent peers who participated in the modeling and role-playing to initiate greetings at other times of the school day and in other settings.
b. Ask other competent peers who did not participate in the modeling or role-playing to initiate greetings at other times of the school day and in other settings.
c. Continue using the self-reporting procedure during the school year with a gradual fading of social praise and finally fading the self-reporting.

    d. For students who continue to perform poorly in making greetings, provide general education classroom teachers and other school staff with description of the skill being worked on. Ask them to provide occasional social praise when the skill is performed appropriately.

    e. Inform families of the skill being taught and ask them to provide encouragement and praise for initiating greetings.

    f. Fade prompts and reinforcements as students become more proficient.

Step 7 Evaluation

After a period of time it is necessary to determine if the skills taught are being sustained and generalized. The following practices are used to determine long-term success of instruction.

    a. Periodically observe the students in general education settings and rate their performance according to the performance criteria listed at the beginning of the lesson.

    b. Ask general education teacher(s)/other support staff to rate students according to the performance criteria.

    c. Collect data using progress-monitoring strategies.

    d. Design individual interventions for students not benefiting from small-group interventions (i.e., students who perform the skill inadequately or fail to generalize the skill to other settings).

LESSON 17
Using Classroom Materials: Sharing, Taking Care of Supplies, and Requesting Materials From Others

Objective

Students will understand shared responsibility for materials, share limited materials, wait to have access to materials, and politely ask for needed materials from peers.

Performance Criteria

This skill will be *performed adequately* when the student:

1. Identifies certain materials that are to be used by others as well as self.
2. Refrains from demanding exclusive possession of any materials that need to be shared.
3. Waits until another student has completed using a material before taking it.
4. Politely requests use of a material while waiting.
5. While waiting, chooses something else to work with.
6. Returns material to a specific location after use.
7. Makes materials available to others when not using them.

Materials Required

Sharing-themed book, such as *The Little Red Hen* (various authors), *Mine! Mine! Mine!* by Shelly Becker (2006), *Sharing How Kindness Grows* by Fran Shaw (2006), or *We Share Everything!* by Robert Munsch (2002)

Pictures/laminated images of classroom items; felt board or Velcro to attach/remove.

Board/poster of "other things to do"

Supplies for sharing practice (Steps 3 and 4)

Other Preparation

A picture or cartoon conversation comic strip may be appropriate for the Steps 2 and 3.

Video modeling is recommended for the role-playing step of this lesson.

Special Considerations

None for this lesson.

Forms and Supplementary Materials (see CD)
Task Analysis form (to use as student self-monitoring form)
Home-School Connection form
Conversation Strip Template

Technology Resources
Software/apps: Comic Life software and app (Plasq.com); Strip Designer app (www.mexircus.com/Strip_Designer/index.html)
Internet: Makebeliefscomix (www.makebeliefscomix.com/), ReadWriteThink Comic Creator (www.readwritethink.org/files/resources/interactives/comic/), StripGenerator (http://stripgenerator.com/), StoryCreator 2 (http://myths.e2bn.org/create/tool527-story-creator-2.html)

Related Lessons
Lesson 6: Saying "Please" and "Thank You"
Lesson 10: Being Patient: Learning How to Wait
Lesson 26: Taking Turns

PROCEDURES 7 STEPS

Step 1 Establish the Need
a. Read a story with the theme of sharing; discuss the story and assist students in understanding the meaning of the term sharing.
b. Ask students to list some of the things that people share. Elicit that children share toys; parents share tools, utensils, and cars; and classmates share materials.
c. Ask students to identify some people in their lives with whom it is necessary to share.

Step 2 Identify Skill Components
a. Tell students that there are some good sharing practices to follow and list the rules:
1) Some things in our class need to be shared; don't keep these things only for yourself.
2) Wait until the other person is done before you take the object.
3) When you are waiting, find something else to do.
4) When you are waiting, ask for what you need while the other person is using it.

5) When you finish with something, put it where others can get it.

b. Present a visual T-chart (felt board or Velcro) of pictures of classroom items to be shared or not-shared. Discuss the different items and have students decide if they can share the items or not. Have students put items in the appropriate column.

c. With students, make a list/poster of words or pictures of other things students can do while waiting to use materials (e.g., work in a seat sack, independent job boxes)

Step 3 Model the Skill

a. Initiate a sharing activity (e.g., preparing a bulletin board where there are only one pair of scissors and one set of marking pens between 2 students). Pair a competent peer with the target student(s).

b. Narrate the skill by using the thinking aloud procedure.

c. Discuss the modeled situation with the class.

Step 4 Role-Play

a. Review the rules for sharing.

b. Have students work in groups of three to demonstrate the skill of sharing, again using limited materials. For example, give each group a coloring or painting task and give each group only one crayon or paint box.

c. Provide feedback to students on how well they shared and have each group evaluate themselves on how well they shared.

Step 5 Practice

a. During the week following introduction of the skill,
   1) Review the rules for sharing.
   2) Set up daily experiences where materials must be shared.
   3) During one sharing experience, give students feedback and be sure to praise or reward correct performance of the skill.

b. Hold a skill review session to review and model the skill.

c. From time to time, create individual challenges where students must demonstrate the skill in front of the class. Provide feedback and praise.

Step 6 Generalization

a. Inform general education teachers/specials teachers/support staff that you are emphasizing sharing. Ask them to set up group activities where sharing is required.

b. Train selected typical peers to interact and engage in sharing activities with the target student(s) ("sharing buddies").

CHAPTER 5

  c. Ask students to self-monitor their progress. Praise them for sharing when in other settings.

  d. Use the Home-School Connection form to ask families to have their children show them how they have learned to share.

  e. If appropriate, ask other classroom teachers reteach this lesson in an abbreviated form and/or post the list of activities students can do while they wait in these other classrooms.

Step 7 Evaluation

After a period of time it is necessary to determine if the skills taught are being sustained and generalized. The following practices are used to determine long-term success of instruction.

  a. Periodically observe the students in general education settings and rate their performance according to the performance criteria listed at the beginning of the lesson.

  b. Ask general education teacher(s)/other support staff to rate students according to the performance criteria.

  c. Collect data using progress-monitoring strategies.

  d. Design individual interventions for students not benefiting from small-group interventions (i.e., students who perform the skill inadequately or fail to generalize the skill to other settings).

LESSON 18
Active Listening to Peers

Objective
Students will listen and respond when peers speak in class and in play situations.

Performance Criteria
This skill will be *performed adequately* when the student:
1. Establishes eye contact/looks at the speaker.
2. Attempts to maintain/regain eye contact.
3. Provides gestural or verbal feedback to speaker.
4. Makes relevant comments on what speaker has said.

Materials Required
Book on the theme, such as *Chatting Cheetahs and Jumping Jellyfish*; *Spotty Dogs and Messy Monsters*; *Cats, Hats, and Hippos*; or *Yakety Yak the Alien's Back*—all by Ruth Thomson (2005).
Posterboard/chalkboard/whiteboard; may use text + icons

Other Preparation
A conversation comic strip may be helpful in presenting the concept.
Video modeling is recommended for the role-playing and practice steps.
Prepare competent peers to participate in modeling and role-playing steps.

Special Considerations
None for this lesson.

Forms and Supplementary Materials (see CD)
Home-School Connection form

Technology Resources
iPad/iPhone app: Functional Skills Systems (Conover): Communication Skills
iPad/iPhone app: Social Skills (MDR)
Internet: The Boardmaker share site has several social stories, cue cards, and pictorial representations of the skill at www.boardmakershare.com/Activities/Search/?SearchText=listening&FileSearchCategoryID=-1; Out on a Limb: A Guide to Getting Along (http://urbanext.illinois.edu/conflict/listening01.html) has a cartoon video on listening to others

Related Lessons

Lesson 3: Active Listening in the Classroom

Lesson 63, Volume 2: Maintaining a Conversation: Active Listening and Joint Attention

PROCEDURES 7 STEPS

Step 1 Establish the Need

a. Introduce the concept of active listening by reading a book on the theme.

b. Discuss with students how listening was important to the characters/plot.

Step 2 Identify Skill Components

a. Elicit from the class or provide the following sequence of skill components (write on posterboard or chalkboard/whiteboard; may use text + icons)
STOP: Face the other person and look them in the eye.
LOOK: Keep looking at the person talking.
LISTEN: Nod your head or say something to let them know you understand.

b. Have the class and individual students restate the rules.

Step 3 Model the Skill

a. Model the skill, listening to a competent peer relating an activity. Ask students to identify the skills you used.

b. Model the skill with a second competent peer, but leaving out a skill component (e.g., not looking at speaker or not responding). Ask students to identify the skills you used and the one(s) you did not.

Step 4 Role-Play

a. Review the skill components.

b. Pair students with a competent peer. Ask the peer to relate an experience or story, and have the target student practice the skill. Give feedback.

c. Have students evaluate their own performance.

d. Prompt students to correct performance, provide feedback, and give praise.

Step 5 Practice

a. Review the listening skill components each day of the week the lesson is introduced.

b. Give feedback and praise when students use the skill spontaneously.

c. During a skill review session, play an active-listening game with a group of students (or class), such as Simon Says OR
  1) Speaker-Listener-Observer: The speaker talks for a few minutes about something important to him. The listener attends quietly, providing cues to the speaker that she is paying attention. When the speaker is finished talking, the listener repeats back, in her own words, the speaker's points. The observer evaluates how well the listener listened.
  2) Identify the Changes: Tell the students a story twice, but change details. Have students identify the differences.

Step 6 Generalization
  a. Give students playground assignments.
  b. Give general education classroom or "specials" teachers feedback cards (e.g., card with a smiley face and picture or an ear) that can be given to students when they demonstrate the skill.
  c. Give students feedback cards (e.g., card with a smiley face and picture or an ear) they can give to each other when they see them demonstrating the skill.
  d. Share the skill component list with general education teachers and playground and cafeteria monitors. Ask that they provide students with feedback on their listening behavior.
  e. Ask students to self-report on how they performed the listening skills.
  f. Use the Home-School Connection form to request that families practice the skill set at home and that they praise their children for following the listening skill steps.

Step 7 Evaluation
After a period of time it is necessary to determine if the skills taught are being sustained and generalized. The following practices are used to determine long-term success of instruction.
  a. Periodically observe the students in general education settings and rate their performance according to the performance criteria listed at the beginning of the lesson.
  b. Ask general education teacher(s)/other support staff to rate students according to the performance criteria.
  c. Collect data using progress-monitoring strategies.
  d. Design individual interventions for students not benefiting from small-group interventions (i.e., students who perform the skill inadequately or fail to generalize the skill to other settings).

LESSON 19
Recognizing and Reporting Emergencies

Objective

Students will understand what constitutes an emergency and how to report.

Performance Criteria

This skill will be *performed adequately* when the student:
1. Recognizes that there is an emergency.
2. Reports the situation to an appropriate adult/resource.

Materials Required

Play phone, books on the theme (optional)

Other Preparation

Develop template for social story (*The New Social Story Book* by Carol Gray, 2010, includes several social stories on school emergencies).
Develop posters/feltboard signs (Emergency/Non-Emergency and Call 911/Tell an Adult) and collect icons/pictures.

Special Considerations

None for this lesson.

Forms and Supplementary Materials (see CD)

None for this lesson.

Technology Resources

Internet: www.911forkids.com has a video ("The Great 911 Adventure") and a 9-1-1 rap song; Autism-PDD.net has a variety of resources on safety issues, including videos, coloring books, and interactive lessons (traffic safety, fire safety, weather emergencies, health emergencies).

Related Lessons

Lesson 20: What to Do if You Get Hurt
Lesson 21: What to Do if You Hurt Someone Else
Lesson 23: Problem Solving
Lesson 52, Volume 2: Interacting With School and Public Authorities

CHAPTER 5

PROCEDURES 7 STEPS

Step 1 Establish the Need

    a. Introduce the theme by showing the class a video or reading a themed book.

    b. Introduce the class to the Emergency/Non-Emergency poster/feltboard; have students apply pictures or icons to the relevant columns.

Step 2 Identify Skill Components

    a. Focusing on the Emergency column of the poster, ask students how they should respond in each of the illustrated events.

    b. Elicit *tell an adult* or *call 911*.

    c. Introduce the class to the Call 911/Tell an Adult poster/feltboard and move the pictures from the Emergency sign to the appropriate column.

    d. Establish the skill steps:

        1) This is an emergency situation.

        2) What kind of emergency is it? Should I tell an adult or call 911?

        3) Take appropriate action.

Step 3 Model the Skill

    a. Use a combination of the pictures/icons from the Emergency/Non-Emergency poster plus pictures of target students to develop a social story.

    b. With students, rehearse the steps of the skill.

Step 4 Role-Play

    a. Suggest various scenarios of emergency and non-emergency situations and have students role-play their response.

Step 5 Practice

    a. Periodically repeat the role-play step and reinforce students for accurate performance of the skill.

    b. Periodically request students to "re-tell" the steps of what to do in an emergency. Coach students to correctly identify the steps.

Step 6 Generalization

    a. Take a field trip to a police station or fire station.

    b. Using the Home-School Connection form, inform families of the lesson topic and have students share the social story with their families. Ask families to review their home emergency procedures with students.

Step 7 Evaluation

After a period of time it is necessary to determine if the skills taught are being sustained and generalized. The following practices are used to determine long-term success of instruction.

a. Periodically observe the students in general education settings and rate their performance according to the performance criteria listed at the beginning of the lesson.

b. Ask general education teacher(s)/other support staff to rate students according to the performance criteria.

c. Collect data using progress-monitoring strategies.

d. Design individual interventions for students not benefiting from small-group interventions (i.e., students who perform the skill inadequately or fail to generalize the skill to other settings).

LESSON 20
What to Do if You Get Hurt

Objective

Students will learn who to tell if they are injured. They will understand intimidation and the importance of not allowing others to do this.

Performance Criteria

This skill will be *performed adequately* when the student:
1. Identifies the appropriate person to whom to report an injury.
2. Is able to relate their experience in a way someone else can understand.
3. Can describe the person who hurt them.
4. Can describe the part of their body that hurts.

Materials Required

None for this lesson.

Other Preparation

Poster with list of steps/icons depicting skills steps
Poster with images of school staff in different settings
Prepare competent peers for role-playing step.

Special Considerations

Nonverbal students may need to use gestures or PECS.

Forms and Supplementary Materials (see CD)

Home-School Connection form

Technology Resources

None for this lesson.

Related Lessons

Lesson 19: Recognizing and Reporting Emergencies
Lesson 21: What to Do if You Hurt Someone Else
Lesson 34: Recognizing and Expressing Bodily Needs

PROCEDURES 7 STEPS

Step 1 Establish the Need

a. Lead a class discussion: Ask students to relate if they have ever been hurt, and what they did when it happened.

b. Ask students who they should go to if they get hurt. Elicit that they should *tell a teacher, parent, or another adult.*

c. Ask students why it is important to tell an adult. Elicit that adults can help, provide bandages, call for medical assistance, or deal with someone who hurt them.

Step 2 Identify Skill Components

a. Introduce the skill steps to the students:
   1) If I'm hurt I need to tell an adult.
   2) I tell them what happened.
   3) I tell them who hurt me.
   4) I tell them where it hurts.

b. Post the poster of the skill steps in the classroom.

c. Post a poster in the classroom with pictures of the responsible adults in each setting to whom students should report an injury (e.g., librarian, playground monitor, cafeteria staff or monitor, school office staff).

Step 3 Model the Skill

a. With another adult, model the skill; specifically say
   1. I'm hurt!
   2. This is what happened:
   3. This is who hurt me:
   4. This is where it hurts:

Step 4 Role-Play

a. Have competent peers model the skill; use different scenarios for the different school settings (e.g., in the library; teacher role-plays the librarian).

b. Have target students model the skill with a competent peer playing the responsible adult. Peer models may prompt target students by asking questions (e.g., "Who hurt you?" "Where does it hurt?").

c. Have target students model the skill in the different settings on the poster.

Step 5 Practice

a. Present students with "what if" situations (not on the poster; e.g., "What if you get hurt in the restroom?") to encourage problem solving.

b. Periodically have students "re-tell" the rules for what to do when they get hurt.

Step 6 Generalization

a. Inform other school staff (especially those identified as the contact adult) of the skill being taught. Ask them to reinforce students when the skill is demonstrated.

b. Take the students to the playground and practice a simulated incident of being hurt. Use examples that include accidents and injury caused by another person.

c. Using the Home-School Connection form, provide families with the content of the lesson on what to do when hurt and ask them to practice the processes for responding to an injury with their children.

d. When real cases where a student is injured either at school or home, have them report to others in the group how they applied the rules.

Step 7 Evaluation

After a period of time it is necessary to determine if the skills taught are being sustained and generalized. The following practices are used to determine long-term success of instruction.

a. Periodically observe the students in general education settings and rate their performance according to the performance criteria listed at the beginning of the lesson.

b. Ask general education teacher(s)/other support staff to rate students according to the performance criteria.

c. Collect data using progress-monitoring strategies.

d. Design individual interventions for students not benefiting from small-group interventions (i.e., students who perform the skill inadequately or fail to generalize the skill to other settings)..

CHAPTER
5

LESSON 21
What to Do if You Hurt Someone Else

Objective

Students will understand what to do if they hurt another person, whether on purpose or by accident.

Performance Criteria

This skill will be *performed adequately* when the student:

1. Recognizes that they have hurt another person.
2. Accepts responsibility.
3. Apologizes.
4. Tells a responsible adult about the injury/event.
5. Makes restitution/accepts punishment or consequences for the behavior.

Materials Required

Book on the theme, such as *The Recess Queen* by Alexis O'Neill (2002) or *Enemy Pie* by Derek Munson (2000).

Other Preparation

Poster with skill steps in text/icons.
Poster with images of school staff responsible in different settings.
Prepare competent peers to participate in role playing.

Special Considerations

Students with ASD often find it difficult to understand other's emotions or feelings as distinct from their own (see Theory of Mind).

Forms and Supplementary Materials (see CD)

Home-School Connection form

Technology Resources

Internet: Speakingofspeech.com has prepared "good friend/not-a-friend" cards that can be used to identify behaviors that are not friendly.

Related Lessons

Lesson 20: What to Do if You Get Hurt

Lesson 50: Being a Friend: Expressing Empathy and Sympathy

Lesson 83, Volume 2: Recognizing and Responding to Teasing, Name Calling, and Bullying

PROCEDURES 7 STEPS

Step 1 Establish the Need

a. Introduce the lesson by reading a book on the theme.

b. Discuss with students how the characters in the book felt when they were being picked on or hurt.

c. Ask students to share times when they have been hurt.

d. Tell students that it is important to be able to recognize when you have hurt someone else.

e. Tell students that when you have hurt someone else, you need to apologize, tell an adult, and accept the consequences of your actions or try to make up with your friend.

Step 2 Identify Skill Components

a. Present the poster to the class; read aloud the skill steps:

    1) Oh no! I hurt someone.

    2) I say I'm sorry.

    3) I tell an adult what happened.

    4) I try to make up with my friend.

b. Explain to the students that sometimes there are consequences or punishments when people hurt someone else.

c. Introduce the poster with images of school staff; note that in different settings, the person in charge is different.

Step 3 Model the Skill

a. With two other adults, model the skill; specifically say

    1) Oh no! I hurt you!

    2) I'm sorry I hurt you.

    3) This is what happened:

    4) What do I need to do?

b. Model the skill for additional scenarios.

Step 4 Role-Play

a. Have competent peers model the skill; use different scenarios for the different school settings (e.g., in the library; teacher role-plays the librarian).

b. Have target students model the skill with a competent peer playing the responsible adult. Peer models may prompt target students by asking questions or making observations about the situation.

c. Have target students model the skill in the different settings on the poster.

Step 5 Practice

a. Present students with "what if" situations (not on the poster; e.g., "What if someone gets hurt in the restroom?") to encourage problem solving.

b. Use a skill challenge at an unexpected time by presenting a scenario to a student and asking them to show you what they would do and how they would do it.

Step 6 Generalization

a. Inform other school staff (especially those identified as the contact adult) of the skill being taught. Ask them to reinforce students when the skill is demonstrated.

b. Take the group to the playground and have them engage in activities where they will be close to one another. Provide targeted students with skill challenges for demonstrating what they would do if they accidentally hurt another child in their proximity. Reinforce correct performance and coach students to correct inappropriate performance by having students repeat the steps accurately.

c. Using the Home-School Connection form, inform families of the skill steps requesting that they practice the skill at home. If siblings are present in the home, request that parents have the students practice with their brothers or sisters.

d. Have the lesson repeated again during the school year with a different instructor.

Step 7 Evaluation

After a period of time it is necessary to determine if the skills taught are being sustained and generalized. The following practices are used to determine long-term success of instruction.

a. Periodically observe the students in general education settings and rate their performance according to the performance criteria listed at the beginning of the lesson.

b. Ask general education teacher(s)/other support staff to rate students according to the performance criteria.

c. Collect data using progress-monitoring strategies.

d. Design individual interventions for students not benefiting from small-group interventions (i.e., students who perform the skill inadequately or fail to generalize the skill to other settings).

LESSON 22
Coping With Sensory Issues

Objective

When on task, students will ignore distractions; students will be able to articulate if something in the environment is disturbing them.

Performance Criteria

This skill will be *performed adequately* when the student:

1. Stays on task during an assignment regardless of activity in the classroom, hallway, or outside.
2. Articulates concern regarding a sensory issue (lights too bright, music too loud, glue too sticky).
3. Assists in identifying a solution to the concern.

Materials Required

Book on the theme, such as *Why Does Izzy Cover Her Ears? Dealing With Sensory Overload* by Jennifer Veenendall (2009) or *The Gooenoughs Get in Sync: 5 Family Members Overcome Their Special Sensory Issues* by Carol Kranowitz (2010)

Other Preparation

Prepare competent peers to support modeling and practice steps; might identify peer buddies who can help redirect target students if they are off-task.

Special Considerations

None for this lesson.

Forms and Supplementary Materials (see CD)

None for this lesson.

Technology Resources

iPad/iPhone app: Time Timer (Time Timer LLC)

Related Lessons

Lesson 1: Classroom Rules: Paying Attention to the Teacher, Getting the Teacher's Attention, Asking Questions
Lesson 34: Recognizing and Expressing Bodily Needs
Lesson 46: Self-Advocacy: What to Do When Someone Is Bothering You

CHAPTER
5

PROCEDURES 7 STEPS

Step 1 Establish the Need

a. Introduce the concept by reading a book on the theme to the class.

b. Ask students what types of things distract or bother them when they're trying to work.

c. Ask students what happens when they are distracted at school; elicit *can't complete assignments, might distract/disrupt other students, do not hear what the teacher says*.

d. Ask students why it is important to learn to "tune out" or work through distractions; elicit *will be able to complete work, will be more comfortable at school*.

Step 2 Identify Skill Components

a. Tell students that every classroom has rules everyone must follow so everyone can learn:
   1) Try not to look out the window or out the classroom door when you are working.
   2) Try not to look at people who are making noise or talking.
   3) Do not respond to questions, teasing, or giggling.
   4) Report behavior to the teacher if necessary.

b. Tell students that there are different ways they can help themselves stay focused on their work:
   1) They can use their finger to follow along/keep track of where they are working.
   2) They can block off the part of the work they are not working on, with another piece of paper.
   3) They can use a task timer.
   4) They can use a visual or written task schedule.
   5) They can have theraputty or some other item to keep their hands busy.

c. Tell students that there are things they ask the teacher for if the distractions are "too much":
   1) They can go to a quiet/safe area in the classroom to work.
   2) They can wear headphones to block out noises.

Step 3 Model the Skill

a. Using competent peers, portray a student working on a task while other students are talking, giggling, or moving around the room. Use the *thinking aloud* procedure to narrate each of the skill steps.

   b. Model the skill with the warning that you may commit an error. Have students identify the errors.

   c. Model skill third time with no errors.

   d. Model using strategies to focus on task at hand.

   e. Model requesting use of quiet/safe area or headphones.

Step 4 Role-Play

   a. Give students a mastery level seatwork task and ask that they demonstrate how well they can ignore distractions.

   b. Create noise in the classroom, have peer models move around, and have a peer model go out into the hall to attempt to distract his or her classmates.

   c. Provide feedback to each student and ask them to relate how they did.

Step 5 Practice

   a. Ask students to model the skill during a skill review session.

   b. At various times during the week following introduction of the lesson, review the steps for ignoring distractions and challenge the class to exhibit the skill. Have some students create some distractions. Give students feedback on their performance.

   c. Give students intermittent praise for correctly performing the skill. Be sure to be explicit with the praise. For example: "John, I am pleased that you kept on working when that student dropped those books in the hall."

   d. Ask various people (principal, another teacher, custodian) to enter your classroom unannounced. Observe the students who were able to stay on task and reward them with reinforcers.

Step 6 Generalization

   a. Inform general education teachers of the skill being taught. Ask them to reinforce the rules for avoiding distractions with their class as a whole and to praise students for ignoring distractions.

   b. Ask general education teachers to identify competent peer "study buddies" who can both model the desired skill and redirect students when off-task.

   c. Have students take an index card with them to their general education classes. Each time that they find themselves consciously trying to ignore distraction, they are to mark the card. Reinforce students for using the cards.

   d. Provide prompts and reinforcement in the general education classes for ignoring distractions.

CHAPTER 5

Step 7 Evaluation

After a period of time it is necessary to determine if the skills taught are being sustained and generalized. The following practices are used to determine long-term success of instruction.

a. Periodically observe the students in general education settings and rate their performance according to the performance criteria listed at the beginning of the lesson.

b. Ask general education teacher(s)/other support staff to rate students according to the performance criteria.

c. Collect data using progress-monitoring strategies.

d. Design individual interventions for students not benefiting from small-group interventions (i.e., students who perform the skill inadequately or fail to generalize the skill to other settings).

LESSON 23
Problem Solving

Objective

Students will be able to identify a situation requiring problem solving and either ask for support from an adult or peer or attempt a solution.

Performance Criteria

This skill will be *performed adequately* when the student:
1. Identifies a situation requiring problem solving.
2. Evaluates possible responses (establishes whether he/she can solve the problem, or needs assistance).
3. Asks for help from an appropriate adult or peer, if the situation requires assistance.
4. Attempts a solution, if appropriate to solving independently.
5. Is able to assess whether the decision was appropriate.

Materials Required

Book on the theme, such as books from the *Kids Can Choose Series* by Elizabeth Crary.

Other Preparation

Prepare a competent peer to assist in modeling the skill.

Investigate using Positive Pragmatics Say and Do game boards (including a problem-solving puzzle, where students match a solution with a problem; www.superduperinc.com/products/view.aspx?pid=bk308)

Special Considerations

Allow students the opportunity to solve problems on their own. Incorporate wait time before stepping in to assist.

Forms and Supplementary Materials (see CD)

Home-School Connection form

Technology Resources

Software: My School Day Enhanced CD (Social Skill Builder) includes videos on socal problem solving, compromising, and conflict resolution.

Internet: It's My Life web site (http://pbskids.org/itsmylife/) has videos and story strips relating to problem solving; Out on a Limb: A Guide to Getting Along (http://urbanext.illinois.edu/conflict/index.html) is an interactive site with different problem-solving episodes.

Related Lessons

Lesson 19: Recognizing and Reporting Emergencies
Lesson 20: What to Do if You Get Hurt
Lesson 21: What to Do if You Hurt Someone Else

PROCEDURES 7 STEPS

Step 1 Establish the Need

a. Prior to formally introducing the lesson, use different games and activities in the classroom that require simple problem solving (e.g., puzzles, Lincoln logs, Legos, constructing simple models).
b. Point out students' successful problem solving during these activities.
c. Introduce the lesson by reading a book on the theme.
d. Link the book content to the classroom activities.

Step 2 Identify Skill Components

a. Discuss with the class scenarios that might require problem solving (e.g., can't unbutton coat, broken pencil, difficulty with an assignment).
b. Tell students that they can become a Master Problem Solver, by learning a few important steps. By mastering these steps, they will develop problem-solving skills.
c. Introduce the steps (may use a poster with text/icons):
   1) Analyze the situation. (What went wrong?)
   2) Can I solve this on my own?
   3) If I can, what different things can I do? (brainstorm solutions)
   4) If I can't, who can I ask to help me? (peer or adult)

Step 3 Model the Skill

a. Using the thinking aloud strategy, model solving a typical problem that a young student might encounter (e.g., finding a lost coat or backpack; forgetting lunch money).
b. Have the skill modeled by a competent peer using a different scenario than the one demonstrated by the teacher.

Step 4 Role-Play

a. Have students make something using atypical materials for the task (e.g., make a building structure using toothpicks and 3 X 5 cards). Have students narrate their problem-solving steps as they engage in the task.

b. Present "what if" scenarios to the students asking them to tell or demonstrate what they would do (e.g., how they would solve the problem of falling into a puddle and getting soaked on the playground). Provide feedback on how well students tell the steps they would take to solve the problems.

Step 5 Practice

a. Periodically review the problem-solving steps.

b. Give students routine problems that are a required part of elementary school instruction. Ask them to complete a checklist or tell how they followed the problem-solving process.

Step 6 Generalization

a. Make a checklist of steps for solving problems for students to use in their general education classrooms. Have students complete the checklists for completing class work or projects.

b. Using the Home-School Connection form, provide families with the four steps and ask them to have their children report on the steps they follow for solving home-related problems.

Step 7 Evaluation

After a period of time it is necessary to determine if the skills taught are being sustained and generalized. The following practices are used to determine long-term success of instruction.

a. Periodically observe the students in general education settings and rate their performance according to the performance criteria listed at the beginning of the lesson.

b. Ask general education teacher(s)/other support staff to rate students according to the performance criteria.

c. Collect data using progress-monitoring strategies.

d. Design individual interventions for students not benefiting from small-group interventions (i.e., students who perform the skill inadequately or fail to generalize the skill to other settings).

LESSON 24
Telling the Truth

Objective
Students will distinguish the truth from fantasy and tell the truth.

Performance Criteria
This skill will be *performed adequately* when the student:
1. Can identify a true fact.
2. Can identify a made-up statement.
3. Can verify a statement of fact.
4. Consistently makes true statements when asked.

CHAPTER
5

Materials Required
Book on the theme, such as *The Boy Who Cried Wolf* (various authors), *Pinky Promise: A Book About Telling the Truth* by Vanita Braver (2004), *The Berenstain Bears and the Truth* by Stan and Jan Berenstain (2004), *Tooth Fairy* by Audrey Wood (2003), or *I'm Telling the Truth: A First Look at Honesty* by Pat Thomas (2006).

Felt storyboard

Two or three hand puppets, dolls, or stuffed animals

Other Preparation
Additional resource: *Unwritten Rules of Social Relationships* by Grandin & Barron (2005), Rule #4 on honesty.

Special Considerations
Some students with ASD are compelled to tell the whole truth, even when it is socially inappropriate. Adapt the lesson to incorporate encouraging restraint in conversations for these students, by teaching them to examine their intent (do not want to embarrass/hurt others) and adjust their response accordingly.

Forms and Supplementary Materials (see CD)
None for this lesson.

Technology Resources
None for this lesson.

Related Lessons

Lesson 37: How to Describe a Personal Experience, Memory, or Dream

PROCEDURES 7 STEPS

Step 1 Establish the Need
a. Use a felt storyboard while reading one or more books on the theme. Ask students to identify the consequences of not telling the truth.
b. Distinguish between telling a lie, an accident, or someone misunderstanding what you say.
c. Present the class with "what if" situations (e.g., "What if you break something and your mom asks you what happened?" "What if you see a friend do something wrong and your teacher asks you what happened?")
d. Establish why it is important to tell the truth: Elicit from students that *it makes them unhappy, it makes others not trust them.*

Step 2 Identify Skill Components
a. Using some very blatant examples, ask students to distinguish fact from fiction (e.g., "It's nighttime," "Susie has orange eyes," etc.).
b. Tell the class a story that is mostly true but includes some "tall tale" elements. Ask students to identify which statements are probably not true.
c. Tell students they must:
   1) Decide what is true and what is not.
   2) Tell the truth.
   3) Be able to show that they are telling the truth.

Step 3 Model the Skill
a. Using the thinking aloud procedure, demonstrate for the children the processes for deciding what truth is and telling the truth. For example, (thinking aloud) "I think I'll tell the class that I have three dollars in my wallet. I know this is true because I counted it this morning." Then show money to verify the true statement.
b. Using puppets, dolls, or stuffed animals, model telling the truth in response to a question. After modeling, ask the class to state what consequences might occur if the character had not told the truth.

Step 4 Role-Play
a. Ask each class member to tell the class something true, tell how they know it is true, and tell what might happen if they told a lie.

b. Give students feedback on their performance.
c. Make sure every student role-plays a different example and not the one they just heard from another student.

Step 5 Practice

a. Play the game Button, Button (Who's Got the Button?): with one person (first a student, then the teacher) covering his or her eyes, the class passes a small object (e.g., button, marble) from hand to hand for a certain amount of time. When time is up, everyone puts their hands behind their back. The "guesser" tries to guess who has the object. Reinforce students for telling the truth.
b. Read scenarios or watch short video clips or movies (e.g., *Sesame Street: Telling the Truth*). Have students identify the true and false statements. Reinforce the importance of telling the truth.
c. During class lessons, have individual students restate a fact in the lesson. Ask them to tell whether or not what they said is true or untrue and how they know it is true.

Step 6 Generalization

a. When students struggle with telling the truth, prompt without accusing (e.g., "Why don't you tell me what happened?" or "Can you tell me that, again?").
b. Use a "not sure" bucket to collect statements that seem out of the ordinary; with the student, conduct Internet research to establish the truthfulness of the statement.
c. Review the skill components on occasion and praise students for telling the truth.
d. Reinforce the skill by calling attention to it when a student tells the truth and praising the behavior (especially if there are consequences).

Step 7 Evaluation

After a period of time it is necessary to determine if the skills taught are being sustained and generalized. The following practices are used to determine long-term success of instruction.

a. Periodically observe the students in general education settings and rate their performance according to the performance criteria listed at the beginning of the lesson.
b. Ask general education teacher(s)/other support staff to rate students according to the performance criteria.

    c. Collect data using progress-monitoring strategies.

    d. Design individual interventions for students not benefiting from small-group interventions (i.e., students who perform the skill inadequately or fail to generalize the skill to other settings).

LESSON 25
Being a Friend: Accepting Ideas Different From Your Own

Objective
Students will listen to the ideas of peers and make appropriate accommodations.

Performance Criteria
This skill will be *performed adequately* when the student:
1. Listens to ideas posed by a peer.
2. Considers idea by weighing advantages and disadvantages.
3. Decides if idea is worthy.
4. Accommodates a worthy idea in peer-associated activity or suggests another alternative.

Materials Required
Chalkboard/whiteboard/posterboard
Selections from *Cooperative Games and Sports: Joyful Activities for Everyone* by Terry Orlick (2006).

Other Preparation
Need assistance from another adult for acting out the concept and initial modeling of the skill.
Prepare competent peers to participate in role-playing and practice steps.
Video modeling is recommended for the modeling and role-playing steps. If used, need to prepare a competent peer to participate with the target student.

Special Considerations
None for this lesson.

Forms and Supplementary Materials (see CD)
Home-School Connection form

Technology Resources
Internet: Out on a Limb: A Guide to Getting Along (http://urbanext.illinois.edu/conflict/listening01.html) has a cartoon video on listening to others

CHAPTER
5

Related Lessons

PROCEDURES 7 STEPS

Step 1 Establish the Need

a. Tell students that you and another school staff member are going to act out a play for them. Perform a conversation where two characters want to play together, but have differing ideas about what to do and will not compromise. Ask students if the two characters were happy about how it ended. Ask how the story might have ended differently.

b. In a class discussion, elicit that being able to compromise or accept a friend's suggestions will mean that *students will be able to play together, be happier, have more opportunities for doing things with others.*

Step 2 Identify Skill Components

a. Tell students that it is important to consider someone else's ideas when working or playing together. Ask them what a person should do to consider someone else's ideas.

b. Elicit steps for considering ideas of others and list on the board (may use text + icons):
   1) Listen to the other person's idea.
   2) Think about what is good and bad about the idea.
   3) Decide if you think the idea is good.
   4) Decide if you think it would be better to compromise.
   5) Change what you do to use the idea or compromise OR suggest another idea.

Step 3 Model the Skill

a. With the same staff member as in Step 1, perform the same conversation but demonstrate compromising.

b. Ask students to identify how each of the skill steps were followed.

c. Model a different scenario using the thinking aloud procedures where two or more people compromise.

Step 4 Role-Play

a. Have students plan a pretend birthday party. Each person gets a set of cards including types of food, activities, types of cake, and so forth. The group must come to a compromise on each decision.

b. On board or chart paper, have students list a variety of school-appropriate joint activities they enjoy doing. Pair students and have them role-play the skill selecting and suggesting different alternatives from the class list. Provide students with feedback and have students evaluate their own performance.

c. Pair students with competent peers and assign them a project where they must cooperate (e.g., making a poster/coloring or painting a picture where each partner has different supplies and ideas). Have other students observe and comment on the skills used or not used.

d. Pair students with competent peers and have them role-play a situation where they are trying to decide what activity to do on a Saturday afternoon (e.g., play a video game vs. play basketball outside).

Step 5 Practice

a. Incorporate partnership tasks/assignments (e.g., pairs of students jointly writing a story or building something) during the week following introduction of the lesson. Provide praise and reinforcement for cooperating and accepting their peers' ideas.

b. Review the skill set prior to naturally occurring opportunities in the general education classroom, PE classes, and so forth.

c. Assign target students a "good friend task" each morning (e.g., cooperating, helping) and have them report at the end of the day how they carried out the task. If they had problems, talk about why another student might not like the actions/words that occurred.

Step 6 Generalization

a. Using the Home-School Connection form, provide families with information on the skill steps. Ask families to reinforce the skill by cooperatively planning a weekend activity. Ask students to report on how well their families followed the procedures.

b. Occasionally have students report when they worked with a partner. Ask them to tell you which skill components they used and how they did. Reinforce students for self-reporting.

c. Suggest that general education teachers incorporate cooperative learning strategies in their classrooms.

d. Ask students to tell you how they might use the skill in other settings (e.g., playground, cafeteria). Ask them to report when they use the skill outside of the classroom.

Step 7 Evaluation

After a period of time it is necessary to determine if the skills taught are being sustained and generalized. The following practices are used to determine long-term success of instruction.

a. Periodically observe the students in general education settings and rate their performance according to the performance criteria listed at the beginning of the lesson.

b. Ask general education teacher(s)/other support staff to rate students according to the performance criteria.

c. Collect data using progress-monitoring strategies.

d. Design individual interventions for students not benefiting from small-group interventions (i.e., students who perform the skill inadequately or fail to generalize the skill to other settings).

LESSON 26
Taking Turns

CHAPTER 5

Objective
Students will take turns in order and wait patiently for their turn during games and activities.

Performance Criteria
This skill will be *performed adequately* when the student:
1. Can verbalize how the order of turns in a game or activity is established (e.g., order of lining up, highest role of dice, etc.).
2. Identifies who has a turn before them.
3. Identifies who has a turn after them.
4. Waits in a specified place.
5. Refrains from intruding on another child's turn.
6. Watches the game or activity while others are taking turns.
7. Takes notice when child goes before is taking turn.
8. Is ready to take turn when time arrives.
9. Takes turn.
10. Relinquishes game or activity toy or equipment when necessary for next child to take turn (e.g. turning over a ball, the dice, etc.).

Materials Required
Book on the theme, such as *Share and Take Turns* by Cheri J. Meiners (2003) or *Take Turns Max and Millie* by Felicity Brooks (2011)
Posterboard/chalkboard/whiteboard
Board game

Other Preparation
Need to select/prepare competent student peers to participate in modeling, role-playing, and practice steps.

Special Considerations
Some students with ASD may need a visual timer when first learning the skill.

Forms and Supplementary Materials (see CD)
None for this lesson.

Technology Resources
iPad/iPhone app: TurnTaker (TouchAutism)

Related Lessons
Lesson 17: Using Classroom Materials
Lesson 41: Playing Games With Peers
Lesson 89, Volume 2: Sportsmanship: Participating in Games

PROCEDURES 7 STEPS

Step 1 Establish the Need
a. Introduce the topic by reading a book on the theme. (May ask students to "take turns" turning the pages.)
b. Lead a group discussion focusing on why it is important to take turns. Elicit from students that *other children will want to play with them*, that *it will make other children happy.*

Step 2 Identify Skill Components
a. Give some examples of games or activities and ask students to tell how turns are taken. For example, on board games, the first one is usually the person to spin a high number or get the highest number on the roll of the dice. Others are determined by where they sit or how they line up.
b. In sequence, list the following steps on the board or on poster paper.
   1) Pick out the person who has a turn before you.
   2) Pick out the person who has the turn after you.
   3) Wait in one place.
   4) Don't get in the way of another child.
   5) Watch while others take turns.
   6) Get ready to take your turn.
   7) Take your turn.
   8) Give whatever is necessary to the next person.

Step 3 Model the Skill
a. Using a simple board game (e.g., Chutes and Ladders), have two competent peers model the skill of taking turns; narrate the steps using the *thinking aloud* process as the students play.

b. Ask students to identify a number of games or activities where taking turns is required. Select one of the games or activities to model. Have students identify which steps were followed.

c. Create a simulated activity or game, then model the skill using the thinking aloud procedure to narrate the activity. Have students identify which steps were followed.

d. Create a second simulated activity and model turn-taking in a different context/setting.

Step 4 Role-Play

a. Tell students that they are going to play a game where they will all have to take turns. (Nonreading board games are most appropriate, e.g., Candyland, Chutes and Ladders, Snoopy's House, or some other appropriate game like throwing bean bags.)

b. Repeat the skill steps for the class and have students repeat in unison.

c. As children get set up for the game, have each one identify who goes first, who proceeds them, and who follows them.

d. Provide feedback to students as the game goes along. Praise them for correct turn taking. Make sure that at least one child is praised for each one of the skill components.

e. Ask students to evaluate how they think they did.

Step 5 Practice

a. During the week of the lesson, point out to students various turn-taking opportunities. Rehearse the steps before an in-class activity and review the skill components.

b. When students are engaged in an activity where turn taking is necessary, reinforce the various skill components.

c. Occasionally ask students if they can tell you the rules for taking turns. Reinforce as necessary.

Step 6 Generalization

a. Inform general education classroom teachers and PE teachers that your social skills group is working hard on learning to take turns. Ask them to provide feedback and reinforcement to students.

b. Send notes home to families describing the turn taking behaviors and ask them to prompt their child to demonstrate turn taking at home.

c. Have students self-report on how they are taking turns.

d. Fade prompts and reinforcements over time.

Step 7 Evaluation

After a period of time it is necessary to determine if the skills taught are being sustained and generalized. The following practices are used to determine long-term success of instruction.

a. Periodically observe the students in general education settings and rate their performance according to the performance criteria listed at the beginning of the lesson.

b. Ask general education teacher(s)/other support staff to rate students according to the performance criteria.

c. Collect data using progress-monitoring strategies.

d. Design individual interventions for students not benefiting from small-group interventions (i.e., students who perform the skill inadequately or fail to generalize the skill to other settings).

LESSON 27
Asking Someone to Play With You

Objective
Students will ask peers to play by suggesting a specific activity.

Performance Criteria
This skill will be *performed adequately* when the student:
1. Identifies a student with whom he/she wants to play.
2. Chooses an activity.
3. Walks up to the selected playmate and addresses him/her by name.
4. Asks the peer to play and suggests one or more specific activities.
5. Asks a second peer to play if the first is not able to participate.

Materials Required
None for this lesson.

Other Preparation
Prepare competent peers to model and role-play; prepare additional peers to respond positively to invitations to play from target students.

Special Considerations
Circle of Friends (see Chapter 3) may be helpful in supporting the target student's acquisition of the skill.

Forms and Supplementary Materials (see CD)
Conversation Strip Template

Technology Resources
Internet: Boardmaker Share site has a social story at www.boardmakershare.com/Activity/65523/asking-someone-to-play-social-story

Related Lessons
Lesson 16: Greeting Peers and Friends
Lesson 28: Joining in an Activity
Lesson 61, Volume 2: Socializing With Peers

PROCEDURES 7 STEPS

Step 1 Establish the Need

a. Ask students to name some activities that cannot be done alone. Elicit things such as playing catch, playing games, pretending to be police and crooks, playing house, and so forth.

b. Demonstrate trying to do these activities alone.

c. Discuss benefits of playing with other children. Elicit that *playing with others is fun.*

d. Tell students that at school,

   1) Recess and free time are for playing with friends. You are not allowed to play alone at school. You must find a friend to play with.

   2) It is the student's responsibility to ask someone to play (with or without prompting).

   3) You must ask friends to play different activities (whether you like that activity or not).

   4) Remember that you are playing with your friend (not just the materials).

Step 2 Identify Skill Components

a. Tell class or group that there are some good ways to ask others to play.

b. Present the following steps:

   1) Pick out a friend you want to play with.

   2) Walk up to them.

   3) Ask if they would like to play.

   4) Tell them what you would like to play.

   5) If they cannot play, ask someone else.

Step 3 Model the Skill

a. Simulate a play situation; have two competent peers model the skill. Use the thinking aloud procedure to narrate the nonverbal steps.

b. Have two competent peers model the skill with an error and ask students to identify the error.

c. Model the skill again, but change the context to include a different child and different activity.

Step 4 Role-Play

a. Pair students with competent peers and role-play the skill.

b. Provide feedback and praise to each student.

c. Have each student evaluate their own performance.

Step 5 Practice

a. Take students to playground; review the skill steps and have them practice asking each other to play.
b. Hold a skill review session and have the skill modeled by proficient peers.
c. Praise students for exhibiting the skill during free time periods in class and recess.
d. Distribute cards listing different activities and practice asking a peer to play.

Step 6 Generalization

a. Make occasional observations on the school grounds and praise students for using the skill appropriately.
b. Ask other school staff members to praise students when they observe them using the skill. Ask them to prompt students to exercise the skill.
c. Send note home to families asking them to encourage their children to exercise the skill. (Note to them that the student must ask another family member to play, specify the activity, and then play with them, not parallel play.)
d. Encourage families to set up after-school play dates.

Step 7 Evaluation

After a period of time it is necessary to determine if the skills taught are being sustained and generalized. The following practices are used to determine long-term success of instruction.

a. Periodically observe the students in general education settings and rate their performance according to the performance criteria listed at the beginning of the lesson.
b. Ask general education teacher(s)/other support staff to rate students according to the performance criteria.
c. Collect data using progress-monitoring strategies.
d. Design individual interventions for students not benefiting from small-group interventions (i.e., students who perform the skill inadequately or fail to generalize the skill to other settings)..

LESSON 28
Joining in an Activity

Objective

Students will have the ability to join in group activities.

Performance Criteria

This skill will be *performed adequately* when the student:
1. Decides he/she wants to join a peer activity.
2. Decides on an appropriate time to approach.
3. Uses a joining-in statement.

CHAPTER
5

Materials Required

Compile pictures of groups doing different activities together (e.g., board games, playground games, sports, student-created puppet shows).

Other Preparation

Prepare competent peers for modeling and role-playing steps.
Prepare competent peers to support the target student at recess or free-play classroom time. Ensure that they will accept the student's request to join.

Special Considerations

Many students with ASD are highly focused on certain favorite topics or activities. For role-playing, first choose scenarios that reflect the target student's area of special interest to encourage desire to participate with others, then identify other activities that might not be of special interest but that are fun to do with a group.

Forms and Supplementary Materials (see CD)

None for this lesson.

Technology Resources

Internet: YouTube has several videos that demonstrate how to play games (e.g., Parachute Troopers, How to Play Jacks); Games for School are available from www.gamesforschool.net

Related Lessons

Lesson 7: Requesting a Preferred Activity
Lesson 27: Asking Someone to Play With You
Lesson 40: Playing Games With Peers

PROCEDURES 7 STEPS

Step 1 Establish the Need

a. Introduce the skill by showing a video (see Technology Resources).
b. Discuss with the class why it is important to learn how to join in an activity with peers. Elicit *it is fun to play with others.*

Step 2 Identify Skill Components

a. Teach students the steps of the skill:
  1) I decide I want to join an activity.
  2) I decide if it's the right time to approach.
  3) I use a joining-in statement.
b. Teach different "joining-in statements" (may post statements with photos of group activities):
  1) Can I play?
  2) Hi! What are you doing?
  3) Do you need another player?
  4) Can I help?

Step 3 Model the Skill

a. Have competent peers model the skill (e.g., two students are playing a game; third student approaches and uses a joining-in statement).
b. Ask students to identify the joining-in statement that was used.

Step 4 Role-Play

a. Have a group of competent peers engage in an activity of interest to the target student; prompt/encourage the target student to join in.
b. Have a group of competent peers engage in an activity of interest to the target student; have the student model the skill without prompting.
c. Discuss other activities that children do that might not be of particular interest, but would be fun to join in.
d. Show the class pictures of groups doing different activities. Have students select activities they would want to join, and role-play the scenario.

Step 5 Practice

a. Encourage target students to join activities at recess or during classroom free-play time. (Prepare competent peers in advance to accept the student's request to join.)

b. Have students set goals for joining in a playground activity and report on their success.

c. Arrange opportunities for free-play in the classroom and reinforce student demonstration of the skill.

Step 6 Generalization

a. Inform other staff/teachers about the skill being taught and ask them to reinforce and to provide praise when they observe students joining in group activities with peers.

b. Re-teach the skill on the playground or just prior to an indoor recess day. (It is often better for a different person to do the re-teaching to avoid stimulus dependence.)

c. Use the Home-School Connection form to inform families of the skill being taught; ask them to reinforce and provide praise when they observe students joining in group activities (e.g., playground, park, family gatherings).

Step 7 Evaluation

After a period of time it is necessary to determine if the skills taught are being sustained and generalized. The following practices are used to determine long-term success of instruction.

a. Periodically observe the students in general education settings and rate their performance according to the performance criteria listed at the beginning of the lesson.

b. Ask general education teacher(s)/other support staff to rate students according to the performance criteria.

c. Collect data using progress-monitoring strategies.

d. Design individual interventions for students not benefiting from small-group interventions (i.e., students who perform the skill inadequately or fail to generalize the skill to other settings).

CHAPTER
5

LESSON 29
Dealing With Stress and Anxiety: Calming Activities

Objective

Students will use calming techniques to relieve stress and remain calm.

Performance Criteria

This skill will be *performed adequately* when the student:
1. Recognizes that a situation is stressful.
2. Chooses a relaxation or calming technique.
3. Is able to adjust to the situation.

Materials Required

Book on the theme, such as *The Worst Day of My Life Ever!* by Julia Cook (2011); *The Worst Day of My Life Ever! Activity and Idea Book* by Julia Cook and Carrie Hartman (2009); or *Angry Octopus* by Lori Lite (2008).
Consequence map; Incredible 5-Point Scale (Dunn Buron & Curtis, 2004) or stress thermometer.

Other Preparation

Create "break" cards (as needed) that students can use in other school settings. Talk to other school staff (i.e., general education classroom teachers) about establishing "chill" or calming areas within their classrooms.

Special Considerations

Some students with ASD may need a sensory choice board or sensory box to incorporate into their calming activities; others may want to use theraputty or a small squishy ball. Some students may benefit from incorporating yoga in their daily schedule.

Forms and Supplementary Materials (see CD)

Home-School Connection form

Technology Resources

Apps: Angry Octopus (Red Piston); Autism Xpress (StudioEmotion); My Choice Board (Good Karma Applications; for nonverbal students)
Internet: www.Speakingofspeech.com has a social story about steps for calming

CHAPTER
5

down; Healthyinfo.com has a template for a stress thermometer (www.healthyinfo. com/consumers/ho/bipolar/Mood.Diaries/thermometer.pdf); Boardmaker share site has a consequence map for calming down as well as a consequence map template (www.boardmakershare.com/Activity/410063/consequence-map)

Related Lessons

Lesson 10: Being Patient: Learning How to Wait

Lesson 22: Coping With Sensory Issues

Lesson 48: Managing Emotions: Dealing With Frustration

PROCEDURES 7 STEPS

Step 1 Establish the Need

a. Introduce the lesson by reading a book on the theme; discuss with students situations or occasions where they have felt upset and needed to calm down.

b. Show students the consequence map and explain how not knowing calming techniques leaves us unhappy, but knowing calming techniques helps us feel better.

c. Tell students that you can help them learn calming activities to *help them feel better so they can participate in school.*

Step 2 Identify Skill Components

a. Using either a 5-point scale or stress thermometer, explain how stress builds up and that it is important to recognize when we are getting stressed.

b. Have students indicate their feelings/stressors on the scale or thermometer.

c. Create small versions of the scale or thermometer that students can keep on their desks for self-monitoring.

d. Discuss different self-calming activities with students (e.g., breathing techniques, talking to self, sensory board/box, manipulatives/theraputty/ therapy ball, secluded or "chill" area in classroom).

e. Elucidate the skill steps:

1) I'm starting to feel stressed or anxious.

2) I need to calm down.

3) I think I will _____ .

4) Now I'm ready to work.

f. With students, brainstorm ideas for calming activities; list them on a chalkboard, whiteboard, or overhead projector (may use icons for nonreading students); this list may be turned into a poster for display in the classroom/use as a choice board.

Step 3 Model the Skill

a. Using a 5-point scale or stress thermometer, demonstrate to the students self-monitoring stress/anxiety.
b. Choose a calming activity and model using it.
c. Ask students whether they would calm down like you do, or whether they would choose another.
d. Have students model the skill steps using their preferred calming activity.

Step 4 Role-Play

a. Have students demonstrate choosing a calming activity for circumstances that may typically cause them stress. Give students individually relevant scenarios for them to practice calming themselves; for example,
   1) Students with ASD may benefit from focusing on unexpected changes in routine.
   2) Students with intellectual disabilities may need to focus on challenging tasks that cause frustration.
b. Provide feedback; prompt to performance as necessary.

Step 5 Practice

a. In real situations, prompt students to exercise their calming strategies. Reinforce them when they engage in the calming activities.
b. Use "what if" scenarios to have students demonstrate or articulate the calming steps.
c. Use skill challenges by creating circumstances that may cause stress (e.g., school assembly, change in routine, substitute teacher) and prompt students through their calming process.

Step 6 Generalization

a. Inform other staff/teachers about the skill being taught and ask them to reinforce and to provide praise when they observe students using their calming strategies.
b. Ask relevant "specials" teachers (i.e., PE, Music) to talk about and present calming activities in their classes.
c. Use the Home-School Connection form to inform families of the skill being taught; ask them to reinforce and provide praise when they observe students using self-monitoring and calming strategies.

Step 7 Evaluation

After a period of time it is necessary to determine if the skills taught are being sustained and generalized. The following practices are used to determine long-term success of instruction.

a. Periodically observe the students in general education settings and rate their performance according to the performance criteria listed at the beginning of the lesson.

b. Ask general education teacher(s)/other support staff to rate students according to the performance criteria.

c. Collect data using progress-monitoring strategies.

d. Design individual interventions for students not benefiting from small-group interventions (i.e., students who perform the skill inadequately or fail to generalize the skill to other settings).

LESSON 30
Reading Facial Expressions

Objective
Students will understand what different facial expressions portray.

Performance Criteria
This skill will be *performed adequately* when the student:
1. Correctly relates a facial expression to an emotion or message.
2. Responds appropriately.

Materials Required
Pictures of individuals demonstrating various facial expressions.

Other Preparation
Prepare another adult to assist with modeling.
Prepare competent peers to assist with role-playing.
Video modeling may be appropriate for the role-playing and practice steps.

Special Considerations
Recognizing and understanding facial expressions is a particular challenge for students with ASD. This lesson is best taught preceding lessons where students will meet significant interaction challenges (e.g., joining a group or asking a friend to play).

Forms and Supplementary Materials (see CD)
Facial expression jpegs (25 photographs of different expressions/emotions)
Reading Facial Expressions PowerPoint

Technology Resources
Software: Mind Reading: The Interactive Guide to Emotions (Jessica Kingsley); Faceland (Do2Learn/Don Johnston Assistive Technology)
Internet: Online facial expression games (www.juliasrainbowcorner.com/html/feelingsgame.html) and (www.do2learn.com/games/facialexpressions/index.htm); do2Learn also has a facial expression bingo PDF (www.do2learn.com/subscription/product_details/facialexpressions_bingo.php); SEN Teacher has free printable expression cards (www.senteacher.org/Worksheet/40/Prosopagnosia.xhtml)
iPad/iPhone app: Smurks (Iconicast)

Related Lessons

Lesson 31: Understanding Nonverbal Communication Cues
Lesson 47: Recognizing and Expressing Emotions
Lesson 69, Volume 2: Using Gestures and Nonverbal Communication
Lesson 73, Volume 2: Reading Facial Expressions and Interpreting Others'
Emotions

PROCEDURES 7 STEPS

Step 1 Establish the Need

a. Introduce the skill by
   1) Playing a facial recognition game with the class;
   2) Using the facial expression graphic files and asking students to guess what the individual is feeling; OR
   3) Reading a book on the theme, such as *Feelings* by Aliki (1986).
b. Have students make different faces when you name different feelings.
c. Make different faces and have students guess the feeling; ask them what they feel in response to different expressions.
d. Make a mad face and ask students "Do I look friendly? Would you like to talk to me?" Explain that our facial expressions tell other people things about us (e.g., a mad face says "stay away," a smile is a greeting).
e. Elicit that the skill is important because it *helps us interact with others.*

Step 2 Identify Skill Components

a. Tell the students that there are two steps to the skill:
   1) Figuring out what someone is feeling based on facial expression.
   2) Responding appropriately to the other person's feeling.
b. Post pictures of different facial expressions in the classroom; have students label the pictures.

Step 3 Model the Skill

a. With another adult, show how facial expressions change during a conversation.
b. Using the thinking aloud procedure, identify the different emotions being modeled.
c. Using the thinking aloud procedure, identify how you are responding to the other adult's changes in facial expression.
d. Model the skill and have students identify the emotions and responses.

Step 4 Role-Play

a. Pair students with competent peers to role-play conversations. Have the peer partner exhibit differing emotions during the conversation and prompt the target student to respond.

b. If videotaping conversations for later review, use thinking aloud and narration to identify elements of the skill.

Step 5 Practice

a. During the week following introduction of the skill, use exaggerated facial expressions when having casual conversations with students. Prompt them to identify and respond.

b. Revisit the facial recognition games; may also use sorting cards to match facial expressions to emotional words.

c. Have students observe a competent peer or yourself as you demonstrate various facial expressions. As they observe, have them mark a pictorial expressions chart consisting of line drawings.

d. Repeat the previous activity using photos rather than line drawings of facial expressions.

Step 6 Generalization

a. Show dramatic video clips where various expressions are depicted and have the students identify and provide an interpretation of their meaning. Stop the video at important places to discuss what the students believe they identified as expressions.

b. Take students to a public place (e.g. a mall or busy plaza) and have them identify facial expressions of the people around them.

Step 7 Evaluation

After a period of time it is necessary to determine if the skills taught are being sustained and generalized. The following practices are used to determine long-term success of instruction.

a. Periodically observe the students in general education settings and rate their performance according to the performance criteria listed at the beginning of the lesson.

b. Ask general education teacher(s)/other support staff to rate students according to the performance criteria.

c. Collect data using progress-monitoring strategies.

d. Design individual interventions for students not benefiting from small-group interventions (i.e., students who perform the skill inadequately or fail to generalize the skill to other settings).

CHAPTER 5

LESSON 31
Understanding Nonverbal Communication Cues

Objective
Students will understand nonverbal communication cues and how to respond appropriately.

Performance Criteria
This skill will be *performed adequately* when the student:
1. Correctly relates a nonverbal cue to an emotion or message.
2. Responds appropriately.

Materials Required
Pictures or videos of body language and gestures.

Other Preparation
Prepare competent peers to assist with role-plays.
Prepare other school staff members to support the generalization step.

Special Considerations
Recognizing and understanding nonverbal communication cues is a particular challenge for students with ASD.

Due to the focus on young students for this lesson, the emphasis on interpreting body language should be restricted to a narrow range of behaviors. Recognition of friendly body language (meaning *approachable*) and interpretation of when to take leave are important for social acceptance. The skills emphasized in this lesson may be blended into the content of other lessons.

Forms and Supplementary Materials (see CD)
None for this lesson.

Technology Resources
None for this lesson.

Related Lessons
Lesson 30: Reading Facial Expressions
Lesson 58, Volume 2: Analyzing Social Situations

CHAPTER
5

Lesson 59, Volume 2: Understanding Unwritten Social Rules
Lesson 69, Volume 2: Using Gestures and Nonverbal Communication

PROCEDURES 7 STEPS

Step 1 Establish the Need
a. Introduce the skill by
   1) Watching a DVD or television show without the sound and point out nonverbal cues; have students create a "script" for what they are seeing; ask them to predict what will happen next in a particular scene; or
   2) Present a comic strip with pictures only depicting nonverbal communication; have students fill in thought or speech bubbles.
b. Elicit that the skill is important because *it is not helpful to engage with people who do not want to associate with you* and *it is not polite to extend contact beyond the other person's interest in being engaged.*

Step 2 Identify Skill Components
a. Tell the students that there are two aspects to understanding and responding to nonverbal communication:
   1) Establishing, based on another person's nonverbal communication, whether you should approach/engage them or not.
   2) During a conversation, deciding, based on another person's nonverbal communication, whether you should keep talking or stop talking.
b. Tell students that they will learn to identify if someone else wants to be friends and is enjoying a conversation, or whether they are bored, tired, or impatient.
c. Inform students of the need to make essential decisions to (1) approach and initiate interaction or not approach, and (2) decide when to stay and when to leave. Make a list of cues they should look for to make decisions and post them. Some of the cues may be gestures (e.g. clenched fist for *anger*, droopy arms for *tired*; looking away for *impatient*).

Step 3 Model the Skill
a. With another adult, model the skill.
b. Using the thinking aloud procedure, identify that the other person is friendly and it's okay to approach them. Specify what they are doing that makes them look friendly.
c. Using the thinking aloud procedure, model recognizing that the other person needs to end the conversation (is impatient) or isn't interested (bored/tired).

d. Using the thinking aloud procedure, model recognizing that the other person is engaged in the conversation so it's okay to keep talking.

e. Model the skill without speaking and have students identify the nonverbal messages and responses.

Step 4 Role-Play

a. Pair students with competent peers to role-play the skill. Give them scenarios and have students act out the nonverbal communication. Provide feedback on performance of the role-plays.

b. Mix the role-play examples between approach/engage situations and stay/leave situations. Have students observe each other and provide feedback on some of the decision cues they observed.

c. Have the target students self-evaluate how they have done on the role-plays.

Step 5 Practice

a. During the week following introduction of the skill, show students a series of pictures and have them decide what the nonverbal messages are. (Alternatively, revisit the cartoon-strip exercise from Step 1.)

b. Use skill challenges over the following weeks by exhibiting a body language gesture and have students identify its meaning and how they should respond. Facial expressions also should be used to provide students with a more holistic experience. For example, demonstrate a smiling face and open-palms gesture and have the students interpret.

Step 6 Generalization

a. Arrange to have other staff members (e.g., school counselor, secretary, custodian, parent volunteer) exhibit previously determined body and facial gestures. If the student demonstrates an adequate response, the staff member should praise and reinforce correct performance.

b. Take the students to different environments within the school and community and have them classify whether certain individuals are approachable or not.

Step 7 Evaluation

After a period of time it is necessary to determine if the skills taught are being sustained and generalized. The following practices are used to determine long-term success of instruction.

a. Periodically observe the students in general education settings and rate their performance according to the performance criteria listed at the beginning of the lesson.

b. Ask general education teacher(s)/other support staff to rate students according to the performance criteria.

c. Collect data using progress-monitoring strategies.

d. Design individual interventions for students not benefiting from small-group interventions (i.e., students who perform the skill inadequately or fail to generalize the skill to other settings).

LESSON 32
Understanding Figures of Speech

Objective
Students will understand that all language does not mean exactly what the words say.

Performance Criteria
This skill will be *performed adequately* when the student:
1. Understands the meaning of *simile, metaphor, hyperbole,* and *personification.*
2. Is able to recognize and use idiomatic expressions and figures of speech.

CHAPTER
5

Materials Required
Prepare T-chart prior to introducing lesson; collect pictures, drawings, or other visuals to use on chart.
Prepare index cards with figures of speech.

Other Preparation
Book on the theme, such as *Bookworm: Discovering Idioms, Sayings and Expressions* by Karen Emigh (2007); *The King Who Rained* by Fred Gwynne (1988); *A Chocolate Moose for Dinner* by Fred Gwynne (2005); *In a Pickle and Other Funny Idioms* by Marvin Terban (2007); or *Crazy Like a Fox: A Simile Story* by Loreen Leedy (2009)

Special Considerations
Students with ASD and those with intellectual disabilities have somewhat different issues related to understanding figures of speech. Whereas students with ASD often interpret language literally, students with intellectual disabilities have difficulty with vocabulary and attaching accurate meaning to phrases. Adjustments may be necessary depending on the type of disability. In addition, the concepts must be limited to high use language. Similes, metaphors, and other types of figurative language are covered again in middle and high school general education English classes.

Forms and Supplementary Materials (see CD)
Home-School Connection form

Technology Resources

Internet: Polyxo.com has 3 social stories on figures of speech at www.polyxo.com/socialstories/toc-language.html; Kids Learning Network has a song introducing figure of speech vocabulary at http://kidslearningnetwork.com/figures-of-speech-song/; portal with online resources on figurative language (games, worksheets, etc.) at www.sturgeon.k12.mo.us/elementary/numphrey/subjectpages/languagearts/figuresofspeech.html; lesson plan on teaching personification and hyperbole using Far Side cartoons at www.speechdrive.net/uploads/5/5/7/1/5571631/far_side_cartoons.pdf

Related Lessons

Lesson 33: Understanding Sarcasm and Irony
Lesson 71, Volume 2: Recognizing and Responding to Jokes and Humor

PROCEDURES 7 STEPS

Step 1 Establish the Need

a. Read exerts from the theme books to engage students in the topic of understanding figures of speech.

b. Discuss with the class the value of understanding when something doesn't mean "what the words say." Provide an example of an idiomatic expression (e.g., *back to square one, spill the beans, under the weather*).

c. Elicit from students that this is an important skill because it *helps you talk with other people*.

Step 2 Identify Skill Components

a. Tell students that this skill requires knowing the names of the different types of language people use to describe things.

b. Explain that the process of identifying the type of language being used leads to understanding the meaning.

c. Introduce and define the terms *simile, metaphor, hyperbole*, and *personification*. Write the terms and their meanings on whiteboard, chalkboard, overhead, or poster.

Step 3 Model the Skill

a. Read a themed book to the class and discuss the imagery provided by the various figures of speech. Provide and discuss examples of similes, metaphors, hyperbole, and personification.

b. Tell students that when they hear a "funny" expression, to think:
  1) Is this a simile? (Did they say *like* or *as*?)
  2) Is this a metaphor? (Are they making a comparison?)
  3) Is this hyperbole? (Are they being dramatic?)
  4) Is this personification? (Are they describing something that's not a person but sounds like it is?)
  5) What do I think it means?

c. Write an example of each type of figure of speech (e.g., *white as a sheet, my computer hates me, hopping mad, time is money*) on overhead, whiteboard, or chalkboard and use the *thinking aloud* procedure to model the skill: identify the type of language being used and demonstrate the process of decoding the meaning.

Step 4 Role-Play

a. Distribute figures of speech index cards and have students read them aloud.
b. As a class, select a half dozen or so examples and affix to T-chart.
c. As a class, go through the process of identifying the type of language being used and decoding its meaning.
d. Write definitions of the figures of speech on the T-chart and add pictures (pictures may either be a literal representation or an image that explains the message).

Step 5 Practice

a. In the week following the lesson, revisit the phrases from the T-chart.
b. A month after the lesson, introduce new phrases and challenge students to demonstrate the skill process.
c. Using the Home-School Connection form, ask families to play an idiom game at home.

Step 6 Generalization

a. Ask other school personnel (e.g., general education classroom teacher, librarian) to support the skills lesson by discussing figures of speech as part of their time with students.
b. Ask other school personnel (e.g., school secretary, principal) to engage target students with conversations that incorporate figures of speech (e.g., "Boy, it sure is raining cats and dogs, isn't it?").
c. Ask students to self-report on figures of speech they discovered people using in other settings.

Step 7 Evaluation

After a period of time it is necessary to determine if the skills taught are being sustained and generalized. The following practices are used to determine long-term success of instruction.

a. Periodically observe the students in general education settings and rate their performance according to the performance criteria listed at the beginning of the lesson.

b. Ask general education teacher(s)/other support staff to rate students according to the performance criteria.

c. Collect data using progress-monitoring strategies.

d. Design individual interventions for students not benefiting from small-group interventions (i.e., students who perform the skill inadequately or fail to generalize the skill to other settings).

LESSON 33
Understanding Sarcasm and Irony

Objective

Students will understand and recognize the use of sarcasm and irony.

Performance Criteria

This skill will be *performed adequately* when the student:
1. Recognizes that a statement is sarcastic or ironic.
2. Is able to grasp the speaker's intention.
3. Responds appropriately.
4. If unsure, asks for clarification.

Materials Required

Comic strip illustrating situations of irony/sarcasm (see possible situations, Step 1).
Situation cards for role-play and practice steps.

Other Preparation

None for this lesson.

Special Considerations

None for this lesson.

Forms and Supplementary Materials (see CD)

None for this lesson.

Technology Resources

iPad/iPhone app: eTOM (Pragmatom); Comic Life software and app (Plasq.com); Strip Designer app (www.mexircus.com/Strip_Designer/index.html)
Internet: Makebeliefscomix (www.makebeliefscomix.com/), ReadWriteThink Comic Creator (www.readwritethink.org/files/resources/interactives/comic/), StripGenerator (http://stripgenerator.com/), StoryCreator 2 (http://myths.e2bn.org/create/tool527-story-creator-2.html); About.com grammar pages for examples of sarcasm (http://grammar.about.com/od/rs/g/sarcasmterm.htm) and irony (http://grammar.about.com/od/il/g/ironyterm.htm)

Related Lessons

Lesson 32: Understanding Figures of Speech

Lesson 71, Volume 2, Volume 2: Recognizing and Responding to Jokes and Humor

Lesson 83, Volume 2: Recognizing and Responding to Teasing, Name Calling, and Bullying

PROCEDURES 7 STEPS

Step 1 Establish the Need

a. Begin a class discussion about the topic; show students the comic strip depicting situations of irony/sarcasm, or relate a story, and discuss the "real" meaning behind the sarcastic/ironic comment, for example:

　1) Joe comes to work, and instead of beginning to work, he sits down and starts checking his e-mail or surfing online. His boss notices his behavior and says, "Joe, don't work too hard." Meaning: "You're a real slacker! Get to work!"

　2) Juan is standing on the curb when his friend Dan walks by, trips, and drops his backpack. Juan says "You dropped your stuff." Dan says "No!" After picking up all his stuff, while Juan stands by, Dan says "Thanks a lot for the help." Meanings: "No" = sarcasm; "of course I did!" and "Thanks" = "I wish you had helped me pick up my stuff."

　3) Amy's father comes home from work. Being polite, she says "How was work?" To which he responds "As much fun as a root canal." Meaning "I had a bad day."

b. Elicit through class discussion that understanding sarcasm and irony will help students *relate to other people* and *understand the real meaning of what people say.*

Step 2 Identify Skill Components

a. Tell students there are specific steps to mastering the skill:

　1) Listen to the phrase.

　2) Does it make sense?

　3) If not, consider the surroundings of the phrase—does it make sense in that context?

　4) If you cannot figure it out, ask the speaker what he or she means.

Step 3 Model the Skill

a. Either through class discussion or by presenting another series of comic strips, revisit the example(s) from Step 1, and model the thinking process for identifying the real meaning/sarcasm/irony, such as, for "Joe and His Boss":

1) Joe stops and thinks: He said don't work too hard, but I'm not working hard.

2) That doesn't make sense.

3) I'm at work, so I should be working hard. My boss was trying to tell me to stop relaxing and start working.

b. With the assistance of another adult, use a variety of phases that include sarcasm or irony. One adult speaks the phrase and the other adult uses the thinking aloud procedure to model interpretation. For example: "That was nice of him." Interpretation: it was not nice at all. Also use the same phrase with a different tone of voice and interpret.

Step 4 Role-Play

a. Distribute situation cards to students. Have them role-play the process of decoding the meaning of the ironic/sarcastic statement.

b. Observe students and provide feedback; have them assess their own performance and that of other students.

Step 5 Practice

a. In the week following the lesson, revisit the phrases from the situation cards.

b. A month after the lesson, introduce new phrases and challenge students to demonstrate the skill process.

c. Have students keep track of and share examples of irony and sarcasm they encounter throughout a school week.

Step 6 Generalization

a. Ask other school personnel (e.g., general education classroom teacher, librarian) to support the skills lesson by discussing figures of speech as part of their time with students.

b. Ask other school personnel (e.g., school secretary, principal) to engage target students with conversations that incorporate figures of speech (e.g., "Boy, it sure is raining cats and dogs, isn't it?").

c. Ask students to self-report on figures of speech they discovered people using in other settings.

Step 7 Evaluation

After a period of time it is necessary to determine if the skills taught are being sustained and generalized. The following practices are used to determine long-term success of instruction.

a. Periodically observe the students in general education settings and rate their performance according to the performance criteria listed at the beginning of the lesson.

b. Ask general education teacher(s)/other support staff to rate students according to the performance criteria.

c. Collect data using progress-monitoring strategies.

d. Design individual interventions for students not benefiting from small-group interventions (i.e., students who perform the skill inadequately or fail to generalize the skill to other settings).

LESSON 34
Recognizing and Expressing Bodily Needs

Objective

Student will recognize body messages and be able to express feeling ill, needing a drink of water/food/to use the restroom.

Performance Criteria

This skill will be *performed adequately* when the student:
1. Can identify which part of his/her body does not feel well.
2. Is able to express/request resolution of the problem, such as,
   a. Will ask for a drink of water if thirsty.
   b. Will ask for food if hungry.
   c. Will ask to use the bathroom when there is a need.

Materials Required

Poster/feltboard with human figure outline, body parts labels, and bodily-need statements.

Other Preparation

Prior to teaching this lesson, it may be necessary to review rules for gaining teacher attention in the settings where the students receive instruction. The rules may be different in the social skills group than when students are included in general education classes. For example, it may be okay for a student to express restroom needs verbally in one setting and only allowed to do so with a physical cue or gesture in another setting.

Special Considerations

None for this lesson.

Forms and Supplementary Materials (see CD)

None for this lesson.

Technology Resources

None for this lesson.

Related Lessons

PROCEDURES 7 STEPS

Step 1 Establish the Need

a. Show students cartoon strips of students with various needs (e.g., need for the restroom, a drink, food, or to report feeling ill).

b. Ask students if they have to use the restroom but felt uncomfortable saying so (it is probable that for some it was an issue).

c. Ask students if they have ever felt sick at school and did not know what to do about it.

d. Inform the students that you will be reviewing how to get teacher attention if you have a personal need.

Step 2 Identify Skill Components

a. Post and tell the students the objective of the lesson is that they will be able to ask or tell of a need for a drink, food, restroom, or feeling sick and relate it to a body part.

b. Create a poster with words and visual symbols of feelings that students may need to express. These may include a restroom symbol, thirsty symbol, hungry symbol, and an illness symbol.

c. Through discussion, create a "How-to" list to express bodily needs, including:

1) A dry throat and mouth for drink.

2) A growing or uncomfortable stomach for hunger.

3) An urgent discomfort for needing to use the restroom.

4) A feeling of nausea (e.g., throwing up) or a high temperature for reporting sickness.

Step 3 Model the Skill

a. Using a poster/feltboard with human figure outline and body parts labels, model identifying and responding to bodily needs:

b. Point to the neck; say "My throat is dry. I need a drink of water. I need to ask for a drink of water."

   c. Point to the stomach; say "My stomach is growling. I'm hungry. I need to ask for something to eat."

   d. Point to the stomach; say "My stomach is full. I need to use the bathroom. I need to ask to use the bathroom."

   e. With students playing the role of teacher, model each of the skills independently of the poster.

Step 4 Role-Play

   a. Have students role-play with the teacher each of the different bodily needs; correct performance as necessary and provide praise and reinforcement.

Step 5 Practice

   a. The week following introduction of the skill, ask general education and "specials" teachers to reinforce/praise student performance of the skill (e.g., praise student when he/she asks for a drink of water).

Step 6 Generalization

   a. Using the body poster, talk about other physical needs (e.g., feeling tired, headache, etc.). Have students practice responding to these "new" bodily needs.

   b. Using the Home-School Connection form, ask families to support skill mastery by discussing and reinforcing at home.

Step 7 Evaluation

After a period of time it is necessary to determine if the skills taught are being sustained and generalized. The following practices are used to determine long-term success of instruction.

   a. Periodically observe the students in general education settings and rate their performance according to the performance criteria listed at the beginning of the lesson.

   b. Ask general education teacher(s)/other support staff to rate students according to the performance criteria.

   c. Collect data using progress-monitoring strategies.

   d. Design individual interventions for students not benefiting from small-group interventions (i.e., students who perform the skill inadequately or fail to generalize the skill to other settings).

CHAPTER 5

LESSON 35
How to Tell a Story

Objective
Students will understand subjects, setting, and sequencing in order to tell a logical story.

Performance Criteria
This skill will be *performed adequately* when the student:
1. Clearly identifies the character(s) in the story.
2. Identifies the setting.
3. Can logically sequence events to make the story clear.
4. Uses the words *first, next,* and *last.*

Materials Required
3-part story sequence mat; story components (words/images). *First, Next, Last* signs or posters.

Other Preparation
None for this lesson.

Special Considerations
Students with ASD and other developmental disabilities often have difficulties in identifying the main ideas or themes from a story; they may be more inclined to focus on details.

Forms and Supplementary Materials (see CD)
Home-School Connection form

Technology Resources
iPad/iPhone app: Storybuilder

Related Lessons
Lesson 36: How to Describe a Movie, Book, or TV Show Episode
Lesson 37: How to Describe a Personal Experience, Memory, or Dream

PROCEDURES 7 STEPS

Step 1 Establish the Need
a. Introduce the lesson by reading a story to the class, preferably a class favorite.
b. Lead a class discussion about the importance of being able to retell a story; elicit that *it's fun to share.*
c. Using the 3-part story mat, mix up the components in a way that is obvious. Discuss with the class that it would be difficult to understand the story if it is told out of order.

Step 2 Identify Skill Components
a. Tell students that you are going to give them a toolbox of words to use to be able to tell a story.
b. Hang up signs or posters (or write on chalkboard, whiteboard, or overhead) of the words *first, next,* and *last.*
c. Discuss the meaning of the words and their place in stories (i.e., 1, 2, 3).
d. Describe the story retelling/sequencing process to students, emphasizing including all steps (i.e., *first, next, last*).

Step 3 Model the Skill
a. Read a story to the class, preferably one with which they are less familiar.
b. Retell the story using the story sequence mat; emphasize use of the words *first, next,* and *last.*

Step 4 Role-Play
a. Pair students. Have one student retell a favorite or familiar story, and the other student (with prompting and reinforcement as necessary) use the story mat to sequence the story.
b. Following the storytelling, discuss details of the story such as setting, that might provide clues to sequencing.
c. Ensure that all students have an opportunity to practice both the story telling and the activity of sequencing a story that is told to them.
d. Provide reinforcement; have students evaluate their performance and that of their partner.

Step 5 Practice
a. Introduce a craft or activity (e.g., making a bird house or a thank-you card) that has 3 clearly defined steps to produce.

b. As the class works on the craft, emphasize the necessity of doing one step *first*, one *next*, and one *last*.

c. The week after introducing the skill, read the class a new story and have them help you sequence the action.

d. Periodically through the school year, ask students to describe what they have just done using the first, next, and last sequence.

Step 6 Generalization

a. Use the Home-School Connection form to ask families to assist by having their child tell a story using the first, next, and last sequence about something that happened that day. Ask parents to provide praise when the skill is accomplished correctly.

b. Arrange with general education teachers to have competent peers tell a story about a shared experience with a target student. A pair/share activity may be the appropriate time for this to occur.

Step 7 Evaluation

After a period of time it is necessary to determine if the skills taught are being sustained and generalized. The following practices are used to determine long-term success of instruction.

a. Periodically observe the students in general education settings and rate their performance according to the performance criteria listed at the beginning of the lesson.

b. Ask general education teacher(s)/other support staff to rate students according to the performance criteria.

c. Collect data using progress-monitoring strategies.

d. Design individual interventions for students not benefiting from small-group interventions (i.e., students who perform the skill inadequately or fail to generalize the skill to other settings).

CHAPTER
5

LESSON 36
How to Describe a Movie, Book, or TV Show Episode

Objective

Students will have the ability to describe a movie, book, or TV episode.

Performance Criteria

This skill will be *performed adequately* when the student:
1. Can pick out the main ideas in a movie, book, or TV episode.
2. Can logically sequence these events.
3. Can relay these events clearly to others, specifying the source.

Materials Required

5-part story sequence mat; story components (words/images).

Other Preparation

None for this lesson.

Special Considerations

It is recommended that this lesson be taught following and in conjunction with Lesson 35.

Forms and Supplementary Materials (see CD)

Homework form
Home-School Connection form

Technology Resources

iPad/iPhone app: Storybuilder

Related Lessons

Lesson 35: How to Tell a Story
Lesson 37: How to Describe a Personal Experience, Memory, or Dream

PROCEDURES 7 STEPS

Step 1 Establish the Need

a. Introduce the lesson by leading a class discussion: Ask students if they watched a movie or a TV show recently and if they ever wanted to talk about it with someone else.

b. Elicit that *it is fun to discuss what they saw with someone who also saw it.* Also elicit that *telling another person about a movie may encourage them to see a movie they would like.*

Step 2 Identify Skill Components

a. Tell the students that they can ask themselves some questions that will help them share a book, movie, or TV show that they like:

1) Was it a book, a movie, or a TV show?
2) What was the big idea?
3) What is important about the characters?
4) Where did the story take place?
5) What things happened *first*, *next*, and *last*?

Step 3 Model the Skill

a. Do a thinking aloud procedure while reading a book, identifying the main characters, setting, main idea, and essential events.

b. Model the difference between providing minor details and providing a "big picture" of the story, with essential events and information.

Step 4 Role-Play

a. Watch a short film, video, or TV show episode with the class.

b. Pair students to work on a 5-event sequence mat. Have the pairs present their retelling of the show to the class. Reinforce and correct skill performance.

Step 5 Practice

a. Using the Home-School Connection form, advise families of the skill being taught. Ask them to watch a movie with the student, to thinking aloud while watching the movie, and to stop it and discuss important events, the setting, the plot sequence, and the main ideas.

b. Assign students the homework of picking out five main events. They should write a short description, draw a picture, or use an icon to represent the event.

c. Have students share their story mats and describe the movie. Reinforce correct sequencing and use of details. Ask questions to correct as necessary.

Step 6 Generalization

   a. In the weeks following introduction of the skill, ask students "Have you seen any good movies lately?" "What book are you reading these days?" or "What did you watch on TV last night?"

   b. Prompt and discuss performance of the skill.

   c. Give the students an assignment to talk with another child and tell them about a movie or TV show they watched at home. Provide the students with a self-evaluation list using the first, next, and last sequence.

Step 7 Evaluation

After a period of time it is necessary to determine if the skills taught are being sustained and generalized. The following practices are used to determine long-term success of instruction.

   a. Periodically observe the students in general education settings and rate their performance according to the performance criteria listed at the beginning of the lesson.

   b. Ask general education teacher(s)/other support staff to rate students according to the performance criteria.

   c. Collect data using progress-monitoring strategies.

   d. Design individual interventions for students not benefiting from small-group interventions (i.e., students who perform the skill inadequately or fail to generalize the skill to other settings).

CHAPTER 5

LESSON 37
How to Describe a Personal Experience, Memory, or Dream

Objective
Students will have the ability to describe a personal experience, memory, or dream.

Performance Criteria
This skill will be *performed adequately* when the student:
1. Identifies whether he/she is sharing a recent experience, a memory, or a dream.
2. Starts at the beginning.
3. Identifies characters and setting.
4. Describes the story in a logical sequence using transition vocabulary.

Materials Required
None for this lesson.

Other Preparation
None for this lesson.

Special Considerations
It is recommended that this lesson be taught in conjunction with Lessons 35 and 36.

Forms and Supplementary Materials (see CD)
Home-School Connection form
Homework form

Technology Resources
None for this lesson.

Related Lessons
Lesson 24: Telling the Truth
Lesson 35: How to Tell a Story
Lesson 36: How to Describe a Movie, Book, or TV Show Episode

PROCEDURES 7 STEPS

Step 1 Establish the Need

a. Introduce the lesson by relating an experience to the class but do not identify whether it happened recently, is a memory, or was a dream.

b. Ask students to guess which they think it was.

c. Discuss that it's important to be able to talk about something that just happened, that happened a long time ago, or that one dreamt or imagined clearly *so other people understand.*

Step 2 Identify Skill Components

a. Tell the students that there are some good rules for sharing an experience, a memory, or a dream or idea:
   1) Which was it? (Experience, memory, or dream?)
   2) What happened *first*?
   3) Who else was involved?
   4) What happened *then, next,* and *finally*?

b. Discuss the importance of sequence words (i.e., *first, next, last*).

c. Tell students that in addition to the steps there are words that give people clues to the story. Write on chalkboard, whiteboard, overhead, or posterboard some transition words (e.g., *then, also, plus, but*).

Step 3 Model the Skill

a. Model the skill by describing a personal experience, memory, or dream; start by saying "I am going to tell you about [something that happened/a memory I have/a dream I had the other night]."

b. Emphasize both sequence words and transition words.

Step 4 Role-Play

a. Pair students and have them share an experience, memory, or dream. Students may need prompting (e.g., "Do you remember your first day of school? What happened?" or "What did your family do last night?").

b. Have students evaluate their own performance and that of their partner.

Step 5 Practice

a. After lunch, recess, or specials class, ask students to tell you their experience.

b. Prompt and reinforce use of sequence and transition words.

Step 6 Generalization

a. Inform general education teachers, special teachers, and other school staff (e.g., librarian) of the skill being taught. Ask them to encourage students to share or describe an experience, memory, or dream. Ask them to reinforce/praise demonstration of the skill.

b. Using the Home-School Connection form, ask families to share memories with their students. Assign students homework of retelling or relating the family story.

c. Have students report on Monday about their activities over the weekend, or dreams they had.

Step 7 Evaluation

After a period of time it is necessary to determine if the skills taught are being sustained and generalized. The following practices are used to determine long-term success of instruction.

a. Periodically observe the students in general education settings and rate their performance according to the performance criteria listed at the beginning of the lesson.

b. Ask general education teacher(s)/other support staff to rate students according to the performance criteria.

c. Collect data using progress-monitoring strategies.

d. Design individual interventions for students not benefiting from small-group interventions (i.e., students who perform the skill inadequately or fail to generalize the skill to other settings).

CHAPTER
5

LESSON 38
Understanding Responsibility: What to Do When You Have to Do Something You Don't Want to Do

Objective
Students will follow classroom rules and participate in activities, even if it is not their preferred activity.

Performance Criteria
This skill will be *performed adequately* when the student:
1. Does not protest or object to assignments or instructions.
2. Refrains from making negative remarks about teachers or school in general.
3. Gathers materials as needed and begins work promptly.
4. Works on assignment or task for allotted time.

Materials Required
Posterboard/whiteboard/chalkboard for T-chart
Poster of procedures for "Doing the Have-to-Dos"

Other Preparation
Solicit the assistance of and prepare another staff member for the modeling step of the lesson.

Special Considerations
None for this lesson.

Forms and Supplementary Materials (see CD)
None for this lesson.

Technology Resources
iPad/iPhone apps: Time Timer (Time Timer LLC); First Then Visual Schedule (Good Karma)
Internet: "Choices and Have-to-Dos at School: A Social Story" (www.speakingofspeech.com/uploads/ChoicesandHaveToDo.pdf)

Related Lessons
Lesson 17: Using Classroom Materials: Sharing, Taking Care of Supplies, and Requesting Materials From Others

PROCEDURES 7 STEPS

Step 1 Establish the Need

    a. Introduce the lesson by discussing with students their responsibilities at home.

        1) What things at home do they have to do? What things do they get to choose?

        2) What do their parents have to do? What do they get to choose?

    b. Tell students that at school there are some things they get to choose to do and some things they have to do.

    c. Set up a T-chart with two categories: "Choices" and "Have to Dos." Put an example (written or picture/icon) in each of the two columns (e.g., choosing which book to read vs. completing a work assignment).

    d. Ask students to provide other examples.

    e. Acknowledge that not everyone will want to do the "Have to Dos."

    f. Elicit from students that when they do the "Have to Dos" *teachers are happy, they will learn more,* and *they are doing their job.*

Step 2 Identify Skill Components

    a. Tell students that there are some school rules about the "Have to Dos":

        1) We don't complain about the "Have to Dos."

        2) We don't say bad things about the teacher or our school.

    b. Tell students that they know how to handle the "Have to Dos":

        1) I figure out what I have to do.

        2) I get my materials together and get started right away.

        3) I check the time and keep working until I'm done or until the time is up.

    c. Post the procedures and have students read aloud along with you as you reread the list. Repeat if necessary.

Step 3 Model the Skill

    a. Have another school staff member play the teacher role and introduce a classroom activity.

    b. Demonstrate making a positive statement about the activity.

    c. Demonstrate following the response to doing a "Have to Do."

    d. Have the "teacher" introduce an activity which many children dislike. Use the thinking aloud procedure to demonstrate not making negative remarks. Follow through beginning the "assignment."

    e. After completing the modeling, review the response to doing a "Have to Do" and the school rules.

Step 4 Role-Play

a. Have students identify things at school that are "Have to Dos" and which they don't enjoy.

b. Have students repeat the school rules for "Have to Dos" and recite or paraphrase the approach or response to such an assignment.

c. Ask students to evaluate their own performance and provide feedback.

Step 5 Practice

a. During the week following introduction of this lesson, whenever a new subject or activity is introduced, challenge a single student to model either saying something positive or avoiding saying something negative.

Step 6 Generalization

a. Inform general education teachers and "specials" teachers (PE, Art, Music) about the skill being taught; ask them to compliment students for successful demonstration.

b. Give students verbal assignments to practice the skill in other settings and to report on their success.

Step 7 Evaluation

After a period of time it is necessary to determine if the skills taught are being sustained and generalized. The following practices are used to determine long-term success of instruction.

a. Periodically observe the students in general education settings and rate their performance according to the performance criteria listed at the beginning of the lesson.

b. Ask general education teacher(s)/other support staff to rate students according to the performance criteria.

c. Collect data using progress-monitoring strategies.

d. Design individual interventions for students not benefiting from small-group interventions (i.e., students who perform the skill inadequately or fail to generalize the skill to other settings).

CHAPTER
5

LESSON 39
Avoiding Inappropriate Contact

Objective
Students will avoid making inappropriate physical contact with peers and adults.

Performance Criteria
This skill will be *performed adequately* when the student:
1. Discriminates which peers and adults may be touched as friends.
2. Identifies times when it may be appropriate to have physical contact.
3. Identifies parts of the body that should not be touched.
4. Touches friends on shoulders or arm to gain attention.
5. Shakes hands with peers and adults when introductions are made (if prompted).
6. Refrains from
   a. Hugging unless invited.
   b. Non-age-appropriate hand-holding (e.g., first graders may hold hands, but this is not typical for sixth graders).
   c. Hanging on to another person's head, arms, midsection, or legs.
   d. Back slapping.
   e. Touching another's face.
   f. Touching private areas of another person's body.

Materials Required
Chalkboard/whiteboard or chart paper
Large doll or stuffed animal

Other Preparation
Book on the theme, such as *The Right Touch: A Read-Aloud Story to Help Prevent Child Sexual Abuse* by Sandy Kleven and Jody Bergsma (1988).

Special Considerations
Do not model inappropriate physical contact with a live subject

Forms and Supplementary Materials (see CD)
None for this lesson.

Technology Resources
None for this lesson.

Related Lessons
Lesson 4: Classroom Rules: Sitting in Your Own Space
Lesson 70, Volume 2: Avoiding Making Inappropriate Comments

PROCEDURES 7 STEPS

Step 1 Establish the Need

a. Tell the students that touching other people has rules that are not written down. Give examples such as when hugging is appropriate and other times when it is not appropriate. For example, it is OK to hug your parents, but not OK to hug someone you do not know. Also share with students that some touching is OK. For example it may be OK to touch someone's elbow to get their attention when they do not see you.

b. Ask students to tell you about different rules of behavior at school (e.g., hallway behavior, answering/asking questions, working, sharing materials, etc.). Ask what it means to keep your hands and feet to yourself.

c. To the discussion, add that there are rules about touching. Explain that some people don't like to be touched, some touches upset people, and there are areas of our bodies other people shouldn't touch.

d. Discuss the consequences for inappropriate touching. Elicit that social rejection occurs for some touching and trouble with school authorities and sometimes the police for other touching.

Step 2 Identify Skill Components

a. Ask students to identify appropriate and inappropriate physical contact (e.g., "Playing football—is it appropriate to grab someone?" "Is it appropriate to hug your grandma?").

b. Through discussion, identify that physical contact should usually be avoided while at school except to gain the attention of someone. The acceptable contacts are tapping on the shoulder or gently taking hold of a person's arm.

c. Using a Venn diagram, discuss and make lists with students of touching that is typically always acceptable, sometimes acceptable, and never or seldom acceptable.

d. Through discussion and often teacher suggestion, create a list of specific examples of when touching is acceptable and with whom. Post the list for use during modeling and practice sessions.

Step 3 Model the Skill

a. Using a mannequin or large doll, model appropriate and inappropriate physical contact. Use the thinking aloud procedure to narrate behaviors that are avoided.

b. Model again, and have students identify which behaviors are inappropriate.

c. Have students participate and model gaining attention by taking hold of an arm and tapping on the shoulder.

Step 4 Role-Play

a. Describe a hypothetical situation and have students role-play the correct and acceptable forms of physical contact by thinking aloud. Some suggested situations:
   1) Student is with best friend on playground.
   2) Student sees old friend he/she hasn't seen for a long time.
   3) Student needs to get attention of a friend.
   4) Student is playing tag with boys and girls.

b. Provide feedback and ask students to provide feedback to each other.

c. Have students evaluate their own performance.

Step 5 Practice

a. In group discussion, ask students to recount the kind of physical contact which is "OK" and "not OK."

b. Have a skills review session and ask students to recount and demonstrate appropriate physical contact.

c. Reinforce students in class for demonstrating appropriate physical contact.

Step 6 Generalization

a. Observe students on the playground and other areas of the school and reinforce students for knowing and following the rules for physical contact.

b. Ask school officials to remind all students to follow rules for physical contact.

c. Ask families to reinforce demonstrations of appropriate physical contact. Identify behaviors that are regarded as inappropriate for public behavior (e.g., hugging, hanging on, leaning on people, unnecessarily rough behavior, etc.).

d. Re-teach the concept but with less specific examples. Reinforce performance when students demonstrate appropriate choices related to physical contact.

Step 7 Evaluation

After a period of time it is necessary to determine if the skills taught are being sustained and generalized. The following practices are used to determine long-term success of instruction.

a. Periodically observe the students in general education settings and rate their performance according to the performance criteria listed at the beginning of the lesson.

b. Ask general education teacher(s)/other support staff to rate students according to the performance criteria.

c. Collect data using progress-monitoring strategies.

d. Design individual interventions for students not benefiting from small-group interventions (i.e., students who perform the skill inadequately or fail to generalize the skill to other settings).

LESSON 40
Playing Games With Peers: Winning and Losing

Objective
Students will understand the rules of game playing and graciously win or lose.

Performance Criteria
This skill will be *performed adequately* when the student:
1. Follows the rules of the game.
2. Waits until appropriate turn.
3. Follows game procedures when taking turn.
4. Stops when turn is finished and allows next player to take turn.
5. Accepts the outcome of the game.
6. Comments on the game.

Materials Required
Games

Other Preparation
Prepare Stop, Go, and Wait cards prior to introducing the lesson.
Prepare another school staff member to assist with modeling the skill.
Prepare competent peers to support and assist with role-playing and practicing.

Special Considerations
Some students may need the added support of a timer or visual aid.

Forms and Supplementary Materials (see CD)
Home-School Connection form

Technology Resources
iPad/iPhone apps: TurnTaker (TouchAutism); Time Timer (Time Timer LLC);
First Then Visual Schedule (Good Karma); iPrompt (Handhold Adaptive)

Related Lessons
Lesson 10: Being Patient: Learning How to Wait
Lesson 26: Taking Turns
Lesson 89, Volume 2: Sportsmanship: Participating in Games

PROCEDURES 7 STEPS

Step 1 Establish the Need

    a. Ask students why some people do not get chosen or invited to play games. Elicit that they *may not be collaborative game players who do not follow the rules, change the rules, don't wait their turn*, or *get angry when they lose.*

    b. Ask students if they can think of what the difference is between a good winner and a bad winner. Elicit that *good winners do not brag about winning or belittle the losers.*

Step 2 Identify Skill Components

    a. Using a T chart, have students identify the characteristics of good and bad game playing. Suggest good behaviors if students are not forthcoming. Post the list and ensure that it includes:

    1) Follow the rules of the game.

    2) Wait for your turn.

    3) Follow the procedures for taking turns.

    4) Stop when your turn is finished and let the next player take a turn.

    5) Accept the outcome of the game.

        a) If a winner, don't brag or say anything mean about the other players.

        b) Accept losing gracefully, and don't blame yourself or someone else.

    6) Comment on the game.

Step 3 Model the Skill

    a. With another adult, play a game and use the thinking aloud procedure to narrate the skill steps, (e.g., "I'm waiting for my turn." "It's my turn, so I'm playing." "I lost, so I say 'good game!'").

    b. Model the procedure playing a different type of game.

Step 4 Role-Play

    a. Distribute Stop, Go, and Wait cards. Explain that they will be a helpful reminder of the steps for playing games.

    b. Set up a game-playing situation. Give students a Go card when it is their turn, a Stop card when they have completed a turn, and a Wait card when it is not their turn.

    c. Pair students with competent peers and role-play the skill using the Stop, Go, and Wait cards.

Step 5 Practice

   a. The week after introduction of the lesson, set up game-playing situations with competent peers. Prompt students with Stop, Go, and Wait cards as necessary.

   b. Fade use of prompts.

Step 6 Generalization

   a. Ask PE teachers to review the skill steps as part of a lesson in their class.

   b. Ask general education teachers/playground monitors to reinforce skill steps on the playground or at recess.

   c. Use the Home-School Connection form to ask families to have a game-playing night and reinforce the skill steps. Have students self-report on how well they performed the skill.

Step 7 Evaluation

After a period of time it is necessary to determine if the skills taught are being sustained and generalized. The following practices are used to determine long-term success of instruction.

   a. Periodically observe the students in general education settings and rate their performance according to the performance criteria listed at the beginning of the lesson.

   b. Ask general education teacher(s)/other support staff to rate students according to the performance criteria.

   c. Collect data using progress-monitoring strategies.

   d. Design individual interventions for students not benefiting from small-group interventions (i.e., students who perform the skill inadequately or fail to generalize the skill to other settings).

CHAPTER
5

LESSON 41
Playing Games With Peers: Following the Rules and What to Do When Someone Cheats

Objective

Students will understand why it is important to follow the rules and will be able to respond appropriately if another player or opponent appears to cheat.

Performance Criteria

This skill will be *performed adequately* when the student:
1. Understands the rules of the game.
2. Follows the rules of the game.
3. Is able to respond appropriately if another player or opponent does not follow the rules or cheats.

Materials Required

Book on the theme, such as *But Why Can't I?* by Sue Graves (2011) or *Clifford's Sports Day* by Norman Bridwell (1996).

Other Preparation

Prepare competent peers to support modeling and role-playing.

Special Considerations

Many students with ASD are extremely literal which can lead to faulty logic; they may misinterpret the nature of *cheating*.

Forms and Supplementary Materials (see CD)

None for this lesson.

Technology Resources

None for this lesson.

Related Lessons

Lesson 24: Telling the Truth
Lesson 89, Volume 2: Sportsmanship: Participating in Games

PROCEDURES 7 STEPS

Step 1 Establish the Need

a. Discuss with students how much fun it is to play with friends on the playground, at home, and in the classroom.

b. Ask students about their favorite games; encourage them to describe the rules of the game.

c. Discuss why it is important to follow the rules when playing games; elicit *it is more fun for everyone, people will not want to play with someone who doesn't follow the rules.*

Step 2 Identify Skill Components

a. Tell the students that you are going to teach them how to deal with someone who fails to follow the rules of games or someone who actually cheats.

b. Engage the students in discussion about what they think constitutes cheating in a game and how they would know it when they see it.

c. Elicit a list of steps they need to follow and provide suggestions on responding. The list should include:
   1) Know the rules of the game.
   2) Follow the rules of the game.
   3) Pay attention to what other players are doing.
   4) Politely correct other players when the rules are broken.
   5) Challenge someone you think is cheating without getting mad.

Step 3 Model the Skill

a. Have two competent peers model the skill while playing a board game. Narrate the skill steps for the class, (e.g.: "Steve is waiting for his turn." "Barry rolls a 7." "It's Steve's turn; he rolled a 1 but he said he rolled a 6!").

b. Provide scripted responses for dealing with cheating/bad sportsmanship.

Step 4 Role-Play

a. Have students role-play scenarios with competent peers where the competent peer inadvertently breaks a rule and, in a second scenario, intentionally cheats. Provide verbal reinforcement when students follow the rules and when they detect and correct inaccurate performance of the game.

b. Have students reflect and self-evaluate how well they followed rules and dealt with cheating.

Step 5 Practice

a. Invent a game with the class; have students develop and articulate the specific rules to play the game.

b. Play cooperative games (e.g., charades, guessing games) as a class to reinforce rule following and rule violation detection.

c. Provide reinforcement for correct practice regarding rule following, detecting and addressing rule breaking, and challenging cheating.

Step 6 Generalization

a. Ask PE teachers to review the skill steps as part of a lesson in their class.

b. Ask general education teachers/playground monitors to reinforce skill steps on the playground or at recess.

c. Use the Home-School Connection form to ask families to have a game-playing night and reinforce the skill steps. Have students self-report on how well they performed the skill.

Step 7 Evaluation

After a period of time it is necessary to determine if the skills taught are being sustained and generalized. The following practices are used to determine long-term success of instruction.

a. Periodically observe the students in general education settings and rate their performance according to the performance criteria listed at the beginning of the lesson.

b. Ask general education teacher(s)/other support staff to rate students according to the performance criteria.

c. Collect data using progress-monitoring strategies.

d. Design individual interventions for students not benefiting from small-group interventions (i.e., students who perform the skill inadequately or fail to generalize the skill to other settings)..

LESSON 42
Classroom Participation: Managing Transitions

Objective
Students will be able to make regular transitions throughout the school day without incident.

Performance Criteria
This skill will be *performed adequately* when the student:
1. Is able to independently follow changes in activities within a daily schedule.
2. Is able to move from one activity to another.
3. Is able to self-calm if anxious or worried about a transition.
4. Is able to adjust or adapt to a sudden change in the schedule.

Materials Required
Materials to create visual schedules, comic strips, and certificates.

Other Preparation
Need to prepare comic strips before presenting lesson.

Special Considerations
Students with ASD may be helped by carrying a reinforcing item with them throughout the day; use a visual timer for students who have difficulty transitioning before finishing an activity. In addition, it may be necessary to have developed individual strategies for students to calm themselves in times of stress before teaching this lesson.

Forms and Supplementary Materials (see CD)
None for this lesson.

Technology Resources
iPad/iPhone app: First-Then Visual Schedule (Good Karma); ASD Timer (In the Round Studios); Stories2Learn (MDR); Comic Life (Plasq.com); Strip Designer (www.mexircus.com/Strip_Designer/index.html)
Internet: "Staying calm when my schedule changes" video (www.youtube.com/watch?v=zzkTTfZMnnE&feature=related); Boardmaker share site has

a social story on transitions at www.boardmakershare.com/Activity/606182/
social-story-for-transitions-zip-file; Makebeliefscomix (www.makebeliefscomix.
com/), ReadWriteThink Comic Creator (www.readwritethink.org/files/resources/
interactives/comic/), StripGenerator (http://stripgenerator.com/), StoryCreator
2 (http://myths.e2bn.org/create/tool527-story-creator-2.html); award certificate
makers at www.teach-nology.com/web_tools/certificates/ and www.senteacher.org/
Worksheet/3/Certificates.xhtml

Related Lessons

Lesson 29: Dealing With Stress and Anxiety: Calming Activities
Lesson 38: Understanding Responsibility: What to Do When You Have to Do
Something You Don't Want to Do
Lesson 57, Volume 2: Adapting to Different Environments

PROCEDURES 7 STEPS

Step 1 Establish the Need

a. Explain to students that changing activities is part of everyday living that we
have to accommodate even when we do not want to. Ask the students to
describe the different but routine changes that occur during the school day.
Elicit times such as *lunch*, *class changes*, and *going home*.

b. Using comic strips, show what kind of consequences occur when students do
not make effective transitions. Discuss other consequences that may impact
students that cannot be depicted on a comic strip.

Step 2 Identify Skill Components

a. Present the following steps to the students that will help them make transitions
to new activities and locations:
   1) Be ready for changing activities by checking the daily schedule.
   2) Talk to yourself about when and how you will make the change.
   3) Move to the next activity and class when the time comes.
   4) Use your calming procedure to make the changes.
   5) Be ready for surprise changes.

Step 3 Model the Skill

a. Demonstrate following the schedule (check off) or changing the schedule
(moving to next activity).

b. Using the *thinking aloud* procedure, model self-talk (e.g., "I checked the schedule. I will be ready to go to my next class. I will not get angry. I will make the change." OR "I will use my calming theraputty during my class change.")

c. Use the thinking aloud procedures to model surprise changes.

Step 4 Role-Play
a. Tell the students in advance that they are going to practice making a surprise activity change and provide students with scripts to follow during the practice change.
b. Make a small change in activity for the group. Prompt and praise students for following the script.
c. Change the scenario and have students role-play individually making a transition. Provide other students with feedback cards to tell the target student what they saw in the role-play.

Step 5 Practice
a. Use the routine schedule changes of the day to role play at first. Ask students to use their thinking aloud process to show they know how to make transitions to new activities and classes. Provide feedback and reinforcement for performing the transitions.
b. Let students know that they are going to get certificates if they can make transitions effectively and that they will have several chances to earn the certificate. Create a change in activity or location and provide students with feedback on their performance.
c. Use schedules and reinforcers.

Step 6 Generalization
a. Provide support in general education classrooms to include coaching for the student (perhaps from a paraprofessional); wean the student from support over time.
b. Prepare a skill monitoring checklist and provide it to general education and specials (art, music, PE, etc.) teachers to rate the performance by target students on making transitions. Request that the general education and specials teachers reinforce the student for making good transitions.
c. Periodically make surprise changes to activities and schedules. Provide reinforcement to the students who engage in the desired behaviors.

Step 7 Evaluation

After a period of time it is necessary to determine if the skills taught are being sustained and generalized. The following practices are used to determine long-term success of instruction.

a. Periodically observe the students in general education settings and rate their performance according to the performance criteria listed at the beginning of the lesson.

b. Ask general education teacher(s)/other support staff to rate students according to the performance criteria.

c. Collect data using progress-monitoring strategies.

d. Design individual interventions for students not benefiting from small-group interventions (i.e., students who perform the skill inadequately or fail to generalize the skill to other settings).

LESSON 43
Hygienic Behavior: Handwashing, Personal Grooming, and Cleanliness

Objective

Students will gain skills needed to keep their hands, face, and body clean.

Performance Criteria

This skill will be *performed adequately* when the student:
1. Can follow a visual schedule of handwashing steps.
2. Checks in the mirror to ensure cleanliness.
3. Follows visual procedures to clean face.
4. Uses a tissue to keep nose free of mucus.
5. Attends to grooming (e.g. brushing/combing hair/dental care).

Materials Required

Hygiene tools, visual guides of procedures.

Other Preparation

Book on the theme, such as *I Am a Booger... Treat Me With Respect* by Julia Cook (2010).

Special Considerations

None for this lesson.

Forms and Supplementary Materials (see CD)

Home-School Connection form

Technology Resources

Internet: Sid the Science Kid episodes "The Journey of a Germ" (www.youtube.com/watch?v=UF3XvCrl75I) and "Clean It Up!" (www.youtube.com/watch?v=uaYluCKcmy0&feature=relmfu); handwashing coloring pages at www.squidoo.com/hand-washing-coloring-pages; Boardmaker share site has a social story on hygiene at www.boardmakershare.com/Activity/815800/social-story-i-wash-away-germs

Related Lessons

Lesson 11: Using the Restroom
Lesson 34: Recognizing and Exprssing Bodily Needs

PROCEDURES 7 STEPS

Step 1 Establish the Need

    a. Introduce the theme by reading a book on the subject or showing a video.

    b. Discuss the importance of general cleanliness (handwashing, clean face, proper use of tissue, and grooming); elicit that *it is important to stay healthy* and *people like it when you are clean.*

    c. Show pictures of individuals with poor grooming and hygiene and those of people with good grooming and hygiene. Lead the students through the process of sorting the pictures into the two categories. Discuss the social consequences of poor grooming and hygiene.

Step 2 Identify Skill Components

    a. Create a chart and lead students though listing "Do's" related to grooming and hygiene.

        1) Washing hands thoroughly

        2) Having a clean face

        3) Checking oneself in mirror for cleanliness and grooming

        4) Using a tissue to clear mucus

        5) Coughing into bend at elbow

        6) Wearing clean clothes

        7) Combing or brushing hair

    b. Elicit for the list of Do's:

Step 3 Model the Skill

    a. Model a self-checking process that includes clean hands, clean face, clean clothes, combed/brushed hair.

    b. Model good hygiene practices including washing hands, checking self in mirror, use of tissue, coughing into elbow bend, and cleaning teeth.

Step 4 Role-Play

    a. Provide either a poster or individual checklists for the students to follow for engaging in self-checks. Take students through a unison process of checking themselves.

    b. Have students demonstrate hand washing, checking self in the mirror, using tissue, and the appropriate way to cough. Provide feedback and verbal praise for correct performance.

Chapter 5   *Social Skills Lesson Plans for Students in Elementary School*

Step 5 Practice

    a. Starting with daily group self-checks of hygiene and grooming and have students evaluate their own status. Reinforce good hygiene and grooming. Thin the use of daily checks to doing it only periodically.

    b. Provide students with reinforcement for naturally occurring needs to use tissues and to cough appropriately.

Step 6 Generalization

    a. Place visual guide to handwashing/face-cleaning procedures at all handwashing sinks in the school.

    b. Ask general education staff and other school employees to reinforce hygienic behavior and good grooming at random times.

    c. Take students into the community and ask them to self-check before, during, and after the outing.

    d. Use the Home-School Connection form to provide families with the self-check sequence and ask that they have their child demonstrate self-checking at home and other settings.

**CHAPTER
5**

Step 7 Evaluation

After a period of time it is necessary to determine if the skills taught are being sustained and generalized. The following practices are used to determine long-term success of instruction.

    a. Periodically observe the students in general education settings and rate their performance according to the performance criteria listed at the beginning of the lesson.

    b. Ask general education teacher(s)/other support staff to rate students according to the performance criteria.

    c. Collect data using progress-monitoring strategies.

    d. Design individual interventions for students not benefiting from small-group interventions (i.e., students who perform the skill inadequately or fail to generalize the skill to other settings).

LESSON 44
Helping a Peer

Objective
When asked, students will help their peers.

Performance Criteria
This skill will be *performed adequately* when the student:
1. Attends to a peer's request for help.
2. Acknowledges the request verbally or by gesture.
3. Decides that giving help is warranted (i.e., not constrained by own task, by prior commitment, by requester's past failure to do own work).
4. Responds verbally or by gesture to the request for help.
5. Provides the help.
6. Refrains from asking for a reward for helping.

Materials Required
Book on the theme, such as *The Hundred Dresses* by Eleanor Estes and Louis Slobodhin (1974), *Frog and Toad are Friends* by Arnold Lobel (1979) or *That's What Friends Do* by Kathryn Cave (2004)
Music reflecting the theme, such as *Lean on Me* (Bill Withers) or *Help!* (The Beatles).
Chalkboard, whiteboard, or chart paper

Other Preparation
If using a conversation comic strip, need to prepare in advance
Need to prepare competent peer to participate in role-playing and practice steps.

Special Considerations
None for this lesson.

Forms and Supplementary Materials (see CD)
Conversation Strip Template

Technology Resources
Software/apps: Comic Life software and app (Plasq.com); Strip Designer app (www.mexircus.com/Strip_Designer/index.html)

Internet: Makebeliefscomix (www.makebeliefscomix.com/), ReadWriteThink Comic Creator (www.readwritethink.org/files/resources/interactives/comic/), StripGenerator (http://stripgenerator.com/), StoryCreator 2 (http://myths.e2bn.org/create/tool527-story-creator-2.html)

Related Lessons

Lesson 45: Asking a Peer for Help

PROCEDURES 7 STEPS

Step 1 Establish the Need

   a. Introduce the concept to the class by showing a video, playing music, or reading a book that relates to the theme; may also prepare and present a conversation comic strip of friends helping each other.

   b. Discuss why it is important to help friends; elicit that *we all need help occasionally* and *people help their friends in need.*

   c. Ask students to identify times when help probably should not be given. Elicit responses such as *during tests, when the person is trying to get out of work,* or *when students are directed to work independently.*

   d. Ask students to identify other things that might prevent them from helping if asked; elicit *working on an assignment, have another commitment,* and so forth.

Step 2 Identify Skill Components

   a. Tell students that they can do some things to be a good helper. List the following on the board or chart paper:

      1) Listen when someone asks for help.

      2) Decide whether or not you can help.

      3) Tell the person you will help.

      4) Help the person.

      5) Don't ask for a favor in return unless you need it.

   b. Have students repeat the list aloud at least two times.

Step 3 Model the Skill

   a. Pair students with a competent peer. Each pair of students should model a helping situation of their own choosing and then switch roles. Students should carry out the thinking aloud procedures while role-playing.

   b. Provide feedback to students on their role-playing.

   c. Ask students to evaluate their own performance.

Step 4 Role-Play

   a. Create a simulated situation where the skill of helping a peer can be modeled (e.g., helping a peer find something lost, helping complete a classroom chore, helping get things out of a locker). Model the skill and narrate the skill components using the thinking aloud procedure.
   b. Create a second simulated situation and repeat the skill without the narrative. Ask pupils to identify the skill components observed.

Step 5 Practice

   a. During the week of the lesson, contrive some helping situations. For example, have a student ask another student for help with an assigned task. Reinforce students for their good helping behavior.
   b. Have one or two pairs of students model the skill during a skill review session.

Step 6 Generalization

   a. Have students report on how they have helped their peers. Praise students for helping. Elicit if they have helped others outside of the classroom.
   b. Inform general education teachers about the lesson on helping, and ask that they reinforce the behavior.
   c. Verbally give students assignments to help someone on the playground or during class activities. These experiences can be contrived by arranging for typical peers to ask for help on some activity.

Step 7 Evaluation

   After a period of time it is necessary to determine if the skills taught are being sustained and generalized. The following practices are used to determine long-term success of instruction.

   a. Periodically observe the students in general education settings and rate their performance according to the performance criteria listed at the beginning of the lesson.
   b. Ask general education teacher(s)/other support staff to rate students according to the performance criteria.
   c. Collect data using progress-monitoring strategies.
   d. Design individual interventions for students not benefiting from small-group interventions (i.e., students who perform the skill inadequately or fail to generalize the skill to other settings).

LESSON 45
Asking a Peer for Help

Objective
Students will be able to ask peers for help.

Performance Criteria
This skill will be *performed adequately* when the student:
1. Decides that help is needed.
2. Considers the most appropriate source for help (peer, teacher, parent, other) and decides that it is appropriate to ask a peer.
3. Approaches a peer who is not otherwise engaged.
4. Tells peer that he/she is having trouble or needs assistance; politely asks peer for help (may use icon system).
5. Says "thank you" after help is provided.

Materials Required
Book on the theme, such as *Help! A Story of Friendship* by Holly Keller (2007).

Other Preparation
Prepare competent peers for modeling and role-playing the skill.

Special Considerations
This lesson should be taught after students have mastered basic classroom procedures (e.g., Lesson 1: Classroom Rules; Lesson 17: Using Classroom Materials).

For students who are especially reluctant to approach other students, identify competent peers to act as "Help Buddies" they can approach any time, who are willing to help and respond.

Forms and Supplementary Materials (see CD)
Conversation Strip Template

Technology Resources
Internet: Goodcharacter.com Teaching Guide: Asking for Help (www.goodcharacter.com/YCC/AskingForHelp.html)

Related Lessons

Lesson 6: Saying "Please" and "Thank You"

Lesson 44: Helping a Peer

Lesson 87, Volume 2: Asking Strangers for Directions or Information

PROCEDURES 7 STEPS

Step 1 Establish the Need

a. Begin a classroom discussion about strengths and challenges. Ask students to name things they are good at. Ask them if there are other things they find difficult to do.

b. Focus the discussion on the need to seek assistance: If you need help but don't ask for it, how can that lead to more problems?

c. Tell students that in addition to the teacher, they can ask their peers for help: "Think about a time when you needed help because you didn't know how to do something. Who did you turn to? How did you feel asking for help?"

d. Ask students to identify examples of when they might need to ask a peer for help. Elicit examples for different settings (e.g., general education classroom, cafeteria, playground).

e. Ask students to identify times when they should not ask for help. Elicit responses such as *during tests*, or when *they are supposed to work independently*.

Step 2 Identify Skill Components

a. Tell students that there are some good ways to ask for help. List and discuss:

1) Try to solve the problem yourself. (Discuss the fact that people don't like to help unless the student tries first.)

2) Decide if you need help and who might be able to help you.

3) If the person is not busy, go to them and tell them that you are having trouble.

4) Explain your problem and ask for help politely.

5) Say "thank you" when the help is given.

b. As the skill steps are introduced, it may be helpful to chain them through an oral read-along procedure (i.e., read Step 1 and 2; then 1, 2, and 3; then 1, 2, 3, and 4, etc.).

Step 3 Model the Skill

a. Model the skill of asking a peer for help in a classroom setting. Use the thinking aloud procedure to narrate each of the skill components.

b. Have students recall the skill components they observed. Then model the skill without narrating the steps. Again, ask students to identify the skill components they observed.

c. Have competent peers model the skill, first using the thinking aloud procedure and then without it.

Step 4 Role-Play

a. Have students role-play a situation of their choosing where they would need to ask for some help. Encourage students to use both in-class and out-of-class examples.

b. Include trained competent peers in the role-play situations.

c. Provide feedback to the students and ask students to provide feedback to each other.

Step 5 Practice

a. Review the skill components frequently during the course of the week following introducing the lesson. Remind students that they may need to ask someone for help and review the steps with students each day.

b. Set up challenge situations where students are given tasks that require help from another individual (e.g., moving a desk or carrying books to another classroom). Be sure to praise students for following correct procedures. Some students will need prompting with statements (e.g., "You might want to find a helper.").

c. At a review session, have students model the skill.

Step 6 Generalization

a. Inform other school staff members about the skill being addressed. Request that they prompt this behavior when needed.

b. Ask students to report on their use of the skill outside the classroom. Some students may benefit from use of skill-monitoring cards.

c. Create practice opportunities for activities outside of the school building (e.g., a cooperative construction or gardening project where students must help each other, challenging recess group games, PE game that relies on students helping each other to achieve a goal).

Step 7 Evaluation

After a period of time it is necessary to determine if the skills taught are being sustained and generalized. The following practices are used to determine long-term success of instruction.

    a. Periodically observe the students in general education settings and rate their performance according to the performance criteria listed at the beginning of the lesson.

    b. Ask general education teacher(s)/other support staff to rate students according to the performance criteria.

    c. Collect data using progress-monitoring strategies.

    d. Design individual interventions for students not benefiting from small-group interventions (i.e., students who perform the skill inadequately or fail to generalize the skill to other settings).

LESSON 46
Self-Advocacy: What to Do When Someone Is Bothering You

Objective

Students will have the skills they need to respond appropriately to being annoyed, pestered, or intimidated by another student.

Performance Criteria

This skill will be *performed adequately* when the student:

1. Is able to identify "safe" adults or peers as sources of aide as needed.
2. Does not use physical means to deflect or resist.
3. Uses appropriate language to defend self and to escape/avoid the situation.

Materials Required

Book on the theme, such as *One* by Kathryn Otoshi (2008), *Howard B. Wigglebottom Learns About Bullies* by Howard Binkow (2008), *The Juice Box Bully* by Bob Sornson (2010), or *Bully BEANS* by Julia Cook (2009).

Other Preparation

Prepare another staff member to assist with modeling the skill.
Prepare competent peers to assist with role-playing and practicing.

Special Considerations

None for this lesson.

Forms and Supplementary Materials (see CD)

None for this lesson.

Technology Resources

Internet: Speakingofspeech.com has "friends behavior labels" and "good-bad friend cards" at www.speakingofspeech.com/Social_Skills_Pragmatics.html; see Out on a Limb's "Guide to Getting Along" at http://urbanext.illinois.edu/conflict/index.html; Nice vs. Mean online game at www.hiyah.net/online_behavior.htm
Software: My School Day Enhanced CD (Social Skill Builder)

Related Lessons

Lesson 80: Saying "No": How to Refuse

Lesson 81, Volume 2: Standing Up for a Friend

Lesson 83, Volume 2: Recognizing and Responding to Teasing, Name Calling, and Bullying

PROCEDURES 7 STEPS

Step 1 Establish the Need

a. Introduce the lesson by reading a book on the subject.

b. Lead a class discussion about the book; elicit experiences from students. If not forthcoming, describe a personal experience and how it can be frustrating to not know what to do.

c. Elicit through discussion a list of examples of being annoyed, pestered, or intimidated by others.

d. Elicit through discussion that the skill is important because *it can help them protect themselves.*

Step 2 Identify Skill Components

a. Tell students that there are steps they can follow to escape or avoid a situation when someone is bothering them:

1) Is there someone who can help? Discuss "helpful" adults (e.g., teachers on playground, another mother at a public park, friendly peer).

2) Don't use hands or feet.

3) Use words. Provide examples, such as "I need to concentrate on what I am doing, could you (or please) give me some time and space?" "I am feeling stressed, can you leave me alone for a while?" "What you are doing (or saying) makes me feel uncomfortable, please stop."

b. For each of the examples elicited in Step 1, write response phrases on chalkboard, whiteboard, or overhead; students may also write on index cards to keep with them. Identify each example as one that might require help from another or would not.

Step 3 Model the Skill

a. With another adult, model a scenario of someone annoying someone else who is trying to work. Use the thinking aloud procedure to identify the problem, identify that one does not need assistance, and choose a phrase to deflect the annoyance.

b. Model a second scenario of being intimidated or pestered and have students identify the skill steps.

Step 4 Role-Play

a. Pair students with competent peers. Have a third peer play the role of bully/annoyance/intimidator. The competent peer should model/support target student role-play of the skill.
b. Prompt and reinforce the skill steps.
c. Have students self-evaluate.

Step 5 Practice

a. In the days following introduction of the lesson, revisit the skill by introducing a what-if scenario and having students describe a response. Vary the scenarios each day.

Step 6 Generalization

a. Monitor students on playground at recess and in cafeteria at lunch time to evaluate generalization and reinforce/prompt appropriate behavior.
b. Ask general education teachers and other school staff to reinforce/praise student demonstration of the skill.

Step 7 Evaluation

After a period of time it is necessary to determine if the skills taught are being sustained and generalized. The following practices are used to determine long-term success of instruction.

a. Periodically observe the students in general education settings and rate their performance according to the performance criteria listed at the beginning of the lesson.
b. Ask general education teacher(s)/other support staff to rate students according to the performance criteria.
c. Collect data using progress-monitoring strategies.
d. Design individual interventions for students not benefiting from small-group interventions (i.e., students who perform the skill inadequately or fail to generalize the skill to other settings).

CHAPTER
5

LESSON 47
Recognizing and Expressing Emotions: Feeling Happy, Sad, Mad, and Excited

Objective
Students will recognize emotions in others and be able to express emotions they feel themselves.

Performance Criteria
This skill will be *performed adequately* when the student:
1. Identifies emotions of others through observing facial expressions, body language, and tone of voice.
2. Considers reasons that cause certain emotions.
3. Explores options for dealing with emotions being felt.
4. Refrains from expressing feelings in an aggressive or inappropriate way.

Materials Required
Book on the theme, such as *Angry Octopus* by Lori Lite (2008), *The Way I Feel* by Janan Cain (2000), *The Feelings Book* by Todd Parr (2000), or *Feelings* by Aliki (1986).
Situation cards for role-playing and practice.

Other Preparation
None for this lesson.

Special Considerations
None for this lesson.

Forms and Supplementary Materials (see CD)
None for this lesson.

Technology Resources
iPad/iPhone app: AutismXpress (StudioEmotion)
Software: MindReading: The Interactive Guide to Emotions (Jessica Kingsley)
Internet: Speakingofspeech.com Emotions Interactive Materials
(www.speakingofspeech.com/Social_Skills_Pragmatics.html); Emotions Bingo
game at Creative Spectrum (http://creativespectrum.blogspot.com/2008/06/
free-printable-emotions-game-for-kids.html)

Related Lessons

Lesson 30: Reading Facial Expressions

Lessons 48–49: Managing Emotions

Lesson 74, Volume 2: Acknowledging and Responding to Others' Feelings

PROCEDURES 7 STEPS

Step 1 Establish the Need

a. Initiate a class discussion about emotions. Present a video or online collection of "feelings," and/or read a themed book.

b. Discuss how different situations and experiences can result in different emotions.

c. With class, brainstorm as many emotions as possible; write on whiteboard, chalkboard, overhead or posterboard; alternatively, have students create and decorate "feelings" posters to hang up in classroom.

d. Discuss that being able to identify and express emotions is important because *when you express positive emotions people want to be around you* and *when you say you have negative emotions people can help you.*

Step 2 Identify Skill Components

a. Describe ways to monitor one's emotions (e.g., emotional collages, wheels of emotions, emotional thermometers, 5-point scale) and to identify emotional response (e.g., increased heart rate, perspiration).

b. Describe the steps of the skill:

1) How are you feeling? (Emotion)

2) What do you want to do? (If negative, why you can't.)

3) What should you do? (Acceptable reaction)

Step 3 Model the Skill

a. Model different techniques to respond to anger, fear, sadness; how to cope.

b. Model acceptable expressions of happiness and excitement.

Step 4 Role-Play

a. Pair students and give each several situation cards to role-play.

b. Have students prompt each other with questions:

1) How are you feeling?

2) What do you want to do?

3) What should you do?

c. Prompt and reinforce as necessary.

Step 5 Practice

a. Have students use a graphic monitoring strategy (e.g., emotional collage, wheel of emotion, emotional thermometer, 5-point scale).

b. Use the strategy over the course of a week and discuss how emotions can change throughout the day.

Step 6 Generalization

a. Inform general education teachers, "specials" teachers, and other school staff of the skill being taught. Ask them to initiate conversations dealing with emotions and that they reinforce/praise students for appropriate expression of emotion.

Step 7 Evaluation

After a period of time it is necessary to determine if the skills taught are being sustained and generalized. The following practices are used to determine long-term success of instruction.

a. Periodically observe the students in general education settings and rate their performance according to the performance criteria listed at the beginning of the lesson.

b. Ask general education teacher(s)/other support staff to rate students according to the performance criteria.

c. Collect data using progress-monitoring strategies.

d. Design individual interventions for students not benefiting from small-group interventions (i.e., students who perform the skill inadequately or fail to generalize the skill to other settings).

CHAPTER
5

LESSON 48
Managing Emotions: Dealing With Frustration

Objective

Students will be able to identify and manage frustration.

Performance Criteria

This skill will be *performed adequately* when the student:
1. Identifies the feeling of frustration.
2. Identifies the source of the frustration.
3. Refrains from expressing frustration aggressively or violently.
4. Uses appropriate methods to self-calm.
5. Chooses an appropriate response (i.e., seeks assistance, tries again, chooses another activity).

Materials Required

Book on the theme, such as *I Just Don't Like the Sound of No!* by Julia Cook (2011).

Other Preparation

See also *I Just Don't Like the Sound of No! Activity Guide for Teachers* by Julia Cook (2011).

Materials/software to create social stories for role-playing and practice steps.

Prepare competent peers to support role-playing, practice, and generalization.

Special Considerations

None for this lesson.

Forms and Supplementary Materials (see CD)

Home-School Connection form

Technology Resources

Internet: "Nigel's 'When I Feel Frustrated' PowerPoint (www.positivelyautism. com/aug07socialstory.ppt); Speakingofspeech.com Emotions Interactive Materials (www.speakingofspeech.com/Social_Skills_Pragmatics.html)

iPad/iPhone app: Angry Octopus (Red Piston); Stories2Learn (MDR) or Pictello (AssistiveWare) for creating social stories

Related Lessons

PROCEDURES 7 STEPS

Step 1 Establish the Need

a. Introduce the lesson topic by reading a book on the theme. Discuss how characters in the story were *frustrated*; elicit from students the source of the frustration and how the characters dealt with it.

b. Lead a class discussion on situations where students become frustrated (e.g., being told "no," difficulty with school work or task).

c. Define *frustration* as the unhappy feeling you get when you can't do something you think you should be able to do or want to do.

d. Explain that everyone feels frustrated sometimes. Point out that learning something new takes patience and practice.

e. Elicit from students that it is important to be able to manage frustration because *people will be more likely to help you*, and *you will feel better about yourself*.

Step 2 Identify Skill Components

a. Tell students that there are ways to respond to frustration that can help them:
    1) Know that you're frustrated.
    2) Figure out what the problem is.
    3) Figure out what to do.
    4) Ask for help.
    5) Try again.
    6) Try something else.

b. Remind students that it is not helpful to respond angrily or physically. Discuss consequences of behaving aggressively or inappropriately.

c. Describe ways that students can manage frustration (use a self-calming technique/reinforcing item, self-talk, take a break, see if there is part of the problem that you can do, remind yourself that you did a good job trying). Write different solutions on whiteboard, chalkboard, overhead, or posterboard.

d. Reinforce the value of making a good effort, of practicing, and of working to improve.

Step 3 Model the Skill

a. Ask students to identify potential situations that cause frustration; model strategies from the list discussed in Step 2 to alleviate or reduce frustration.
b. Use the thinking aloud procedure to narrate the skill steps of identifying and responding to a source of frustration.
c. Model without narration and have students identify the problem-solving process.

Step 4 Role-Play

a. Using student-identified situations from Step 3, create social stories with students that provide guidance in responding to frustration.
b. Pair students with competent peers and role-play different scenarios from the student-identified situations in Step 3. Prompt and reinforce as necessary.
c. Have students evaluate their own performance and that of other students.

Step 5 Practice

a. Pair individual students with positive peers who can serve as role models and provide support during potentially frustrating situations.
b. Provide support, encouragement, and prompting of strategies during potentially frustrating situations.
c. Teach, practice, and review strategies before potentially stressful times of the year (e.g., holidays, exam time).
d. Use descriptive feedback to reinforce students when they demonstrate effective strategies to deal with frustration.

Step 6 Generalization

a. Inform general education teachers and "specials" teachers of the skill being taught and ask them to prompt and provide feedback to students.
b. Using the Home-School Connection form, ask families to support student acquisition of the skill by prompting and reinforcing coping strategies at home and in the community.

Step 7 Evaluation

After a period of time it is necessary to determine if the skills taught are being sustained and generalized. The following practices are used to determine long-term success of instruction.

a. Periodically observe the students in general education settings and rate their performance according to the performance criteria listed at the beginning of the lesson.

b. Ask general education teacher(s)/other support staff to rate students according to the performance criteria.

c. Collect data using progress-monitoring strategies.

d. Design individual interventions for students not benefiting from small-group interventions (i.e., students who perform the skill inadequately or fail to generalize the skill to other settings).

LESSON 49
Managing Emotions: Dealing With Boredom

Objective
Students will maintain expected behavior when bored and demonstrate socially acceptable strategies to alleviate boredom.

Performance Criteria
This skill will be *performed adequately* when the student:
1. Maintains joint attention or focus even when uninterested in topic being taught or discussed.
2. Maintains focus on speaker.
3. As needed, uses materials that support focus and are unobtrusive (e.g., theraputty, taking notes, doodle pad, texture pad).

Materials Required
Theraputty, doodle pad, Velcro texture pad or other tactile object.
Materials/software to create social stories and visual guides.
Video clips of appropriate learning behavior.

Other Preparation
Prepare another staff member to assist in modeling the skill.

Special Considerations
Students with ASD often have special or unique interests, at times it will be necessary to link curricular-based activities to those interests to maintain their engagement. In some cases using a preferred activity as a contingency for engagement is effective. For students with intellectual disabilities, maintaining attention is a significant challenge. This can be the result of not understanding the content of instruction.

Forms and Supplementary Materials (see CD)
Homework form

Technology Resources
Software: Boardmaker (Mayer-Johnson) for creating visual guides
iPad/iPhone app: Stories2Learn (MDR) or Pictello (AssistiveWare) for creating social stories

Related Lessons
Lesson 10: Being Patient: Learning How to Wait
Lesson 12: Appropriate Classroom Participation
Lesson 42: Classroom Participation: Managing Transitions

PROCEDURES 7 STEPS

Step 1 Establish the Need
a. Ask students if they ever get bored in class. Allow for some discussion of what students find boring. Given the likely response that they will say they have been bored, ask what they do to maintain attention to task or work at hand.
b. Ask students what happens or what are the consequences of not paying attention in school. Elicit that they lose learning, their parents or the teacher become unhappy.
c. Share some strategies for maintaining attention in class with the students. Ask if they think these ideas might help. Elicit that the positive outcomes of learning the skill include pleasing parents/teachers and learning more.

Step 2 Identify Skill Components
a. List the skill steps on overhead, whiteboard, chalkboard, or posterboard:
   1) Keep my mind focused.
   2) Keep my eyes forward.
   3) Keep my hands busy.
b. Create visual guides for student desks with words/icons representing the steps.

Step 3 Model the Skill
a. Have another staff member "teach" a unit to the class. Use the thinking aloud procedure to narrate the skill steps, from recognizing that the topic is not of personal interest to occupying self until the lesson is over.
b. Ask students to evaluate your performance, and to provide suggestions for responding to situations where one might be bored.
c. Show video clips of students appropriately engaged in learning tasks and instruction. (Optional)

Step 4 Role-Play
a. Group students in threes to role-play; one student plays the teacher, one the student, and the third student is the observer. Encourage the "student" to thinking aloud and narrate the skill steps. Have the observer give feedback

to the role players. For some students, use of feedback cards will help the observer identify the relevant components of the task.

b. Have students rotate the roles.

c. Have students evaluate their performance and each others'.

Step 5 Practice

a. During the days following the original lesson, periodically tell the students that they will receive reward tickets (or whatever is typically used in the school) for demonstrating appropriate work behavior and dealing with boredom. Pair the reward tickets with explicit descriptions of how students performed correctly.

b. Periodically review the skill components and have students self-report on how they followed the skill steps and used their various strategies and tools (e.g. theraputty) to maintain attention.

Step 6 Generalization

a. Inform general education teachers of the skill being taught; ensure that students have access to appropriate tactile supports as needed in their classrooms. Ask teachers to reinforce and praise student demonstration of the skill.

b. Ask students to self-report on their success using the skill at different times throughout the school day.

c. As homework, have students keep a log of times during the school day when they needed to use the skill.

Step 7 Evaluation

After a period of time it is necessary to determine if the skills taught are being sustained and generalized. The following practices are used to determine long-term success of instruction.

a. Periodically observe the students in general education settings and rate their performance according to the performance criteria listed at the beginning of the lesson.

b. Ask general education teacher(s)/other support staff to rate students according to the performance criteria.

c. Collect data using progress-monitoring strategies.

d. Design individual interventions for students not benefiting from small-group interventions (i.e., students who perform the skill inadequately or fail to generalize the skill to other settings).

LESSON 50
Being a Friend: Expressing Empathy and Sympathy

Objective
Students will express empathy and/or sympathy to peers who are having a bad day, injured, have been ill, or have suffered a loss.

Performance Criteria
This skill will be *performed adequately* when the student:
1. Identifies that a peer or familiar adult has a need for an expression of empathy or sympathy.
2. Decides what type of expression is appropriate (e.g., verbal, physical gesture, make a card).
3. Chooses an appropriate time to express empathy or sympathy.
4. Makes appropriate expression of empathy or sympathy.

Materials Required
Book on the theme, such as *Hey, Little Ant* by Phillip Hoose and Hannah Hoose (1998), *Alexander and the Terrible, Horrible, No Good, Very Bad Day* by Judith Viorst (1972), *Miss Bindergarten Stays Home From Kindergarten* by Joseph Slate (2004), or *A Story for Hippo: A Book About Loss* by Simon Puttock (2001).

Other Preparation
Prepare competent peers for modeling, role-playing, and practice steps.

Special Considerations
None for this lesson.

Forms and Supplementary Materials (see CD)
Home-School Connection form
Conversation Strip Template

Technology Resources
Software: You Are a Social Detective (Social Skill Builder)

Related Lessons

PROCEDURES 7 STEPS

Step 1 Establish the Need

a. Introduce the concept by reading two or more themed books that illustrate, variously, someone who has suffered a loss/understanding how someone else is feeling.

b. Discuss the books with the class, eliciting that the characters are *sad, having a hard time,* or *sick.*

c. Explain that *sympathy* means feeling sorry; *empathy* means feeling what the other person would feel. Ask students to identify which response is appropriate for the different characters' situations.

d. Lead the class through an empathy exercise: Just Like Me! Students stand up and offer a fact about themselves; other students say "Just like me!" if they can relate.

e. Discuss with the class why it is helpful to offer sympathy and empathy to friends; elicit *it comforts them, makes them feel better.*

Step 2 Identify Skill Components

a. Tell the class that it is an important friendship skill to know how to express empathy and sympathy. The way we do this is we See, Think, Say:

1) We see that someone is hurt, sad, feeling bad, or was sick. (Provide examples of how they would know/recognize this: student has been absent, is looking sad, expresses a worry/concern/problem.)

2) We think of something we could say or do (e.g., for sympathy, "I'm sorry about…" or make a card; for empathy, "I know how you feel because…").

3) We express empathy or sympathy.

b. Have students make posters based on See, Think, Say; they may draw pictures or write the words.

Step 3 Model the Skill

a. To model the skill, distribute situation cards to students describing a concern/problem/loss; have the student read the situation to you, then model the expression of appropriate sympathy or empathy, using the thinking aloud procedure: "I see.... I think.... So, I say...."

b. Repeat the process, without using the thinking aloud procedure. Ask students to identify the skill components.

c. Model the skill again, and ask students what other gestures/expressions might be appropriate.

d. To exercise empathy skills, ask students to "make a face" depicting what someone else is feeling in a given situation.

Step 4 Role-Play

a. Pair students with competent peers and have them describe a concern/problem/loss. Encourage students to use examples different from the preceding modeling situations; use situation cards if necessary.

b. Be sure that students role-play both the giver and the receiver of empathy/sympathy. Prompt the students to think aloud while demonstrating the steps.

c. Provide students with feedback and ask them to evaluate their performance.

d. Have students give feedback to each other.

Step 5 Practice

a. During the week subsequent to introducing the lesson, set up challenge situations where individual students are in situations where expressing empathy or sympathy is appropriate. Coach students who fail to respond to the situation and reinforce correct skill performance.

b. Hold a skill review session and have one or two students model the skill. Provide feedback and review the skill steps.

Step 6 Generalization

a. Ask students' families to reinforce expressing empathy and sympathy at home and in different settings.

b. Have students self-report on situations where they offered sympathy or empathy to a peer.

c. When supporting students in general education classes or on the playground, reinforce students for expressing sympathy or empathy.

Step 7 Evaluation

After a period of time it is necessary to determine if the skills taught are being sustained and generalized. The following practices are used to determine long-term success of instruction.

a. Periodically observe the students in general education settings and rate their performance according to the performance criteria listed at the beginning of the lesson.

b. Ask general education teacher(s)/other support staff to rate students according to the performance criteria.

c. Collect data using progress-monitoring strategies.

d. Design individual interventions for students not benefiting from small-group interventions (i.e., students who perform the skill inadequately or fail to generalize the skill to other settings).

Appendix
Forms

Social Skills Assessment (Preintervention)		
Student:	Birth Date: ❑ M ❑ F	
Grade/Teacher:	Special education eligibility classification, if any:	
Date(s) of observation:	Observer:	

Use the scale below to rate the student's behavior in each skill set.

4	The student possesses the skill and performs it adequately and with sufficient frequency.
3	The student possesses the skill and performs it adequately but not with sufficient frequency.
2	The student possesses the skill but is not fluent in its performance
1	The student possesses the skill but performs it inadequately (e.g., leaves out part of the skill or uses incorrect language when performing the skill).
0	The student does not have the skill.
N/A	The rater has no knowledge/cannot assess the student's ability in this skill area.
N/A	The skill is not age appropriate.

Lesson	Social Skill Assessed/Elementary (1-50)	Rating
1	Classroom Rules: Paying Attention to the Teacher, Getting the Teacher's Attention, Asking Questions	
2	Responding to Questions From a Teacher or Other Adult	
3	Active Listening in the Classroom	
4	Classroom Rules: Sitting in Your Own Space	
5	Keeping Your Desk in Order	
6	Saying "Please" and "Thank You"	
7	Requesting a Preferred Activity	
8	Hallway Etiquette: Staying in LIne, Entering a Room/Area	
9	Riding the School Bus	
10	Being Patient: Learning How to Wait	
11	Using the Restroom	
12	Appropriate Classroom Participation	
13	Cafeteria Rules: Going Through the Lunch Line and Sitting With Peers	
14	Cafeteria Rules: Table Manners and Having a Conversation	
15	Greeting Teachers and Other Adults	
16	Greeting Peers and Friends	
17	Using Classroom Materials: Sharing, Taking Care of Supplies, and Requesting Materials From Others	
18	Active Listening to Peers	
19	Recognizing and Reporting Emergencies	
20	What to Do if You Get Hurt	
21	What to Do if You Hurt Someone Else	
22	Coping With Sensory Issues	
23	Problem Solving	
24	Telling the Truth	
25	Being a Friend: Accepting Ideas Different From Your Own	

APPENDIX

26	Taking Turns	
27	Asking Someone to Play With You	
28	Joining in an Activity	
29	Dealing With Stress and Anxiety: Calming Activities	
30	Reading Facial Expressions	
31	Understanding Nonverbal Communication Cues	
32	Understanding Figures of Speech	
33	Understanding Sarcasm and Irony	
34	Recognizing and Expressing Bodily Needs	
35	How to Tell a Story	
36	How to Describe a Movie, Book, or TV show Episode	
37	How to Describe a Personal Experience, Memory, or Dream	
38	Understanding Responsibility: What to Do When You Have to Do Something You Don't Want to Do	
39	Avoiding Inappropriate Contact	
40	Playing Games With Peers: Winning and Losing	
41	Playing Games With Peers: Following the Rules and What to Do	
42	Classroom Participation: Managing Transitions	
43	Hygienic Behavior: Handwashing, Personal Grooming, and Cleanliness	
44	Helping a Peer	
45	Asking a Peer for Help	
46	Self-Advocacy: What to Do When Someone Is Bothering You	
47	Recognizing and Expressing Emotions: Feeling Happy, Sad, Mad,	
48	Managing Emotions: Dealing With Frustration	
49	Managing Emotions: Dealing With Boredom	
50	Being a Friend: Expressing Empathy and Sympathy	

Student's Social Skills Strength Score

| Step 1 | Divide the total of all rating points by the number of items rated to obtain the quotient. Total, rating points (all sections): _____ ÷ Total # of items rated: _____ = | |
| Step 2 | Multiply the quotient by 100 to derive the Composite Strength Score (CSS). Quotient: _____ x 100 = | |

Note: Highlight lowest scores (0–2) and check against Table 4-3. This analysis will provide information relating to the student's area of greatest need (i.e., prosocial skill development, personal skill development, or personal interaction skill development), and can assist in the development and prioritization of social skills goals.

Social Skills Assessment (Postintervention)		
Student:	Birth Date: ❑ M ❑ F	
Grade/Teacher:	Special education eligibility classification, if any:	
Date(s) of observation:	Observer:	

Use the scale below to rate the student's behavior in each skill set.

4	The student possesses the skill and performs it adequately and with sufficient frequency.
3	The student possesses the skill and performs it adequately but not with sufficient frequency.
2	The student possesses the skill but is not fluent in its performance
1	The student possesses the skill but performs it inadequately (e.g., leaves out part of the skill or uses incorrect language when performing the skill).
0	The student does not have the skill.
N/A	The rater has no knowledge/cannot assess the student's ability in this skill area.
N/A	The skill is not age appropriate.

Lesson	Social Skill Assessed/Elementary (1-50)	Rating
1	Classroom Rules: Paying Attention to the Teacher, Getting the Teacher's Attention, Asking Questions	
2	Responding to Questions From a Teacher or Other Adult	
3	Active Listening in the Classroom	
4	Classroom Rules: Sitting in Your Own Space	
5	Keeping Your Desk in Order	
6	Saying "Please" and "Thank You"	
7	Requesting a Preferred Activity	
8	Hallway Etiquette: Staying in LIne, Entering a Room/Area	
9	Riding the School Bus	
10	Being Patient: Learning How to Wait	
11	Using the Restroom	
12	Appropriate Classroom Participation	
13	Cafeteria Rules: Going Through the Lunch Line and Sitting With Peers	
14	Cafeteria Rules: Table Manners and Having a Conversation	
15	Greeting Teachers and Other Adults	
16	Greeting Peers and Friends	
17	Using Classroom Materials: Sharing, Taking Care of Supplies, and Requesting Materials From Others	
18	Active Listening to Peers	
19	Recognizing and Reporting Emergencies	
20	What to Do if You Get Hurt	
21	What to Do if You Hurt Someone Else	
22	Coping With Sensory Issues	
23	Problem Solving	
24	Telling the Truth	
25	Being a Friend: Accepting Ideas Different From Your Own	

APPENDIX

26	Taking Turns	
27	Asking Someone to Play With You	
28	Joining in an Activity	
29	Dealing With Stress and Anxiety: Calming Activities	
30	Reading Facial Expressions	
31	Understanding Nonverbal Communication Cues	
32	Understanding Figures of Speech	
33	Understanding Sarcasm and Irony	
34	Recognizing and Expressing Bodily Needs	
35	How to Tell a Story	
36	How to Describe a Movie, Book, or TV show Episode	
37	How to Describe a Personal Experience, Memory, or Dream	
38	Understanding Responsibility: What to Do When You Have to Do Something You Don't Want to Do	
39	Avoiding Inappropriate Contact	
40	Playing Games With Peers: Winning and Losing	
41	Playing Games With Peers: Following the Rules and What to Do	
42	Classroom Participation: Managing Transitions	
43	Hygienic Behavior: Handwashing, Personal Grooming, and Cleanliness	
44	Helping a Peer	
45	Asking a Peer for Help	
46	Self-Advocacy: What to Do When Someone Is Bothering You	
47	Recognizing and Expressing Emotions: Feeling Happy, Sad, Mad,	
48	Managing Emotions: Dealing With Frustration	
49	Managing Emotions: Dealing With Boredom	
50	Being a Friend: Expressing Empathy and Sympathy	

Student's Social Skills Strength Score

| Step 1 | Divide the total of all rating points by the number of items rated to obtain the quotient.

Total, rating points (all sections): _____ ÷ Total # of items rated: _____ = | |
| Step 2 | Multiply the quotient by 100 to derive the Composite Strength Score (CSS).

Quotient: _____ x 100 = | |

Note: Compare student's postintervention CSS to preintervention CSS to determine overall improvement/progress.

Social Skills Task Analysis	
Lesson:	Date(s) observed:
	Observer:

Mark a + when the individual skill step is performed consistently and independently, "I" when performed inconsistently or requires prompting, and "0" if never demonstrated.

Skill steps	Rating
1	
2	
3	
4	
5	
6	
7	
8	
9	
10	

Additional comments/observations:

APPENDIX

Homework Assignment for: _____

Lesson:	Date:

The steps for this skill are:

I practiced this skill on [date]

Did I follow all the steps?	Yes	No
Do you think you did a good job practicing this skill?		

If you don't think you did a good job, what will you do differently next time?

Home-School Connection	
To the family of:	Date:
We are currently working on the following social skill at school:	
The steps for this skill are:	
It would be great if you could help reinforce this skill at home. Some suggestions for practicing/reinforcement:	
We did it! Parent/guardian signature:	Date:
To practice/reinforce the skill, we…	
Feedback/ideas:	

APPENDIX

Individual Progress Monitoring		
Student:	Grade:	Date:
Staff:		
Domain:		
Objective:		
Data collection:		
Teaching environments:		
Natural cues and consequences:		
Natural environments outside of school:		
Correction procedures:		
Materials:		
Planned reinforcers:		
Location codes:		

Skill steps:	Dates													

Trend Graph for Social Skill Progress Monitoring

Student:	Grade:
	Teacher:

Social skill goal:

Skill measures:

Success criterion:

Target dates and location:

Baseline

Skill Steps																			
10																			
9																			
8																			
7																			
6																			
5																			
4																			
3																			
2																			
1																			
0																			
Dates																			
Score																			

Positive Behavior Support Plan		
Student:	Grade/Teacher:	Date:
Meeting participants Name:	Position/Title/Role:	
Description of the student's problem behaviors:		
Description of antecedent conditions:		
What typically follows the behavior?		
Previous interventions implemented: Description of intervention(s)		Date(s)
Problem analysis: 1. What is the function and communicative intent of the behavior? 2. What sustains the behavior? 3. Does the student have medical and/or neurological issues? 4. Is the behavior a skill or performance deficit issue?		
Hypothesis:		
Solutions brainstormed and considered:		

Action Plan			
Behavioral goal/objective:			
Behavior	Criterion	Start date	Completion date
Description of intervention:			
Action/activity	Person(s) responsible	Start date	Completion date
Method of evaluation:			
Data collection plan and data evaluation procedures:			
Review date schedule:			

References

Adams, L., Gouvousis, A., VanLue, M., & Waldron C. (2004). Social story intervention: Improving communication skills in a child with an autism spectrum disorder. *Focus on Autism and Other Developmental Disabilities, 19*, 87–94. doi:10.1177/10883576040190020301

Adders, C. (2006). *ADD/ADHD social stories: Personal hygiene'*. Retrieved from http://www.adders.org/socialstories5.htm

Autism Spectrum Institute. (n.d.). *Power card strategies*. Normal, IL: Illinois State University Special Education Department. Retrieved from http://www.autismspectrum.ilstu.edu/resources/factsheets/powercard.shtml

Ballard, M., Corman, L., Gottlieb, J., & Kaufman, M. J. (1977). Improving the social status of mainstreamed retarded children. *Journal of Educational Psychology, 69*, 605–611.

Barratt, P., Joy, H., Potter, M., Thomas, G. & Whitaker, P. (n.d.) *Circle of friends: A peer based approach to supporting children with autistic spectrum disorders in school*. Leicestershire, England: Leicestershire County Council Special Teaching Service, Autism Outreach Team. Retrieved from http://www.leics.gov.uk/index/education/special_education_needs/specialist_teaching_service/service_teams/autism_outreach_team/autism_team_resources/circle_of_friends.htm

Barry, T. D., Klinger, L. G., Lee, J. M., Palardy, N., Gilmore, T., & Bodin, S. D. (2003). Examining the effectiveness of an outpatient clinic–based social skills group for high-functioning children with autism. *Journal of Autism and Developmental Disorders, 33*, 685–701. doi:10.1023/B:JADD.0000006004.86556.e0

Bash, M. A., & Camp, B. W. (1980). Teacher training in the think aloud classroom program. In G. Carledge & J. F. Milburn (Eds.), *Teaching social skills to children* (pp. 143–178). New York, NY: Pergamon.

Batchelor, D., & Taylor, H. (2005). Social inclusion—The next step: User-friendly strategies to promote social interaction and peer acceptance of children with disabilities. *Australian Journal of Early Childhood, 30*(4), 10–18.

Bauminger, N., Solomon, M., Aviezer, A., Heung, K., Brown, J., & Rogers, S. J. (2008). Friendship in high-functioning children with autism spectrum disorder: Mixed and non-mixed dyads. *Journal of Autism and Developmental Disorders, 38*, 1211–1229. doi:10.1007/s10803-007-0501-2

Bear, G. G., Minke, K., & Manning, M. (2002). Self-concept of students with learning disabilities: A meta analysis. *School Psychology Review*, 31, 405-427.

Bellini, S. (2004). Social skill deficits and anxiety in high-functioning adolescents with autism spectrum disorders. *Focus on Autism and Other Developmental Disabilities, 19*, 78–86. doi:10.1177/10883576040190020201

Bellini, S. (2006a). The development of anxiety in adolescents with autism spectrum disorders. *Focus on Autism and Other Developmental Disabilities, 21*, 138–145. doi:10. 1177/10883576060210030201

Bellini, S. (2006b). *Building social relationships: A systematic approach to teaching social interaction skills to children and adolescents with autism spectrum disorders and other social difficulties.* Shawnee Mission, KS: Autism Asperger Publishing.

Bellini, S., & Hopf, A. (2007). The development of the autism social skills profile: A preliminary analysis of psychometric properties. *Focus on Autism and Other Developmental Disabilities, 22*, 80–87. doi:10.1177/10883576070220020801

Bernad-Ripoll, S. (2007). Using a self-as-model video combined with social stories to help a child with Asperger syndrome understand emotions. *Focus on Autism and Other Developmental Disabilities, 22*, 100–106. doi:10.1177/10883576070220020101

Bernard-Opitz, V., Sriram, N., & Nakhoda-Sapuan, S. (2001). Enhancing social problem solving in children with autism and normal children through computer-assisted instruction. *Journal of Autism and Developmental Disorders, 31*, 377–384. doi:10.1023/A:1010660502130

Black, D., Downs, J., Bastien, J., & Brown, L. (1984). *Motivation systems workshop manual.* Omaha, NE: Boys Town.

Bock, M. A. (2007). The impact of social-behavioral learning strategy training on the social interaction skills of four students with Asperger syndrome. *Focus on Autism and Other Developmental Disabilities, 22,* 88–95. doi:10.1177/10883576070220020901

Bond, R., & Castagnera, E. (2005). Peer supports and inclusive education an underutilized resource. *Theory into Practice, 45,* 224–229. Retrieved from http://exchange.guhsd.net/teacher_objects/TIP%20article.pdf

Brigman, G. A., & Webb, L. D. (2003). Ready to learn: Teaching kindergarten student school success skills. *Journal of Educational Research,* 96, 286-292. doi:10.1080/00220670309597641

Brown v. Board of Education of Topeka, 347 U.S. 483 (1954).

Browning, P., & Nave, G. (1993). Teaching social problem solving to learners with mild disabilities. *Education and Training in Mental Retardation, 28,* 309–317.

Browning, P., & White, W. (1986). Teaching life enhancement skills with interactive video-based curricula. *Education and Training of the Mentally Retarded, 21,* 236–244.

Bryan, T. S. (1974). An observational analysis of classroom behaviors of children with learning disabilities. *Journal of Learning Disabilities, 7,* 26–34. doi:10.1177/002221947400700106

Burstein, N., Sears, S., Wilcoxen, A., Cabello, B., & Spagna, M. (2004). Moving toward inclusive practices. *Remedial and Special Education, 25,* 104–116. doi:10.1177/07419325040250020501

California Department of Education. (2005). Instructional planning. In *Inclusive education starter kit, manual 2: Classroom-based strategies.* San Francisco, CA: WestEd. Retrieved from http://www.wested.org/cpei/10Manual2Chapter2.pdf

Carter, E. W., Cushing, L. S., Clark, N. M., & Kennedy, C. H. (2005). Effects of peer support interventions on students' access to the general curriculum and social interactions. *Research and Practice for Persons with Severe Disabilities, 30,* 15–25.

Carter, E. W., & Kennedy, C. H. (2006). Promoting access to the general curriculum using peer support strategies. *Research and Practice for Persons with Severe Disabilities, 31,* 284–292.

Cartledge, G., & Milburn, J. F. (1980). *Teaching social skills to children.* New York, NY: Pergamon.

REFERENCES

Castles, E., & Glass, C. (1986). Training in social and interpersonal problem-solving skills for mildly and moderately mentally retarded adults. *American Journal of Mental Deficiency, 91,* 35–42.

Causton-Theoharis, J. N., & Malmgren, K. W. (2005). Increasing peer interactions for students with severe disabilities via paraprofessional training. *Exceptional Children, 71,* 431–444.

Center for Effective Collaboration and Practice. (n.d.). *Functional behavior assessment.* Retrieved from http://cecp.air.org/fba/default.asp

Chadsey, J., & Han K. G. (2005). Friendship-facilitation strategies: What do students in middle school tell us? *TEACHING Exceptional Children, 38*(2), 52–57.

Charlop, M. H., & Milstein, J. P. (1989). Teaching autistic children conversational speech using video modeling. *Journal of Applied Behavior Analysis, 22,* 275–285. doi:10.1901/jaba.1989.22-275

Close, D. W., Irvin, L. K., Taylor, V. E., & Agosta, J. (1981). Community living skills instruction for mildly retarded persons. *Exceptional Education Quarterly, 2,* 75–86.

Collet-Klingenberg, L., & Chadsey-Rusch, J. (1991). Using a cognitive-process approach to teach social skills. *Education and Training in Mental Retardation, 26,* 258–270.

Cooke, T. P., & Apolloni, T. (1976). Developing positive social-emotional behaviors: A study of training and generalization effects. *Journal of Applied Behavior Analysis, 9,* 65–78. doi:10.1901/jaba.1976.9-65

Cooper, M. J., Griffith, K. G., & Filer, J. (1999). School intervention for inclusion of students with and without disabilities. *Focus On Autism and Other Developmental Disabilities, 14,* 110–115. doi:10.1177/108835769901400207

Crawford, C., & Porter, G. L. (2004). *Supporting teachers: A foundation for advancing inclusive education.* Toronto, Ontario: The Roeher Institute.

Crites, S. A., & Dunn, C. (2004). Teaching social problem solving to individuals with mental retardation. *Education and Training in Developmental Disabilities, 39,* 301–309.

Crozier, S., & Tincani, M. J. (2005). Using a modified social story to decrease disruptive behavior of a child with autism. *Focus on Autism and Other Developmental Disabilities, 20,* 150–157. doi:10.1177/10883576050200030301

Cushing, L. S., Kennedy, C. H., Shukla, S., Davis, J., & Meyer, K. A. (1997). Disentangling the effects of curricular revision and social grouping within cooperative learning arrangements. *Focus on Autism and Other Developmental Disabilities, 12,* 231–240. doi:10.1177/108835769701200405

Deterline, W. A. (1970). *Training and management of student tutors: Final Report.* Palo Alto, CA: General Programmed Teaching. (ERIC Document Reproduction Service No. ED048133)

DiSalvo, C. A., & Oswald, D. P. (2002). Peer-mediated interventions to increase the social interaction of children with autism: Consideration of peer expectancies. *Focus on Autism and Other Developmental Disabilities, 17,* 198–207. doi:10.1177/1088357602 0170040201

Downing, J. (2006). On peer support, universal design, and access to the core curriculum for students with severe disabilities: A personnel preparation perspective. *Research and Practice for Persons with Severe Disabilities, 31,* 327–330.

Downing, J. E. (2001). Meeting the communication needs of students with severe and multiple disabilities in general education classrooms. *Exceptionality, 9,* 147–156.

Downing, J. E., & Eichinger, J. (2003). Creating learning opportunities for students with severe disabilities in inclusive classrooms. *TEACHING Exceptional Children, 36*(1), 26–31.

Downing, J. E., & Peckham-Hardin, K. D. (2007). Inclusive education: What makes it a good education for students with moderate to severe disabilities? *Research and Practice for Persons with Severe Disabilities, 32,* 16–30.

Eddas, M. (2002). Circles of friends: A qualitative study of this technique with a ten-year-old child with an autistic spectrum disorder. *Good Autism Practice, 3*(1), 31-36.

Elias, M., & Maher, C. (1983). Social and effective development of children: A programmatic perspective. *Exceptional Children, 49,* 339–346.

Ellis, D. N., Wright, M., & Cronis, T. G. (1996). A description of the instructional and social interactions of students with mental retardation in regular physical education settings. *Education and Training in Mental Retardation and Developmental Disabilities, 31,* 235–241.

Ellis, N. (Ed.). (1963). *Handbook on mental deficiency.* New York, NY: McGraw Hill.

Embregts, P. (2003). Using self-management, video feedback, and graphic feedback to improve social behavior of youth with mild mental retardation. *Education and Training in Developmental Disabilities, 38,* 283–295.

Falvey, M. A. (2004). Toward realization of the least restrictive educational environments for severely handicapped students. *Research and Practice for Persons with Severe Disabilities, 32*, 16–30.

Fisher, M., & Meyer, L. H. (2002). Development and social competence after two years for students enrolled in inclusive and self-contained educational programs. *Research and Practice for Persons with Severe Disabilities, 27*, 165–174.

Fisher, M. A., & Zeaman, D. (1973). An attention-retention theory of retardate discrimination learning. In N. R. Ellis (Ed.), *The international review of research in mental retardation* (Vol. 6, pp. 169–256), New York, NY: Academic Press.

Flores, M. M., & Ganz, J. B. (2007). Effectiveness of direct instruction for teaching statement inference, use of facts and analogies to student with developmental disabilities and reading delays. *Focus on Autism and Other Developmental Disabilities, 22*, 244–251. doi:10.1177/10883576070220040601

Foreman, P., Arthur-Kelly, M., Pascoe, S., & Smyth King, B. (2004). Evaluating the educational experiences of students with profound and multiple disabilities in inclusive and segregated classroom settings: An Australian perspective. *Research and Practice for Persons with Severe Disabilities, 29*, 183–193.

Forest, M., & Lusthaus, E. (1988). *The kaleidoscope: Each belongs—quality education for all.* Unpublished manuscript, Frontier College, Toronto, Canada.

Forrest, M., Pearpoint, J., & O'Brien, J. (1996). "MAPS": Educators, parents, young people, and their friends planning together. *Educational Psychology in Practice, 11*(4): 41–48.

Frederickson, N., & Turner, J. (2003). Utilizing the classroom peer group to address children's social needs: An evaluation of the circle of friends intervention approach. *The Journal of Special Education, 36*, 234–245. doi:10.1177/002246690303600404

Freedman, B., & Silverman, W. (2008). Improving social skills for children with high functioning autism. *Exceptional Parent, 38*(5), 64–66.

Fuchs, D., Fuchs, L.S., Mathes, P.G., & Martinez, E. (2002). Preliminary evidence on the social standing of students with learning disabilities in PALS and No-PALS classrooms. *Learning Disabilities Research and Practice, 17*, 205–215. doi:10.1111/1540-5826.00046

Fuchs, D., Fuchs, L. S., Mathes, P. G., & Simmons, D. C. (1997). Peer-assisted learning strategies: Making classrooms more responsive to diversity. *American Educational Research Journal, 34*, 174–206.

Gagnon, E. (2001). *Power cards: Using special interests to motive children and youth with Asperger Syndrome and autism.* Shawnee Mission, KS: Autism Asperger Publishing.

Giangreco, M, F. (1997) Key lessons learned about inclusive education: Summary of the 1996 Schonell memorial lecture. *International Journal of Disability, Development and Education, 44,* 193–206.

Giangreco, M. F., & Broer, S. (2005). Questionable utilization of paraprofessionals in inclusive schools: Are we addressing symptoms or causes? *Focus on Autism and Other Developmental Disabilities, 20,* 10–26. doi:10.1177/10883576050200010201

Giangreco, M. F., Cloninger, C., & Iverson, V. S. (1998). *Choosing outcomes and accommodations for children (COACH): A guide to educational planning for students with disabilities* (2nd ed.). Baltimore, MA: Brookes.

Glaeser, B. C., Pierson, M. R., & Fristschman, N. (2003). Comic strip conversations: A positive behavioral support strategy. *TEACHING Exceptional Children, 36*(2), 14–19.

Goldstein, H. (1974). *Social learning curriculum.* Columbus, OH: Merrill.

Goldstein, A. P., Sprafkin, R. P., Gershaw, N. J., & Klein, P. (1980). *Skill-streaming the adolescent: A structured learing approach to teaching prosocial skills.* Champaign, IL: Research Press.

Gordon, P. A., Feldman, D., & Chiriboga, J. (2005). Helping children with disabilities develop and maintain friendships. *Teacher Education and Special Education, 28,* 1–9. doi:10.1177/088840640502800101

Gottlieb, J., Semmel, M. I., & Veldman, D. J. (1978). Correlates of social status among mainstreamed mentally retarded children. *Journal of Educational Psychology, 70,* 396–405.

Gottman, J., Gonso, J., & Rasmussen, B. (1975). Social interaction, social competence, and friendship in children. *Child Development, 46,* 707–718.

Graetz, J. E., Mastropieri, M., & Scruggs, T. E. (2009). Decreasing inappropriate behaviors for adolescents with autism spectrum disorders using modified social stories. *Education and Training in Developmental Disabilities, 44,* 91-104.

Grandin, T. (2008). *The way I see it: A personal look at autism and Asperger's.* Arlington, TX: Future Horizons.

Gray, C. A. (2000). *The new social story book: Illustrated edition.* Arlington, TX: Future Horizons.

REFERENCES

Gray, C. A., & Garand, J. D. (1993). Social stories: Improving responses of students with autism with accurate social information. *Focus on Autistic Behavior, 8*(1), 1–10.

Greenspan, S. (1979). Social intelligence in the retarded. In Ellis, N. (Ed.), *Handbook of mental deficiency: Psychological theory and research* (2nd ed., pp. 483–531), Hillsdale, NJ: Erlbaum.

Gresham, F. M. (1981). Social skills training with handicapped children: A review. *Review of Educational Research, 51*, 139-176. doi:10.3102/00346543051001139

Gresham, F. M. (1982). Misguided mainstreaming: The case for social skills training with handicapped children. *Exceptional Children, 48*, 422–435.

Gresham, F. M. (2002). Teaching social skills to high-risk children and youth: Preventive and remedial strategies. In M. Shinn, H. Walker, & G. Stoner (Eds.), *Interventions for Academic and behavior problems II: Preventive and remedial approaches* (pp 403–432). Bethesda, MD: National Association of School Psychologists

Gresham, F .M., & Elliot, S. N. (1990). *Social skills rating system manual.* Circle Pines, MN: American Guidance Service.

Gresham, F. M., Sugai, G., & Horner, R. H. (2001). Interpreting outcomes of social skills training for students with high-incidence disabilities. *Exceptional Children, 67*, 331-344.

Gronlund, H., & Anderson, L. (1963). Personality characteristics of socially accepted, socially neglected and socially rejected junior high school pupils. In J. M. Seidman (Ed.), *Educating for Mental Health.* New York, NY: Crowell.

Gumpel, T. P., Tappe, P., & Arki, C. (2000). Comparison of social problem solving abilities among adults with and without developmental disabilities. *Education and Training in Mental Retardation and Developmental Disabilities, 35*, 259–268.

Harper, L., & McCluskey, K. (2003). Teacher-child and child-child interactions in inclusive preschool settings: Do adults inhibit peer interactions? *Early Childhood Research Quarterly, 18*, 163–184.

Helgeson, D. C., Fatuzzo, J. W., Smith, C., & Barr, D. (1989). Eye-contact skill training for adolescents with developmental disabilities and severe behavior problems. *Education and Training in Mental Retardation, 24*(1), 56–62.

Hendrickson, J. M., Shokoohi-Yekta, M., Hame-Nietupski, S., & Gable, R. A. (1996). Middle and high school students' perceptions on being friends with peers with disabilities. *Exceptional Children, 63*, 19–28.

Heron, T. E., Villareal, D. M., Yao, M., Christianson, R. J., & Heron, K. M. (2006). Peer tutoring systems: Applications in classroom and specialized environments. *Reading & Writing Quarterly, 22*(1), 27–45.

Hodge, S. R., Yahiku, K., Murata, N. M., & Von Vange, M. V. (2003, January). Social inclusion or social isolation: How can teachers promote social inclusion of students with disabilities? *Teaching Elementary Physical Education*, 29–32.

Hughes, C., & Carter, E. W. (2008). Peer buddy programs: For successful secondary school inclusion. Baltimore, MA: Brookes.

Hume, K., Bellini, S., & Pratt, C. (2005). The usage and perceived outcomes of early intervention and early childhood programs for young children with autism spectrum disorder. *Topics in Early Childhood Special Education, 25*, 195-207. doi:10.1177/0271 1214050250040101

Hundert, J. & van Delft, S. (2009). Teaching children with autism spectrum disorders to answer inferential "why" questions. *Focus on Autism and Other Developmental Disabilities*, 24, 67-76. doi:10.1177/1088357609332984

Hunt, P., Hirose-Hatae, A., Doering, K., Karasoff, P., & Goetz, L. (2000). "Community" is what I think everyone is talking about. *Remedial and Special Education, 21*, 305–317. doi:10.1177/074193250002100507

Hyatt, K. J., & Filler, J. W. (2007). A comparison of the effects of two social skill training approaches on teacher and child behavior. *Journal of Research in Childhood Education, 22*(1), 85–87.

Idol, L. (2006). Toward inclusion of special education students in general education. *Remedial and Special Education, 27*, 77–94. doi:10.1177/07419325060270020601

Individuals With Disabilities Education Act, 20 U.S.C. §§ 1400 *et seq.* (2006).

Ivey, M. L., Hellin, L. J., & Aberto, P. (2004). The use of social stories to promote independent behaviors in novel events for children with PDD-NOS. *Focus on Autism and Other Developmental Disabilities, 19*, 164–176. doi:10.1177/1088357604019003 0401

James Stanfield. (2010). Being with people: 100 essential social skills. *The James Stanfield basic social skills library* [DVD/VHS]. Available from http://stanfield.com/being-with-people.html

Jenkins, J., Speltz, M., & Odom, S. (1986). Integrating normal and handicapped preschoolers: Effects on child development and social interaction. *Exceptional Children, 52*, 7–17.

Johnson, D., Johnson, R., & Holubec, E. (1998). *Cooperation in the classroom* (7th ed.). Edina, MN: Interaction.

Johnson, D., Johnson, R., & Holubec, E. (2002). *Circles of learning* (5th ed.). Edina, MN: Interaction.

Johnson, D., Johnson, R., & Maruyamma, G. (1983). Interdependence and interpersonal attractions among heterogeneous and homogeneous individuals: A theoretical formulation and meta analysis. *Review of Educational Research, 53*, 5–54. doi:10.3102/00346543053001005

Johnson, D. W., & Johnson, R. T. (1994). *Leading the cooperative school* (2nd ed.). Edina, MN: Interaction.

Johnson, R., & Johnson, D. (1983). Effects of cooperative, competitive, and individualistic learning experiences on social development. *Exceptional Children, 49*, 323–329.

Jones, M. (1998). *Within our reach*. Arlington, VA: Council for Exceptional Children.

Kagan, S. (1994). *Cooperative learning*. San Clemente, CA: Kagan.

Kamps, D. M., Leonard, B. R., Vernon, S., Dugan, E. P., Delquadri, J. C., Gershon, B., . . . Folk, L. (1992). Teaching social skills to students with autism to increase peer interactions in an integrated first-grade classroom. *Journal of Applied Behavior Analysis, 25*, 281–288.

Katz, J., Mirenda, P., & Auerbach, S. (2002). Instructional strategies and educational outcomes for students with developmental disabilities in inclusive "multiple intelligences" and typical inclusive classrooms. *Research and Practice for Persons with Severe Disabilities, 27*, 227–238.

Kirk, S. A., & Johnson, G. O. (1951). *Educating the retarded child*. Cambridge, MA: Houghton Mifflin.

Knapczyk, D., & Rodes, P. (2001). *Teaching social competence: Social skills and academic success* [DVD]. Verona, WI: Attainment. Available from http://www.attainmentcompany.com/

Kroeger, K. A., Schultz, J. R., & Newsom, C. (2006). A comparison of two group-delivered social skills programs for young children with autism. *Journal of Autism and Developmental Disorders, 37*, 808–817. doi:10.1007/s10803-006-0207-x

Kunda, M., & Goel, A. K. (2011). Thinking in pictures as a cognitive account of autism. *Journal of Autism and Developmental Disorders, 31*, 1157–1177. doi:10.1007/s10803-010-1137-1

Kugelmass, J. W. (2006). Sustaining cultures of inclusion: The limits of cultural analyses. *European Journal of Psychology of Education, 21*, 279–292

Kuoch, H., & Mirenda, P. (2003). Social story interventions for young children with autism spectrum disorders. *Focus on Autism and Other Developmental Disabilities, 18*, 219–227. doi:10.1177/10883576030180040301

Kuttler, S., Myles, B. S., & Carlson, J. (1998). The use of social stories to reduce precursors to tantrum behavior in a student with autism. *Focus on Autism and other Developmental Disabilities, 13*, 176–182. doi:10.1177/108835769801300306

La Greca, A., Stone, W., & Bell, C. (1983). Facilitating the vocational-interpersonal skills of mentally retarded individuals. *American Journal of Mental Deficiency, 88*, 270–278.

Laushey, K. M., & Heflin, L. J. (2000). Enhancing social skills of kindergarten children with autism through training of multiple peers as tutors. *Journal of Autism and Developmental Disorders, 30*, 183–193. doi:10.1023/A:1005558101038

Lloyd, J., & Carnine, D. W. (1981). Forward. *Exceptional Education Quarterly, 2*, viii-ix.

Lopata, C, Thomeer, M. L., Volker, M. A., & Nida, R. E. (2006). Effectiveness of a cognitive-behavioral treatment on the social behaviors of children with Asperger disorder. *Focus on Autism and Other Developmental Disabilities, 21*, 237–244. doi:10.1177/10883576060210040501

MacMillan, D. L., & Morrison, G. M. (1980). Correlates of social status among mildly handicapped learners in self-contained special classes. *Journal of Educational Psychology, 72*, 437–444.

Maheady, L., Harper, G. F., & Mallette, B. (2001). Peer-mediated instruction and interventions and students with mild disabilities. *Remedial and Special Education, 22*, 4–14. doi:10.1177/074193250102200102

Marzano, R. J. (2007). *The art and science of teaching*. Alexandria, VA: Association for Supervision and Curriculum Development.

McCormick, L., & Kawate, J., (1982). Kindergarten survival skills: New directions for preschool special education. *Education and Training of the Mentally Retarded, 17*, 247–252.

McDonnell, J., Mathot-Buckner, C., Thorson, N., & Fister, S. (2001). Supporting the inclusion of students with moderate and severe disabilities in junior high school general education classes: The effects of classwide peer tutoring, multi-element curriculum, and accommodations. *Education and Treatment of Children, 24*, 141–160.

McGinnis, E., & Goldstein, A. (1984). *Skillstreaming the elementary child*. Champaign, IL: Research Press.

McMahon, C. M., Wacker, D. P., Sasso, G. M., Berg, W. K., & Newton, S. M. (1996). Analysis of frequency and type of interactions in a peer-mediated social skills intervention: Instructional vs. social interactions. *Education and Training in Mental Retardation and Developmental Disabilities, 31*, 339–352.

Meadan, H., & Monda-Amaya, L. (2008). Collaboration to promote social competence for students with mild disabilities in the general classroom: A structure for providing social support. *Intervention in School and Clinic, 43*, 158–167. doi:10.1177/1053451207311617

Meichenbaum, D. (1977). *Cognitive behavior modification*. New York, NY: Springer.

Mesibov, G. B., & La Greca, A. M. (1981). A social skills instructional module. *The Directive Teacher, 3*, 6–7.

Metzke, L., & Berghoff, P. (1999). Cooperative learning in the classroom. In A. S. Canter & S. A. Carroll (Eds.), *Helping children at home and school: Handouts from your school psychologist* (pp. 147–150). Bethesda, MD: National Association of School Psychologists.

Midland County Educational Service Agency. (2009). *Sample social stories*. Midland, MI: Author. Retrieved from http://www.autism-pdd.net/testdump/test14154.htm

Miller, M. A. (2005). Using peer tutoring in the classroom: Applications for students with emotional/behavioral disorders. *Beyond Behavior, 15*(1), 25-30. Retrieved from http://www.ccbd.net/documents/bb/Fall2005vol15no1pp25-30.pdf

Milsom, A. (2006). Creating positive school experiences for students with disabilities. *Professional School Counseling, 10*(1), 66–71.

National Association of School Psychologists. (2002). *Social skills: Promoting positive behavior, academic success and school safety.* Bethesda, MD: Author.

National Center on Educational Restructuring and Inclusion. (1994). *National survey on inclusive education.* (Bulletin No. 1). New York, NY: The Graduate Schools and University Center.

Newton, C., Taylor, G., & Wilson, D. (1996). Circles of friends: An inclusive approach to meeting emotional and behavioural needs. *Educational Psychology in Practice, 11*(4), 41–49.

Nikopoulos, C. N., & Keenan, M. (2007). Using video modeling to teach complex social sequences to children with autism. *Journal of Autism and Developmental Disorders, 37*, 678–693. doi:10.1007/s10803-006-0195-x

Nirje, B. (1969). The normalization principle and its human management implications. In R. B. Kugel & W. Wolfensberger (Eds.), *Changing patterns in residential services for the mentally retarded* (pp. 179–195). Washington, DC: President's Committee on Mental Retardation.

No Child Left Behind Act of 2001, 20 U.S.C. § 6301 *et seq.* (2006).

Odom, S., & Asher, S. (1977). Coaching children in social skills for making friendships. *Child Development, 48*, 495–506.

Odom, S. L., & Strain, P. S. (1986). A comparison of peer-initiation and teacher-antecedent interventions for promoting reciprocal social interaction of autistic preschoolers. *Journal of Applied Behavior Analysis, 19*(1), 59–71.

Ogilvie, C. R. (2011). Step by step: Social skills instruction for students with autism spectrum disorder using video models and peer mentors. *TEACHING Exceptional Children, 43*(6), 20–26.

Owen-DeSchryver, J. S., Carr, E. G., Cale, S. I., & Blakely-Smith, A. (2008). Promoting social interactions between students with autism spectrum disorders and their peers in inclusive school settings. *Focus on Autism and Other Developmental Disabilities, 23*, 15–28. doi:10.1177/1088357608314370

Palilis, B. (2008, October 14). A "circle of friends" for students with disabilities. ASHA Leader, 13(14), 53.

Perner D. (2004). *Changing teaching practices: Using curriculum differentiation to respond to students' diversity.* Paris, France: Author. Retrieved from http://unesdoc.unesco.org/images/0013/001365/136583e.pdf

Perner, D. (2008). Creating inclusive schools: Strategies for change, administrators and teachers. In P. Parette, G. Peterson-Karlan, & R. Ringlaben (Eds.), *Research-based and emerging best practices in developmental disabilities* (2nd ed., pp. 543–565). Austin, TX: PRO-ED.

Perner, D., & Porter, G. (2008). Creating inclusive schools: Changing roles and strategies. In P. Parette, G. Peterson-Karlan, & R. Ringlaben (Eds.), *Research-based and emerging best practices in developmental disabilities* (2nd ed., pp. 521–541). Austin, TX: PRO-ED.

Phillips, E. L., Fixsen, D., Phillips, E. E., & Wolf, M. (1970). The teaching-family model: A comprehensive approach to residential treatment of youth. In D. Cullinan & M. H. Epstein (Eds.), *Special education for adolescents, issues and perspective.* Columbus, OH: Merrill.

Pierce, K., & Schreibman, L. (1997). Using peer trainers to promote social behavior in autism: Are they effective at enhancing multiple social modalities? *Focus on Autism and Other Developmental Disabilities, 12,* 207–218. doi:10.1177/108835769701200403

Pierson, M. R., & Glaeser, B. C. (2005). Extension of research on social skills training using comic strip conversation to student without autism. *Education and Training in Developmental Disabilities, 40,* 279–284.

Polloway, E. A., Patton, J. R., & Serna, L. (2008). *Strategies for teaching learners with special needs* (9th ed.). Upper Saddle, NJ: Prentice Hall.

Prizant, B. M., Wetherby, A. M., Rubin, E., Laurent, A. C., & Rydell, P. J. (2006). *The SCERTS model: A comprehensive educational approach for children with autism spectrum disorders, Vol. I. Assessment.* Baltimore, MD: Brookes.

Putnam, J. W. (1998). *Cooperative learning and strategies for inclusion: Celebrating diversity in the classroom.* Baltimore, MD: Brookes.

Reynhout, G., & Carter, M. (2006). Social stories for children with disabilities. *Journal of Autism and Developmental Disorders, 36,* 445–469. doi:10.1007/s10803-006-0086-1

Robinson, J. E. (2008). *Look me in the eye: My life with Asperger's.* New York, NY: Three Rivers Press.

Roeyers, H. (1996). The influence of nonhandicapped peers on social interaction of children with pervasive developmental disorder. *Journal of Autism and Developmental Disorders, 26*, 303–320. doi:10.1007/BF02172476

Rogers, S. J. (2000). Interventions that facilitate socialization in children with autism. *Journal of Autism and Developmental Disorders, 30*, 399–409. doi:10.1023/A:1005543321840

Rohrbeck, C., Ginsburg-Block, M., Fantuzzo, J. & Miller, T. (2003). Peer assisted learning interventions with elementary school students: A meta-analytic review. *Journal of Educational Psychology, 95*, 240–257.

Rosenthal-Malek, A. L, & Yoshida, R. K. (1994). The effects of metacognitive strategy training on the acquisition and generalization of social skills. *Education and Training in Mental Retardation and Developmental Disabilities, 29*, 213–221.

Sailor, W., & Roger, B. (2005). Rethinking inclusion: Schoolwide applications. *Phi Delta Kappan, 86*, 503-509.

Sargent, L. R. (1983). *Project SISS (systematic instruction of social skills).* Des Moines, IA: Iowa Department of Public Instruction.

Sargent, L. R. (1998). *Social skills for school and community.* Arlington, VA: Council for Exceptional Children.

Sasso, G. M., Mundschenk, N. A., Melloy, K. J., & Casey, S. D. (1998). A comparison of the effects of organismic and setting variables on the social interaction behaviors of children with developmental disabilities and autism. *Focus on Autism and Other Developmental Disabilities, 13*, 2–16. doi:10.1177/108835769801300101

Scattone, D., Tingstrom, D., & Wilczynski, S. (2006). Increasing appropriate social interactions of children with autism spectrum disorders using social stories. *Focus on Autism and Other Developmental Disabilities, 21*, 211–222. doi:10.1177/1088357606 0210040201

Scattone, D., Wilczynski, S. M., Edwards, R. P., & Rabian, B. (2004). Decreasing disruptive behaviors of children with autism using social stories. *Journal of Autism and Developmental Disorders, 32*, 535–543. doi:10.1023/A:1021250813367

Simpson, R. L. (2005). Autism spectrum disorders: Interventions and treatments for children and youth. Thousand Oaks, CA: Corwin.

Siperstein, G. N., Leffert, J. S., & Widaman, K. (1996). Social behavior and social acceptance and rejection of children with mental retardation. *Education and Training in Mental Retardation and Developmental Disabilities, 31*, 271–281.

REFERENCES

Slavin, R. E. (1995). *Cooperative learning: Theory, research and practice* (2nd ed.). Boston, MA: Allyn & Bacon.

Spencer, V. G., Simpson, C. G., Day, M., & Buster, E. (2008). Using the power card strategy to teach social skills to a child with autism. *TEACHING Exceptional Children Plus, 5*(1). Retrieved from http://escholarship.bc.edu/cgi/viewcontent.cgi?article=1539&context=education/tecplus

Stephens, T. M. (1978). *Social skills in the classroom.* Columbus, OH: Cedars Press.

Stevens, R., & Rosenshine, B. (1981). Advances in research on teaching. *Exceptional Education Quarterly, 2,* 1–9.

Strain, P., & Odom, S. (1986). Peer social initiations: An effective intervention for social skill deficits of preschool handicapped children. *Exceptional Children, 52,* 543–552.

Strain, P., Shores, R., & Timm, M. (1977). Effects of peer social initiations on the behavior of withdrawn preschool children. *Journal of Applied Behavior Analysis, 10,* 289–298.

Strain, P., & Timm, M. (1974). An experimental analysis of social interaction between a behaviorally disordered preschool child and her classroom peers. *Journal of Applied Behavior Analysis, 7,* 583–590.

Strain, P., & Wiegerink, R. (1976). The effects of sociodramatic activities on social interaction among behaviorally disordered preschool children. *The Journal of Special Education, 10,* 71–75. doi:10.1177/002246697601000109

Sugai, G. (2006, February). *Positive behavior support: Trainer-of-trainers.* Presentation at Colorado Department of Education workshop, Denver.

Test, D. W., Richter, S., Knight, V., & Spooner, F. (2011). A comprehensive review and meta-analysis of the social stories literature. *Focus on Autism and Other Developmental Disabilities, 26*(1), 49–62. doi:10.1177/1088357609351573

Thiemann, K. S., & Goldstein, H. (2004). Effects of peer training and written text cueing on social communication of school-age children with pervasive developmental disorder. *Journal of Speech, Language, and Hearing Research, 47,* 126–144. doi:10.1044/1092-4388(2004/012)

Travis, L., Sigman, M., & Ruskin, E. (2001). Links between social understanding and social behavior in verbally able children with autism. *Journal of Autism and Developmental Disorders, 31,* 119–130. doi:10.1023/A:1010705912731

Utley, C. A., Mortweet, S. L., & Greenwood, C. R. (1997). Peer-mediated instruction and interventions. *Focus on Exceptional Children, 29*, 1–23.

Vaughn, S., Bos, C. S., & Schumm, J. S. (2007). *Teaching students who are exceptional, diverse, and at risk in the general education classroom* (4th ed.). Boston, MA: Allyn & Bacon.

Vaughn, S., Kim, A., Sloan, C. V. M., Hughes, M. T., Elbaum, B., & Sridhar, D. (2003). Social skills interventions for young children with disabilities: A synthesis of group design studies. *Remedial and Special Education, 24*, 2–15. doi:10.1177/074193250302400101

Vaughn, S., Ridley, C., & Cox, J. (1983). Evaluating the efficacy of an interpersonal skills training program with children who are mentally retarded. *Education and Training of the Mentally Retarded, 18*, 191–196.

Villa, R. A. (2005). Everything about Bob was cool, including the cookies. In R. A. Villa & J. S. Thousand (Eds.), *Creating an inclusive school* (2nd ed., pp. 156–168). Alexandria, VA: Association for Supervision and Curriculum Development.

Villa, R. A., & Thousand, J. S. (2005). The rationales for creating and maintaining inclusive schools. In R. A. Villa & J. S. Thousand (Eds.), *Creating an inclusive school* (2nd ed., pp. 41–56). Alexandria, VA: Association for Supervision and Curriculum Development.

Walther-Thomas, C., Korinek, L., McLaughlin, V. L., & Williams, B. (2000). *Collaboration for inclusive education: Developing successful programs.* Boston, MA: Allyn & Bacon.

Wang, P., & Spillane, A. (2009). Evidence based social skills interventions for children with autism: A meta-analysis. *Education and Training in Developmental Disabilities, 44*, 318–342.

Webb, B. J., Miller, S. P., Peirce, T. B., Strawser, S., & Jones, W. P. (2004). Effects of social skill instruction for high-functioning adolescents with autism spectrum disorders. *Focus on Autism and Other Developmental Disabilities, 19*, 53–62. doi:10.1177/10883 576040190010701

Wolfberg, P. J., & Schuler, A. L. (1993). Integrated play groups: A model for promoting the social and cognitive dimensions of play in children with autism. *Journal of Autism and Developmental Disorders, 23*, 467–489. doi:10.1007/BF01046051

REFERENCES

Working Forum on Inclusive Schools. (1994). *Creating schools for all our students: What twelve schools have to say.* Arlington, VA: Council for Exceptional Children.

Wright, J. (2004). *Kids as reading helpers: A peer tutor training manual* (Rev. ed.). New York, NY: Author. Retrieved from http://www.jimwrightonline.com/pdfdocs/prtutor/ peerTutorManual.pdf

Yang, N. K., Schaller, J. L., Hang, T., Wang, M. H., & Tsai, S. (2003). Enhancing appropriate social behaviors for children with autism in general education classrooms: An analysis of six cases. *Education and Training in Developmental Disabilities, 38,* 405–416.

Zeaman, D., & House, B. J. (1963). The role of attention in retardate discrimination learning. In N. R. Ellis (Ed.), *Handbook of mental deficiency* (pp. 159–223) New York, NY: McGraw-Hill.

Zionts, P. (2005). Inclusion. In P. Zionts (Ed.), Inclusion strategies for students with learning and behavior problems: Perspectives, experiences, and best practices (2nd ed., pp. 3–27). Austin, Texas: PRO-ED.